Unravelling Sustainability and Resilience in the Built Environment

In this timely book, Emilio Jose Garcia and Brenda Vale explore what sustainability and resilience might mean when applied to the built environment. Conceived as a primer for students and professionals, it defines what the terms sustainability and resilience mean and how they are related to each other and to the design of the built environment. After discussion of the origins of the terms, these definitions are then compared and applied to case studies, including Whitehill and Bordon, UK, Tianjin Eco-city, China, and San Miguel de Tucuman, Argentina, which highlight the principles of both concepts. Essentially, the authors champion the case that sustainability in the built environment would benefit from a proper understanding of resilience.

Emilio Jose Garcia, originally from Argentina, is a Lecturer in Sustainability in the School of Architecture and Planning at the University of Auckland, New Zealand. His current research is about the application of ecological resilience to the analysis of the morphology and context of urban landscapes. He is interested in the research of resilience in relationship with compactness, adaptability, and inequality in the built environment.

Brenda Vale is a Professorial Research Fellow at the University of Wellington in Victoria, New Zealand. Since her first publication (with Robert Vale) in 1975, *The Autonomous House*, she has been an influential figure in the area of sustainability as it relates to the built environment.

'In this book, Garcia and Vale question conventional wisdom about the rhetorical shibboleths that clutter discussions of "sustainable" and "resilient" built environments like redundant scaffolding. They're right to do it, and they do it well as they abandon designer hubris in favour of factual analysis and rational argument as the basis for understanding and reshaping the "manageable complexity" of our cities so they can work for everyone.'

– Paul Downton, Ecocity Design Institute, Australia

Unravelling Sustainability and Resilience in the Built Environment

Emilio Jose Garcia and Brenda Vale

LONDON AND NEW YORK

First published 2017
by Routledge
2 Park Square, Milton Park, Abingdon, Oxon OX14 4RN

and by Routledge
711 Third Avenue, New York, NY 10017

Routledge is an imprint of the Taylor & Francis Group, an informa business

© 2017 Emilio Jose Garcia and Brenda Vale

The right of Emilio Garcia and Brenda Vale to be identified as authors of this work has been asserted by them in accordance with sections 77 and 78 of the Copyright, Designs and Patents Act 1988.

All rights reserved. No part of this book may be reprinted or reproduced or utilised in any form or by any electronic, mechanical, or other means, now known or hereafter invented, including photocopying and recording, or in any information storage or retrieval system, without permission in writing from the publishers.

Trademark notice: Product or corporate names may be trademarks or registered trademarks, and are used only for identification and explanation without intent to infringe.

British Library Cataloguing-in-Publication Data
A catalogue record for this book is available from the British Library

Library of Congress Cataloging-in-Publication Data
Names: Garcia, Emilio (Emilio Jose), author. | Vale, Brenda, author.
Title: Unravelling sustainability and resilience in the built environment / Emilio Garcia and Brenda Vale.
Description: New York: Routledge, 2017. | Includes bibliographical references and index.
Identifiers: LCCN 2016036623| ISBN 9781138644021 (hb) | ISBN 9781138644045 (pb) | ISBN 9781315629087 (ebook)
Subjects: LCSH: Urban ecology (Sociology) | Sustainable urban development. | Sustainable architecture. | Resilience (Ecology)
Classification: LCC HT241.G37 2017 | DDC 307.76–dc23
LC record available at https://lccn.loc.gov/2016036623

ISBN: 978-1-138-64402-1 (hbk)
ISBN: 978-1-138-64404-5 (pbk)
ISBN: 978-1-315-62908-7 (ebk)

Typeset in Sabon LT Std
by Out of House Publishing

Contents

Figures and tables   viii

PART 1
Definitions   1

1 Unravelling   3
    1.1 The built environment 4
    1.2 Environmentalism and the built environment 7
    1.3 A resilient built environment 8
    1.4 Institutionalization of definitions: sustainability 8
    1.5 Institutionalization of definitions: resilience 11
    1.6 Unravelling sustainability and resilience 12

2 Defining sustainability   15
    2.1 Living within one's means 15
    2.2 The emergence of modern sustainability 18
    2.3 Sustainability thinking: continuity within limits 19
    2.4 What is to be sustained? 19
    2.5 Development, evolution and sustainability 20
    2.6 Technological development and sustainability 24
    2.7 Sustainability and economics 25
    2.8 Sustainable design 26
    2.9 Happiness: the ultimate goal of sustainability? 26
    2.10 A sustainable society 27

3 Defining resilience   31
    3.1 Why bother with resilience? 31
    3.2 Why architects, urban and landscape designers should care about resilience 32
    3.3 Why bother with the definition of resilience? 32
    3.4 Early definitions 33
    3.5 The consolidation of ecological resilience 36
    3.6 The expansion of ecological resilience: from ecology to social science 41

vi Contents

    3.7 What resilience is not: misunderstandings 46
    3.8 Critics of the concept of resilience 47
    3.9 Conclusions 50

4 Mapping sustainability and resilience   58
    4.1 Introduction 58
    4.2 Similarities 59
    4.3 Differences 61
    4.4 Emergent themes 65

PART 2
Case studies   69

    Introduction   69

5 Eco-cities   71
    5.1 Why eco-cities? 71
    5.2 Whitehill and Bordon, Hampshire: a UK eco-town 77
    5.3 Tianjin Eco-city, China 80
    5.4 Conclusions 88

6 Heritage   94
    6.1 Persistence 94
    6.2 Identity 95
    6.3 Why link heritage and sustainability? 97
    6.4 Why link heritage and resilience? 97
    6.5 The built heritage is more than old buildings 98
    6.6 Braudel and Waisman 99
    6.7 Case study: the inheritance of San Miguel de Tucuman in Argentina 101
    6.8 Humble heritage: the tube houses of Hanoi 110
    6.9 Conclusions 112

7 Compact cities   116
    7.1 Introduction 116
    7.2 Density 117
    7.3 Intensity 120
    7.4 Compactness 120
    7.5 The example of Auckland 127
    7.6 Sustainability and a compact built environment 129
    7.7 Compaction and resilience 132
    7.8 Conclusions 135

    Conclusion to Part 2 136

PART 3
Measuring sustainability and resilience in the built environment 141

    Introduction 141

8 Measuring sustainability 143
    8.1 The issues 143
    8.2 Measuring sustainability with carbon footprint 145
    8.3 Measuring sustainability with the ecological footprint 147
    8.4 Measuring sustainability with indicators 149
    8.5 Measuring the sustainability of the built environment 151
    8.6 Measuring the sustainability of buildings 153
    8.7 Measuring the sustainability of people 154

9 Measuring resilience 159
    9.1 State of the art in the measurement of resilience 159
    9.2 How to build an urban Panarchy 164
    9.3 Assessing the texture of urban landscapes 173
    9.4 Conclusions 178

10 Assessing resilience and sustainability 180
    10.1 Assessing an urban Panarchy in the Auckland CBD 180
    10.2 Assessing relative resilience in urban landscapes using discontinuities and aggregations 189
    10.3 Measuring relative resilience 192
    10.4 Measuring sustainability and resilience together 198
    10.5 Conclusions 199

11 Conclusion 201
    11.1 Confusion in sustainability and resilience 201
    11.2 Sustainability and resilience 202
    11.3 Applying ecological resilience to the built environment 203
    11.4 Why it might be worth applying resilience in built environments 205

Index 208

Figures and tables

Figures

1.1	Buildings, plots, blocks and streets	6
1.2	Plots, blocks and streets and urban texture	7
2.1	Weak and strong sustainability models	16
3.1	Diagram of the adaptive cycle (based on Gunderson and Holling, 2002)	38
3.2	A Panarchy (based on Gunderson and Holling, 2002)	39
5.1	Diagram of current master plan (based on http://whitehillbordon.com/home/the-revised-masterplan/)	79
5.2	Eco-cells and eco-communities (after Government of Singapore, 2012)	82
5.3	Diagram of Tianjin Eco-city master plan (after Government of Singapore, 2012)	84
6.1	Early development of San Miguel de Tucuman	102
6.2	Development of San Miguel de Tucuman	103
6.3	Pattern of development of the city centre and land subdivisions within blocks	104
6.4	Development of the sausage house in Buenos Aires	106
6.5	Development from *inquilinatos* to apartments units in SMdT	107
6.6	Change at different scales	109
7.1	Site coverage and plot ratios	118
7.2	Site coverage and plot ratios	119
7.3	Changes in buildings, plots and streets	121
7.4	Development of large and small blocks over time	122
7.5	Development of compaction in terms of incremental plot subdivisions and an increase in built area	133
8.1	Inputs and outputs	144
8.2	2005 EF of a citizen of Cardiff broken into components (based on Collins *et al.*, 2005)	149
8.3	Weak sustainability model and indicator sets	150
9.1	The burgage and the adaptive cycles	168
9.2	Development of total areas (sum) of building footprints, plots and blocks over time	169
9.3	Development of the total number (*N*) of building footprints, plots and streets over time	169
9.4	The cost–benefits of complexity (after Tainter, 2000)	171
9.5	A hypothetical urban Panarchy	173

Figures and tables ix

9.6	Aggregations and discontinuities in an urban landscape	175
9.7	Example of the use of discontinuities to assess resilience	177
10.1	The case study area in the CBD of Auckland, New Zealand	181
10.2	Timeline post-1840 at the scale of New Zealand	181
10.3	Timeline at the scale of Auckland	184
10.4	Auckland timelines at country, city and CBD scale	186
10.5	Plot of the average change per period and the rate of change per element in the case study area	189
10.6	Visualization of a cluster analysis	191
10.7	Illustration of the aggregations and discontinuities found in the cluster analysis of the elements of the urban landscape	193
10.8	Mapping of clusters in green spaces, streets, blocks and plots	194

Tables

3.1	Walker's framework for the assessment of resilience, based on Walker and Salt (2012)	44
3.2	Properties of general resilience	44
4.1	Comparisons of themes in sustainability and resilience	65
4.2	Strengths and weaknesses of linking sustainability and resilience	66
7.1	Definitions of Auckland, New Zealand	128
8.1	Carbon emissions for electricity generation in New Zealand	146
8.2	Carbon footprint of electricity generation based on 2004–06 global data, adapted from Baldwin (2006)	146
8.3	Comparative ecological footprints	147
9.1	Criteria and assessment used in the Resilience Alliance theoretical framework	161
9.2	Summary of the Stockholm Resilience Centre framework	162
9.3	Key qualities of a resilient city by the 100 Resilient Cities project	162
9.4	The City Resilience Framework (CRF) dimensions, drivers and measurements	163
9.5	Institutions and their frameworks compared with key topics in ecological resilience	164
10.1	Percentage of change in number of elements from 1866 to 2008	187
10.2	Percentage of change in the numbers of elements in the urban landscape	188
10.3	Average annual rate of change in the number of elements in the urban landscape	188
10.4	Measurements for assessing the relative resilience of the Auckland case study	196
10.5	Averages for assessing relative resilience in the Auckland case study	197
10.6	Relative resilience of elements of the urban landscape	197
10.7	Variance in relative resilience of the elements of the urban landscape	197

Part 1
Definitions

1 Unravelling

'Ce que l'on conçoit bien s'énonce clairement.'
['What is well conceived can be said clearly'.]

Boileau (Art poét., I, 53)

We all know if you stretch a rubber band and then let go it will rebound, probably sting you, and return to its original shape. This is what engineers call resilience, the ability of something to be distorted under a force and then return to what it was. So how can a city be resilient? Unlike rubber, bricks and mortar tend to collapse into a heap when force is applied and most built environments are made of these materials, not rubber. Nevertheless, there are league tables of city resilience (100 Resilient Cities, 2015) and these also reveal paradoxes. Top of the list is Toronto and bottom Dhaka. However, in 1998 the ecological footprint (EF) of Toronto was 7.6 gha/person, just below the Canadian average of 7.7 gha/person (Onisto et al., 1998). EF is a tool for measuring how sustainable something is, by assessing the area of land in hectares of average productivity – 'global hectares' or gha – needed to support it. So if you build a house totally of wood its EF would be the land taken to grow all the timber, plus the land needed to 'grow' the energy for the power tools and to make the nails and other fixings, etc. Although the average EF in Canada is now a somewhat lower 6.4 gha/person (WWF, 2012: 144), this is still more than twice the world average EF of 2.7 gha/person, whereas the EF of Bangladesh (Dhaka) is 0.7 gha/person, well below the average EF. More importantly, the EF of Pakistan is below available global capacity, which is all the productive land and which amounts to about 1.8 gha/person (WWF, 2012: 140). Since EF is a measure of sustainability, the message is that you cannot be a sustainable and resilient city at the same time. To be a really resilient city, like Toronto, it seems that, like Toronto, you have to consume many more resources than your fair share of what the planet can supply on a sustained basis. At the same time, the terms sustainable and resilient are often used as if they are interchangeable. This stems from the other view of resilience, which comes from the science of ecology (Holling, 1973). Put simply, the Canadian ecologist C. S. Holling argued that ecosystems adapt to changing circumstances and the availability of resources, and this property of being able to adapt he termed resilience. However, because resilience in this sense is to do with adaptation in the face of changing resources, it sounds like sustainability, which has been focused on how to live well while consuming fewer resources, especially carbon-based fossil fuels. So why is Toronto, which is consuming far more than its fair share of global resources, deemed to be the most resilient city in the world? This is the paradox that the book sets out to unravel. Are sustainability and resilience compatible or incompatible? Are the meaning and use of these two concepts mismatched to the point that they can represent both similar and opposite concepts? Can resilience be applied to the human-made built environment? The objective of this book is to make these concepts plain and free from complications without losing both their complexity and their potential for use.

Despite the wealth of written material and talk about the idea of sustainability, what it means and what needs to be done to achieve it remain elusive. The goal of being more sustainable is virtually a global talking point but the quest to achieve the goal is normally at the expense of a real understanding of what sustainability means. This is reflected in the built environment where a 'sustainable' office building is often no more than a conventional but slightly more energy-efficient office building, which then becomes 'very sustainable' if it has a grass roof. More rarely is the sustainable office designed without car parking, like the Shard in London built on top of a railway station and with only forty-eight car parking spaces for guests in the hotel part of the building, to force office workers to use less resource-intensive public transport. Even more rarely is the whole concept of having an office building to which people come to work questioned. Is this the sustainable way of organizing work? Rather than answering these hard questions, which potentially turn the built environment of the modern developed world with its central CBDs on its head, the quest for sustainability has been replaced with the quest for resilience. Sometimes resilience is confused with sustainability, sometimes the term is used instead of sustainability. As a result designers are supposed to build in resilience but without agreement over what it is. Meanwhile, the world goes on overreaching global biocapacity and we continue to build and rebuild cities in the image of the industrial revolution, when resources seemed limitless. Given that buildings and infrastructure are long-life assets this seems short-sighted at best. It is timely, therefore, to attempt to unravel both sustainability and resilience for designers of the built environment in the hope they can use and understand these concepts to rethink and re-imagine better cities.

This introduction looks forward to the next two chapters where the definitions of first sustainability and then resilience are explored. It explores why definitions are needed and why both sustainability and resilience are important for the built environment. It shows that at present these two concepts are often treated as being interchangeable, whereas our premise is that they are different but related (see Chapter 4).

1.1 The built environment

As the human population grows it becomes increasingly difficult to talk about a 'natural world'. When we say this we usually mean natural habitat for species other than human beings as opposed to an environment, whether rural or urban, constructed by people for people. However, this constructed land also includes uses that seem more natural than man-made, like sheep safely grazing on hillsides. The World Wildlife Fund (WWF) (2015) states that more than half of all habitable land has been converted to farmland, which now forms 38 per cent of the land area of the planet. The term built environment thus could include this human-formed rural land as well as the more obvious cities and towns, where buildings and hard infrastructure for people dominate. In this book we use built environment to mean the latter, the material representation of the urban.

Human experience is built on the human view of the world so by definition it is not possible ever to see or hear untouched nature. Yet everything is 'nature', including people, since human beings have evolved on the planet along with all the other species. From this point of view, 'nature' is the entire physical environment (Benton-Short and Short, 2008). The view of the so-called natural world in this book is the relationship between what people do and create and the effect this has on the one environment from which we all come. This means that the built environment may be dominated by buildings but the resources to make and maintain these will have to come from outside the urban area. It is not possible, for example, to grow enough food for a household in a typical urban private garden; food has to be brought in from agricultural areas. A long time ago the town planner Thomas Sharp (1940: 19) recognized human beings as the creators and adapters of landscapes, noting that civilization, which often implies what comes out of urban areas, means human activities in both rural and urban areas. The writer Jane Jacobs also highlighted the dependency of cities on their rural areas, to the point of implying that rural landscapes were the creation of cities, rather than the other way (Jacobs, 1969). Without agriculture there could not be towns and cities. Without towns and cities there would not have been advances in agriculture. Sharp (1940: 20) goes on to point out that human change to the landscape is fundamentally the result of the economic imperative, or the need to grow food and other resources, such as wood for ship-building, although doing these things can also produce an aesthetic effect, such as the forests and woods which have inspired poets from Byron (1818) to Frost (1923/1969). On occasion, a predominating aesthetic motive produces monumental changes to the landscape for the sake of effect, such as the spectacle of the palace and gardens of Versailles, where squiggly patterns of path and lawn have been superimposed on what was once wood and marsh.

As designers we tend to think that making buildings and urban areas is an aesthetic activity but the definition of a city has been largely linked with density and closeness around a market place (Kostof, 1991). It is the place where people can live when doing things other than agricultural activities (Weber, 1966) and also where power is concentrated and social forces have converged (Mumford, 1961). What designers often forget when composing an urban elevation is the underlying economic motive for what they are doing, since it has been claimed that economic growth depends on urbanization (Spence et al., 2009: 1). Although the poor migrate to the city in search of better prospects and the economic motive of rural migrants coming into the city in search of a better life was acknowledged during the nineteenth century (Carlyle, 1839), it not just the poor who benefit from this. In Britain during Victorian industrialization and urban expansion the gap between rich and poor also grew bigger (Hobsbawm, 1962/1996: 206), something that is still happening in modern developed economies (Yalnizyan, 2000). As the poor get a little richer, the rich tend to get much richer. Because designers only do what clients ask them to, they tend to ignore their contribution to the visible disparity in cities through the contrast created between the large houses of the rich and the smaller and less desirable houses of the poor.

The built environment consists of many systems, such as the economic and class systems (Hobsbawm, 1962/1996: 203) and not just the built fabric and infrastructure. This inclusive view is the definition taken here. Defining what we mean by the built environment is important as globally more people live in urban areas every

6 Definitions

year, in 2014 reaching 54 per cent of the human population (WHO, 2015). However, although planners, architects, urban designers and developers are obviously responsible for what this built environment looks like, in a way we are all designers of the built environment. Pulling up a weed from the garden is an action that has an effect on the local ecosystem, just as laying down a new road with an impervious surface affects the local hydrological cycle because water is no longer absorbed by the soil but drained away to be dealt with somewhere else. This impact is universal and the effect we all have on the ecosystems of the Earth, like the hydrological cycle and the carbon cycle, cannot be ignored wherever we live. It is this impact that both sustainability and resilience thinking aim to influence.

The urban landscape also has a texture, or way in which it is made up, that is important to define to recognize its elements. The texture is given by the interactions between the series of interrelated elements in the town plan, like building footprints, plots, blocks and streets and the building fabric, that represents the three-dimensional form of the urban landscape (Conzen, 1960). At the smallest scale is the building with its footprint (the area of land directly underneath the building). Buildings generally sit on plots, which are the parcels of land that contain a building and any surrounding open space, whether used for a garden or a car park. Plots generally align with ownership, and where multiple owners occupy a single plot, as in the case of a block of private apartments, special legal arrangements have to be put in place over plot ownership. Most plots have street access, streets being another element in the urban texture. Where streets surround land made up of several plots this is called a block, and blocks can be both big or small, depending upon whether streets are large and far apart or narrow and close together (Figures 1.1 and 1.2). A number of blocks together can be assembled into bigger units like a neighbourhood, which is defined by council policies, or by a natural boundary such as a river. Neighbourhoods might have different histories, street patterns and functions. A city contains a series of neighbourhoods, many of which will be residential, while others relate to business (central business district or CBD) or industry.

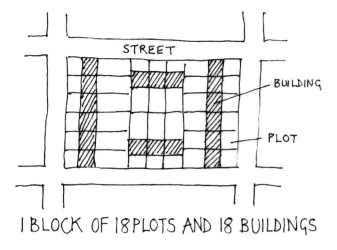

Figure 1.1 Buildings, plots, blocks and streets

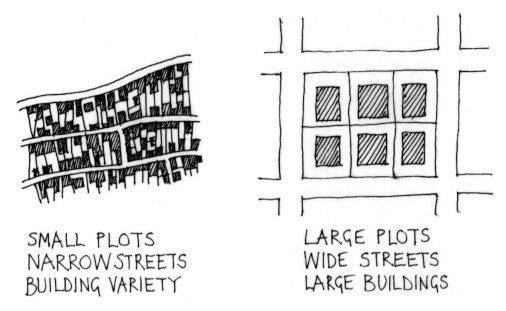

Figure 1.2 Plots, blocks and streets and urban texture

1.2 Environmentalism and the built environment

Rachel Carson's book *Silent Spring* (1962) showed how industrialized society had affected ecosystems. This realization, coupled with the 1970s' energy crisis, gave rise to the not unsurprising idea that how we live depends on the resources available and that maybe we need to be smarter in how we use resources so as not to destroy the systems on which we depend. From this has come the call to create a sustainable built environment. Essentially, this would minimize human effects on ecosystems and also use as few non-renewable resources as possible, and where these had to be used, making sure they lasted as long as possible. This means building with materials that grow, like wood, and designing buildings that are only powered by wind and sun. In the 1970s architecture involved discussion of how using only renewable resources would change the way buildings looked and how they operated. Graham Caine's Eco-house in a corner of a playing field in south London not only looked weird and homemade (which it was) but also involved sharing the conservatory with ducks. For a while it looked as if the nature of architecture would be changed by engaging with alternative sources of energy but this was short-lived. What we now have are buildings that are constructed and function in a more or less conventional way, whether labelled sustainable, green, zero energy or even energyplus because they generate more energy than they consume, though these latter are few and far between. There are attempts at green or sustainable urban design, for example, Tianjin Eco-city in China and Freiburg solar city in Germany, and these look comfortingly familiar but with a few more solar panels attached. There is no agreement as to what a sustainable built environment really means, not just for the building fabric but for other urban systems, such as the economic system. Another issue is how the design of a built environment enables or discourages a sustainable urban way of living. Putting more people in apartments in the CBD to reduce the impact of commuting may not be more sustainable if the same people drive long distances at the weekends to get out of the city for recreation. At the same time, the lifestyle of urban people in developing economies could be described as more or less sustainable in terms of a low environmental impact, even if it might not appear desirable to Western eyes. The issue in the developing world is one of raising living standards without increasing this low environmental impact, whereas the developed world wants to hang on to an ever-rising standard of living and concurrently reduce environmental impact significantly. The problem for sustainability is to sort out whether you can have a sustainable product, like a building or city, without also having sustainable people to use and live in it.

1.3 A resilient built environment

Not only is the global urban population expanding but by 2050 more than half of the world's human population will be living in coastal territories where cities will be more exposed to natural hazards and more dependent on their capacities to adapt to these. Consequently, coastal cities have become habitats where the significant social and economic capital invested is at risk. With fourteen of the seventeen largest cities in the world being coastal (eleven are in Asia) this risk is significant (Tibbetts, 2002). This along with tsunamis, earthquakes and volcanic eruptions that have caused and continue to cause the destruction of cities are the reasons why designers are starting to care about resilience. The aim is to find ways of making new built environments or remaking the existing, so if and when such crises occur, life can resume with minimal disruption. However, this is where the rubber band and ecosystem definitions of resilience come into conflict. It is not enough just to design for bouncing back after natural disasters, which is the rubber band or engineering approach. Ordinary 'crises', such as economic crashes, social inequalities, rapid growth of city peripheries, loss of urban identity with globalization or unreasonable densification of an urban area, are seldom or never considered when resilience is attached to design. Nevertheless, these ordinary crises affect the resilience capacity of the built environment because they are linked with everyday life, which is the scale of focus for any designer. The implications and opportunities that emerge from a better understanding of resilience need to be grasped if designers are going to build resilience into the urban fabric.

1.4 Institutionalization of definitions: sustainability

These dual interests of sustainability and resilience have, to an extent, already become institutionalized, though the definitions adopted by institutions do not always seem to be about the same thing, as will be discussed further in Chapters 2 and 3. By definitions we mean that what the terms mean can be determined by what the related institutions do and publish. For example, the Global Footprint Network (GFN), established in 2003, aims for a sustainable future where all human beings can have a 'satisfying' life within the limits of the Earth's resources (GFN, 2014). Their use of the ecological footprint as a measure of this human impact has caused debate over exactly how immeasurables, such as the amount of land given to tigers, aardvarks and any other creature that is not *homo sapiens*, should be calculated (Lenzen and Murray, 2001; Harbel *et al.*, 2005). The definition of sustainability from this institution thus emphasizes what can be measured. This is helpful in terms of knowing the impact of humanity on resource use but does not offer guidance on how that resource use could be reduced, or how policies might be devised for this to happen. It is like being given a target and a quiver of arrows (my personal will to change) but no bow. I can see the need to get the arrow into the target but cannot throw it there by myself. This leads to another set of institutionalized definitions of sustainability which underpin political institutions such as Agenda 21 and the Kyoto Protocol. These are about making some sort of bow so as to be able to get the arrows into the target.

Agenda 21, which came out of the 1992 Earth Summit conference and which is both voluntary and non-binding, is a plan for implementing sustainable development at the level of local, national and global government (UN, 1992). Its definition of sustainability is for industrialized societies to be more efficient to reduce resource use and environmental pollution and thus reduce poverty by freeing the resources to allow for at least a basic standard of living for all people. These are fine words but unlike the EF, they do not offer a clear and measurable goal. This is also an optimistic definition of sustainability which relies on the myths of technological efficiency and trickle-down economics (see Chapter 2) and ignores the ever-widening gap between rich and poor, which, as mentioned above, has been with us since the onset of industrialization. It also suggests that sustainability is going to be difficult to achieve but not uncomfortable, unlike GFN which suggests that living within the planet's resources is going to be very difficult to achieve and will mean living very different lives from those in modern developed societies. Although strictly more concerned with climate change mitigation through greenhouse gas reduction than general sustainability, the Kyoto Protocol is also predicated on industrialized societies being efficient in how energy is used rather than on a dramatic reconstruction of human society. Its Clean Development Protocol has two strands: the first is to aid the sustainable development of poorer societies and the second to help developed societies achieve their greenhouse gas reduction targets (UNFCC, 2010), in anticipation that sustainability will somehow be achieved when these two ideas merge. So although now equipped with the bow of efficiency and the arrows of will, I am not sure what I am shooting at. How efficient do I need to be to reach the target? Will swapping incandescent bulbs for LEDs be sufficient or should I build an autonomous house and collect my own rainwater off the roof? The target is somewhat veiled in the mist.

Another important set of institutions with their own definition of sustainability, especially when it comes to the built environment, are the various building accreditation schemes. These include LEED (Leadership in Energy and Environmental Design), BREEAM (Building Research Establishment Environmental Assessment Method), CASBEE (Comprehensive Assessment System for Built Environment Efficiency) and the more recent LBC (Living Building Challenge). For most designers engaging with these institutions and their various schemes the risk is falling asleep before even shooting the arrow. They are just not very exciting. LEED opens by stating that it represents '… a mark of quality and achievement in green building' (US Green Building Council, 2015). It goes on to state that its aim is to encourage 'energy and resource efficient buildings', but couples this with noting that it is also concerned with 'savings from increased building value, higher lease rates and decreased utility costs'. This is a different definition of sustainability, where you are directly rewarded for your efforts rather than undertaking the making of an energy and resource efficient building because this is what is needed to decarbonize society and avoid global warming and sea-level rise. Here for every arrow you lose you are rewarded, either by getting more money when you let your building or by saving money in running it. What you do with this additional money is never stated. Will you give it to those that have less or will you spend it on something, like a cruise or a big car that will add to your own personal impact? LEED is also predicated on a checklist approach, suggesting that if you achieve the listed targets then your building will be more sustainable. This ignores the need to think holistically and the need to think about changing the way we do things – changing our whole social system – not just the things we make. However, the key issue with rating systems is that they are themselves a product that is sold. The UK-developed BREEAM can thus claim to be the '… world's leading design and assessment method for sustainable buildings' (BRE, 2015) because it is in competition with other systems that have different checklists and differently weighted scoring systems for the awards they give. There is no comparability between these rating system products and therefore no agreement about what makes a sustainable building. This suggests that maybe no-one knows what a sustainable building is. CASBEE, a product of Japanese thinking, describes its building rating system as a measure to promote sustainability (good) (Japan GreenBuild Council (JaGBC)/Japan Sustainable Building Consortium (JSBC), nd(a)) and in its later developments considers the building and its site as a whole, so the assessment deals with the effects of this building both within and beyond the boundary. This sounds more holistic until we note they say: 'the space beyond is public (non-private) space, which is largely beyond control' (Japan GreenBuild Council (JaGBC)/Japan Sustainable Building Consortium (JSBC), n.d.(b)). Both BREEAM and LEED now offer larger neighbourhood-based rating systems but most of the focus has been and remains on the single building. NABERS (National Australian Built Environment Rating System) (NSW Office of Environment and Heritage, n.d.) was the first system to rate buildings in use rather than in terms of design, but both BREEAM and CASBEE now also do this, thus acknowledging the big difference between design intentions and what happens when the built environment is built and used. LBC is a relative newcomer and aims at buildings that contribute to ecosystem regeneration, not just buildings that are more efficient in their non-renewable resource use, although it is unclear how this contribution to regeneration is measured. It also rates buildings in use (International Living Future Institute, 2014). However, the sting is that all these rating systems charge for assessment leading to certification. They are additional products in economies that are already using resources beyond their means. Additionally, these rating systems fail to make the sustainable building process more understandable for the majority of society, since, as noted, there is no agreement between rating systems as to what makes a sustainable building. Unlike the vernacular building tradition that was both more sustainable and open to everybody, these certifications tend to create a complicated language that can only be shared between those privileged to understand the rating system.

All these rating systems are also competing for money in the market and are effectively selling sustainability to the well off. The benefit for the buyer is a building that can be advertised as being more environmentally friendly, which in turns gives them an edge in a competitive market, whether competing for rent dollars, students or home buyers. The underlying definition of sustainability is that developed world life with its market economics is recognizable if a shade greener. There now seem to be various targets and there is a charge for shooting arrows.

1.5 Institutionalization of definitions: resilience

Although resilience is a younger and perhaps less developed concept than sustainability, its definition has also been institutionalized, partly because the institutions have been driving its study and setting out its themes. Consequently, their publications affect present and future research and our current understanding of resilience. Additionally, many of the members of these institutions are the most published authors in the resilience field (Janssen et al., 2006). This is neither a negative or positive situation as what happens will depend on the people and intentions behind the particular organization. What is of interest here is to highlight the contributions of some of the most popular institutions to an understanding of resilience.

Since Holling's original work in proposing that ecosystems exhibit resilience (1973) he has attracted fellow scholars including Gunderson, Folke, Walker, Carpenter and Allen, who are now clustered in the organization named Resilience Alliance (2015). Formed in 1999, this organization has a focus on ecology and has been diffusing knowledge about resilience and collecting and comparing case studies. It has also tried to develop around Holling's original definition a theoretical framework that is intended for practitioners and scientists inside and outside ecology. Through the journal *Ecology and Society*, the Resilience Alliance has openly diffused knowledge about resilience by integrating work from scholars, mainly from ecology, environmental sciences and biology, supplemented by a little from social sciences. Urban designers and architects are so far absent, which is unfortunate considering the impact and importance that built environments have for the planet.

Created by the Swedish government in 2006, the Stockholm Resilience Centre has strong connections with the Resilience Alliance. Some Stockholm Resilience Centre members are on the board of the Resilience Alliance and serve as editors of *Ecology and Society*. The Stockholm Resilience Centre has a broader approach to resilience research focused on 'the understanding of complex social-ecological systems', and thus deals with ecosystems that involve people. This concept has been developed by Resilience Alliance member Carl Folke, illustrating the close connections between these two organizations. The Stockholm Resilience Centre has a preoccupation with urban issues, and one of its main themes relates to 'urban social-ecological systems'. Despite this, there is not one architect, landscape architect or urban designer in the whole team. The Stockholm Resilience Centre (2014) defines resilience as 'the capacity of a system, be it an individual, a forest, a city or an economy, to deal with change and continue to develop. It is about the capacity to use shocks and disturbances like a financial crisis or climate change to spur renewal and innovative thinking'. This definition of resilience recognizes that bad things can be turned to good providing the system has the capacity to cope and adapt. I discover that my seventy-year-old roof tiles are becoming porous and are letting in the rain (a bad thing). Luckily I have enough savings (a financial buffer) to pay for re-roofing. However, because the ceilings follow the line of the roof rather than being flat, re-roofing gives me the opportunity to insulate the roof (a good thing) from outside, without having to suffer the mess inside of ripping down the ceilings. Basically I can turn something negative into something positive. This has echoes in Chinese where the word 'crisis' is formed from the characters that represent danger and opportunity. In the Stockholm Resilience Centre online book *What is Resilience?* other definitions of resilience appear, including '…

the long-term capacity of a system to deal with change and continue to develop' (Stockholm Resilience Centre, 2014: 6). Assuming that development is something positive (see chapter 2), the only issue with this definition is to know what *capacity* and *development* mean in this sentence. This suggests that to understand this definition of resilience you have to know a lot about the topic in order to understand the definition.

The Rockefeller Foundation is another institution with an increasing presence on the resilience map. Since Judith Rodin, the author of *The Resilience Dividend* (2014), became its president in 2005, the Foundation has focused on four subjects: ecosystems, cities, security and health. The vision is to build resilience in these and the objective is 'to be prepared for, withstand, and emerge stronger from shocks and chronic stresses' (The Rockefeller Foundation, 2015). The project 100 Resilient Cities (2015) has 100 million dollars to build resilience into the cities across the globe. The website defines the resilience of cities 'in terms of numerous factors that influence their ability (cities) to continue to function in the face of challenging circumstances, to recover quickly from disruptions, and the relationship between these factors' (in other words, 'to keep on going').

None of these institutions rely on the participation of urban designers and architects, which seems an oversight given the emphasis on the link between social and ecological systems. Is the lack of involvement of built environment professionals because the institutions think we have nothing to offer because we are not interested or just that we fail to understand what these clever ecologists are talking about? Is it because ecologists and resource managers assume the built environment is as passive as an inert rock? In answer, this book is attempting to be the first architectural toe dipped into the cold water of resilience.

The progressive institutionalization of resilience could mark the intellectual end to research into its nature and definition, which would be a pity if those responsible for designing the built environment fail to make a contribution. Resilience so far seems to have become a good cause that encapsulates a desire for survival, and in the last few years there has been a shift from talking about understanding what resilience is to talking about building resilience. This is a particular problem for designers because governments are starting to demand resilience in the built environment even though nobody knows what has to be built or if it is even possible to do it.

1.6 Unravelling sustainability and resilience

Because of the lack of a consistent definition of the terms sustainability and resilience the next two chapters will explore how these terms came into being and how the meanings of both have changed. The subsequent chapter will then map the similarities and differences between the two terms to see how they are related. The first case study chapter examines eco-cities and whether and how these fit with the definitions of sustainability and resilience developed here. The second case study looks at heritage and how the idea of preserving the built environment might fit both with sustainability and resilience. The third case study examines urban compaction and whether this is a move that will enhance both sustainability and resilience. The final part of the book deals with how we might be able to measure sustainability and resilience in the built environment. The hope is to offer a way in which designers could assess the impact of their latest castle in the air before it becomes a castle on the ground.

Bibliography

100 Resilient Cities. (2015). *Helping cities around the world become more resilient to the physical, social and economic challenges that are a growing part of the 21st century*, available at www.100resilientcities.org/#/-_/, accessed 21 April 2015.

Benton-Short, L. and Short, J. (2008). *Cities and Nature*. London and New York: Routledge.

BRE (Building Research Establishment) (2015). *BREEAM*, available at www.breeam.org/, accessed 5 April 2015.

Byron, Lord G. (1818). Childe Harold's Pilgrimage, Stanza XXV, available at www.gutenberg.org/files/5131/5131-h/5131-h.htm, accessed 7 April 2015.

Carlyle, T. (1839). Chartism. Reprinted in *Thomas Carlyle, Selected Essays*. London: Dent.

Carson, R. (1962). *Silent Spring*. Boston, MA: Houghton Mifflin.

Conzen, M. R. G. (1960). Alnwick, Northumberland: a study in town-plan analysis. *Transactions and Papers (Institute of British Geographers)* 27, pp. iii–122.

Frost, R. (1923/1969). Stopping by woods on a snowy evening. In E. C. Latham (ed.), *The Poetry of Robert Frost*. New York: Henry Holt and Co. Inc.

Global Footprint Network (GFN). (2014). *At a Glance*, available at www.footprintnetwork.org/en/index.php/GFN/page/at_a_glance/, accessed March 2015.

Harbel, H., Pltzar, C., Erb, K.–H., Gaube, V., Pollheimer, M. and Schulz, N. B. (2005). Human appropriation of net primary production as a determinant of avifauna diversity in Austria. *Agriculture, Ecosystems and Environment* 110, pp. 119–131.

Hobsbawm, E. (1962/1996). *The Age of Revolution 1789–1848*. New York: Vintage Books.

Holling, C. S. (1973). Resilience and stability of ecological systems. *Annual Review of Ecology and Systematics* 4(1), pp. 1–23.

International Living Future Institute. (2014). *Living Building Challenge 3.0*, available at https://living-future.org/sites/default/files/reports/FINAL%20LBC%203_0_WebOptimized_low.pdf, accessed 7 April 2015.

Jacobs, J. (1969). *The Economy of Cities*. New York: Random House.

Janssen, M., Schoon, M., Ke, W. and Börner, K. (2006). Scholarly networks on resilience, vulnerability and adaptation within the human dimensions of global environmental change. *Global Environmental Change* 16(3), pp. 240–252.

Japan GreenBuild Council (JaGBC)/Japan Sustainable Building Consortium (JSBC). (n.d.(a)). *CASBEE: Comprehensive Assessment System for Built Environment Efficiency*, available at www.ibec.or.jp/CASBEE/english/overviewE.htm, accessed 7 April 2015.

Japan GreenBuild Council (JaGBC)/Japan Sustainable Building Consortium (JSBC). (n.d.(b)). *CASBEE: Comprehensive Assessment System for Built Environment Efficiency*, available at www.ibec.or.jp/CASBEE/english/backgroundE.htm, accessed 7 April 2015.

Kostof, S. (1991). *The City Shaped: Urban Patterns and Meanings through History* (1st North American edn). Boston, MA: Little, Brown and Co.

Lenzen, M. and Murray, S. A. (2001). A modified ecological footprint method and its application to Australia. *Ecological Economics* 37, pp. 229–255.

Mumford, L. (1961). *The City in History: Its Origins, Its Transformations, and Its Prospects* (1st edn). New York: Harcourt.

NSW (New South Wales) Office of Environment and Heritage. (n.d.). *NABERS*, available at www.nabers.gov.au/public/WebPages/Home.aspx, accessed 7 April 2015.

Onisto, L. J., Krause, E. and Wackernagel, M. (1998). *How Big is Toronto's Ecological Footprint?*, available at http://portalsostenibilitat.upc.edu/archivos/fichas/informes/huellaecol% F3gicadetoronto.pdf, accessed 18 May 2015.

Resilience Alliance. (2015). *Resilience Alliance*, available at www.resalliance.org/, accessed 21 April 2015.

Rockefeller Foundation. (2015). *Resilience*, available at www.rockefellerfoundation.org/our-work/topics/resilience/, accessed 21 April 2015.

Rodin J. (2014). *The Resilience Dividend*. New York: The Rockefeller Foundation.
Sharp, T. (1940). *Town Planning*. Harmondsworth: Penguin Books.
Spence, A., Annez, P. C. and Buckley, R. M. (eds) (2009). *Urbanization and Growth*. Washington, DC: The International Bank for Reconstruction and Development/Commission on Growth and Development.
Stockholm Resilience Centre. (2014). What is Resilience?, available at www.stockholmresilience.org/download/18.10119fc11455d3c557d6d21/1398172490555/SU_SRC_whatisresilience_sidaApril2014.pdf, accessed 25 February 2015.
Tibbetts, J. (2002). Coastal cities: living on the edge. *Environmental Health Perspectives* 110(11), pp. 674–681.
UN (United Nations). (1992). *Agenda 21: the United Nations programme of action from Rio*. United Nations.
UNFCC (United Nations Framework Convention on Climate Change). (2010). The Kyoto Protocol Mechanisms, available at https://cdm.unfccc.int/about/cdm_kpm.pdf, accessed 5 April 2015.
US Green Building Council. (2015). This is LEED, available at http://leed.usgbc.org/leed.html, accessed 7 April 2015.
Weber, M. (1966). *The City*. New York: Free Press.
World Health Organisation (WHO). (2015). Urban Population Growth, available at www.who.int/gho/urban_health/situation_trends/urban_population_growth_text/en/, accessed 10 March 2015.
World Wildlife Fund (WWF). (2012). Living Planet Report 2012, available at http://awsassets.wwf.ca/downloads/lpr_2012_1.pdf, accessed 11 May 2015.
World Wildlife Fund (WWF). (2015). Farming: habitat conversion and loss, available at http://wwf.panda.org/what_we_do/footprint/agriculture/impacts/habitat_loss/, accessed 10 March 2015.
Yalnizyan, A. (2000). *Canada's Great Divide: The Politics of the Growing Gap between Rich and Poor in the 1990s*. Toronto: Centre for Social Justice.

2 Defining sustainability

'Do all your work as though you had a thousand years to live; and as you would if you knew you must die tomorrow.'

Shaker proverb

Like many ideas the meaning of sustainability has changed with time. Different meanings also exist concurrently, such as the ideas of weak and strong sustainability (Figure 2.1) (see also Chapter 8). Here sustainability is pictured as three circles denoting society, the economy and the environment. In the overlapping or weak model sustainability only occurs where each is given equal importance at the overlap in the centre. In contrast, the strong model assumes that everything depends on the environment, so society and its economy have to be contained with this.

The purpose of this chapter is to explore the different meanings of sustainability and evolve a definition for this book that will then be compared with a definition of resilience that will be developed in a similar manner. The chapter begins by considering what sustainability means and how and when the concept emerged. It continues by considering how sustainability has been used and is being used more recently, and ends with considering what a sustainable society might be.

This approach is necessary because sustainability has come to mean different things to different people. It has also become an adjective applied to modern products, an example being the new Scotch-Brite cleaner from 3M which is made of 100 per cent agave fibre, which it is claimed is mostly a waste product once the agave juice has been extracted for making tequila (Sustainable Life Media, 2013). Agave fibre is, however, a valuable product in rural areas of Mexico for making into ropes for local binding of building structures and cords for mats and bags but cannot be produced on a commercial scale (Rios, 2015). Thus a situation where the agave was harvested for local use and all parts were used (a sustainable situation) has in the commercial manufacture of tequila resulted in a 'waste' product because of the increased scale of manufacture and the non-cost-effective uses for the waste. However, when a new use is found for this, the result is a 'sustainable product', which can attract a premium price in the market because of this, emerging from what might be described as an unsustainable situation. This phenomenon makes any attempt to define sustainability difficult.

2.1 Living within one's means

Historically, humanity has had an intrinsic understanding of what sustainability is – living within the means to hand. The more recent investigation of sustainability has

16 *Definitions*

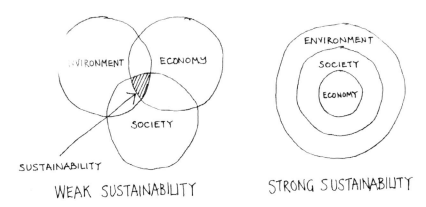

Figure 2.1 Weak and strong sustainability models

come about because those means, rather than being visible and tangible resources like land, seeds, timber, animals, have become replaced by purchasing resources, such as energy and food, with money or, strictly speaking, capital.[1] Thus work, once the hours needed for the direct transformation of local resources into the means to support life, has with industrialization become a system of swapping hours of work for money, which becomes the means to purchase the resources needed. Living within means today means living within an earned income, or as Mr Micawber in *David Copperfield* by Dickens (1850: 117) memorably stated: 'Annual income twenty pounds, annual expenditure nineteen [pounds] nineteen [shillings] and six [pence], result happiness. Annual income twenty pounds, annual expenditure twenty pounds [n]ought and six, result misery.' Ignoring for the moment the link between living within one's means and happiness (the latter is discussed later), the problem with earned money as a measure is that it is at a considerable remove from tangible resources. When we buy a pair of jeans, for instance, we have no idea this represents on average the purchase of nearly 11,000 litres of water (Chapagain *et al.*, 2006). Husbanding tangible resources leads to a different set of behaviours compared with reliance on monetary means. The traditional subsistence farmer was (and is) aware of the need to care for the land and not over-crop in order to maintain soil fertility, not just for the next year, but for all years to come. Similarly, some harvest would have to be saved as seeds to be sown to provide the next harvest. Before the industrialization of agriculture this led to methods like crop rotation for natural control of pests and for nitrogen-fixing crops for fertility, and also to growing green manures and leaving land fallow to improve the latter. To modern eyes, some of these practices would seem to be inefficient through not maximizing the transformation of resources and hence profit at any one time. When it comes to money, however, the disassociation from resources means consumers will not be aware of what they are buying. If you cannot buy jeans with cotton coming from USA (5,967m^3 of water consumed per ton of cotton), you could have cotton from Egypt (10,787m^3/ton) (Chapagain *et al.*, 2006) without realizing you have almost doubled your consumption of virtual water, that is if you are even aware of where the cotton comes from when you buy your jeans or have given thought to how sustainable the agricultural processes are that produced this cotton.

This traditional view of one aspect of sustainability, setting up a system of human living that can be sustained, leads to one possible definition, which is that any system that yields a product needs to be set up in such a way that the production can be maintained long term, not just short term. This is what the famous definition of sustainability in the Brundtland Report (World Commission on Environment and Development, 1987: 43) was hinting at: 'Sustainable development is development that meets the needs of the present without compromising the ability of future generations to meet their own needs.' Again, leaving aside the idea of development, which will also be explored later in this chapter, the Brundtland definition contains the idea that a human system has to be able to be sustained over a long time, indeed for generations, although without explaining how this might be achieved in current industrialized human society. The traditional subsistence farmer would, however, understand this implicitly. With urbanization the link between the products of agriculture, which are needed in the cities, and the processes by which these products are created becomes broken. The essence of sustainability, therefore, may be more obvious in rural than in urban societies.

Husbanding tangible resources also leads to another set of short-term behaviours. As Mr Micawber hinted, over a year there is a need to live within one's personal resources. The year is a key idea here, since in many traditional rural societies the year was the timeframe for producing through growing the food resources that would sustain a way of living. Many traditions celebrate harvest as a time of plenty but then stored resources have to be husbanded by the keeper of the household to make sure that they last through the coming year, with sufficient not just for the household but for guests (number unknown), and with some put by against a bad harvest the following year. This was a difficult balancing act, since the aim was to maintain the flow of resources within two systems – the natural world and a fluctuating household – that were both inevitably different from one year to the next.

> Traditionally, the world over, the woman in a house has been known as the 'keeper of the keys.' To hold the keys to the household, to its storerooms, attics, chests and cupboards, was a position of great responsibility…In a season of impoverishment it was the woman's wise allocation of limited supplies that would see the family through, and in times of plenty, it was her foresight that provided for future needs.
>
> (Robertson *et al.*, 1976/1981: 51)

This image is a long way from modern urbanized Western habits, where supermarkets source the globe in order to stock the same product whether it is locally in season or not. For the consumer the only hint that food might have been grown outside rather than in heated glasshouses (tomatoes, cucumbers) is that the outdoor crops will be cheaper when 'in season'. Effectively, the keys have been handed over by the housekeeper to the corporation behind the supermarket whose aim is to make a profit. Balancing the household resources now depends on budgeting to stay within income. If you can afford it, you buy it, without thought to where the foodstuffs have come from or how they were grown. Effectively, sustainability in terms of the responsibilities of creating a system that can be maintained have been handed over from the individual household to the big corporations. Whereas in the past the limits of the system were clear to those who used its products, now few people are even aware that there might be limits.

18 Definitions

Other common human requirements, such as clothing and buildings, were also produced on a sustainable basis in the past, although the timeframes of their production systems were much longer than the annual food cycle. As an example, the vernacular architecture in the village of Kampung Naga in Java, Indonesia, where life has not changes for centuries (Pamungkas, 2013: 215–223), has simple rectangular thatched houses made of local materials (wood, bamboo, rattan and palm). The woven walls are made by the women and replaced approximately every twenty years. There is, however, no 'waste' in this process since the natural materials of the old walls will biodegrade, returning their substance to the local ecosystem. It is these traditions that produce the wide variety within vernacular architecture (and also within clothing), something that has largely been lost in modern urbanized societies. Differences in modern urban environments are now related to changes in fashion rather than cultural differences emanating from the available local resources.

2.2 The emergence of modern sustainability

Having described sustainability as something, like death and taxes, that has always been with us, it is necessary to trace the modern interest in this concept. Bosselmann (2008: 18–19) dates the emergence of the term 'sustainability' to von Carlowitz's book of 1714 *Sylvicultura oeconomica*, which talked about how to grow timber for a continuing and sustained (*nachhaltend*) use. Von Carlowitz argued that all human endeavour depended on nature and nature's systems and for the need to work with nature rather than seeing it as a repository of resources to be exploited and even wasted in the name of progress. The full term *Nachhaltigkeitsprinzip* is credited to eighteenth-century German forestry (Wiersum, 1995). This translates as lastingness or persistence (*Nachhaltigkeit*) principle (*prinzip*), although more recently it is translated as sustainability. In 1804, Hartig, lecturing on forestry, defined *Nachhaltigkeit* in terms of forest management: 'Every wise forest director has to have evaluated the forest stands to utilize them to the greatest possible extent, but still in a way that future generations will have at least as much benefit as the living generation' (Reynolds *et al.*, 2007: 185). This thought for the future is admirably illustrated by the story of New College, Oxford who needed new sizeable oak beams to replace the beetle-infested ones in the hall ceiling. In the search for these the College Forester was contacted and was reported to have said he wondered when someone would be asking about the mature oaks. The trees had been planted at the time the hall roof was first built as a future replacement, with each succeeding forester being told not to cut them until needed (Brand, 1994: 131–132). Sustainability is here equated with forward-thinking and the good management of resources.

What is of particular use for defining sustainability in Hartig's (1804) definition is the concept of persistence. The production of the forest was to be such that the profits from growing and selling the timber would not benefit just one generation but that the same level of profits should be available for each generation in turn. This is different from the clear felling in a country like New Zealand, where land was cleared for growing crops, first by the Maori to grow kumara (sweet potato) (Buck, 1952: 89) and later and to a much greater extent by mid-nineteenth-century European settlers (Crosby, 1986: 263). Using Hartig's definition the current use of fossil fuels such as oil and coal to the point of exhaustion of some supplies is not in accordance with *Nachhaltigkeit* or sustainability. This also implies that any social system that depends on resources like fossil fuels that are not being used at a rate that makes them available for future generations can never be sustainable. Thus the idea of somehow making modern industrialized societies 'sustainable' without fundamental change to the way they are organized is, by definition, impossible. The sustainable organization of a society implies addressing its economic systems (modern capitalism in the developed world) and social behaviour (consumerism).

2.3 Sustainability thinking: continuity within limits

Obviously things have to change if there is really going to be an attempt to live within the regeneration capacities of the Earth's systems. To be sustainable, not only do these unpalatable limits have to be calculated and agreed, they also have to become the fundamental givens of change towards sustainability.

The fact there might be limits is hard to admit. However, the idea that technological advances will make life more sustainable without the need to rethink the current economic systems or change our social behaviour is problematic for Hartig's definition of sustainability. A clear example of that idiosyncrasy can be found in the economic success of all sorts of mechanical and electronic 'sustainable' devices to the detriment of a better management and sensitive consumption of natural resources. The diversity and volume of 'sustainable' products for consumer purchase has increased substantially in recent decades (Vadicheria and Saravanan, 2015: 109–135), however, CO_2 emissions continue to increase every year (Raupach *et al.*, 2007; IPCC, 2013). The results are obvious but still neglected: technological gadgets to save energy, such as better insulated refrigerators with improved compressor technology, have increased and have diversified but modern life has become more complicated, unequal and expensive, so people in the developed world not only have a refrigerator in the kitchen, but may also have a wine refrigerator and one for fishing bait out in the garage. The effect of having more appliances cancels out any gain from their being more efficient.[2] What Hartig's definition unravels is that sustainable thinking is not simply about persisting but about the persistence of a principle, or way of thinking, that can benefit an entire generation and this provides continuity. However, to think in this way, behaviour has to be holistically considered by each individual so that each acts in order to reduce their impact on the environment.

2.4 What is to be sustained?

The definition of what has to be sustained seems to be crucial, particularly when modern life has not produced the promised 'trickle down' economics that have been shown to be a myth (Arndt, 1983). In fact, the gap between rich and poor has increased (Vale and Vale, 2009: 22). So what lifestyle is to be sustained? Again, this has been widely discussed and there seems to be some agreement in that ecosystems and their services should be sustained (or persist) and that development implies moving to a more equitable society where every human has access to resources to meet their needs and potential. However, these basic needs must be specified and quantified in order to redefine sustainability in the present. In addition, Böhringer and Jochem (2006) observed that the measures of sustainability that are being used to guide policy and assess progress towards sustainability, such as Ecological Footprint (Global Footprint Network, 2015), Human Development Index (UNDP, n.d.) and Genuine

20 *Definitions*

Savings Indicator (Hamilton, 2000), have been independently developed based on the data available with no consistent application of weightings within the various indicators. Inevitably, this means each locality is measuring progress to sustainability of its existing lifestyle, without considering whether in fact, taking a global perspective, radical change to at least some lifestyles, especially those of the developing world, is required to approach sustainability for all. This leads on to a discussion of human development and what goals for this should be in the move to living sustainably on the planet.

2.5 Development, evolution and sustainability

The concept of evolution needs discussing here, as generally evolution tends to be aligned with the idea of making progress and is seen as something positive, whereas in biology it means something different. The biological definition of evolution is posited on the idea that somewhere in a population a gene has changed, the individual has been selected and the population has evolved to something different. In biology this is usually a very slow process. This is different from observing that people are larger now than in Victorian times. This has nothing to do with evolution and everything to do with better diets and better medicine and has happened relatively quickly. Genetically, we are the same people as the Victorians. Evolution is also a very long-term process whereas development normally implies short-term goals; for example, you might 'develop' new building regulations to reduce energy use by going through a process of drafting and commentary until agreement is reached, which might take several years, but you do not evolve building regulations over centuries.

In ecology, the difference between development and evolution is clearer, although there is still not total agreement about how and why some of the processes occur. An ecosystem undergoes change in the form and distribution of its population and resources; therefore it goes through ecological succession. Odum (1997) explained that ecological succession can be understood as the development of a community, meaning the population of individuals of any species living in the same area, in the 'short term' of around 1,000 years. Golley (1993) suggests that because ecosystems do not have genetic structures, it is not possible talk about their evolution. Only changes that spread over geological times (millions of years) fall under the category of organic evolution, referring to changes in organisms with time (Odum, 1997) toward more complex and better adapted forms. This is what Darwin (1859/2009) explained through his process of natural selection, where the influence of environmental factors and the competition between organisms are major drivers of change.

Progress

The problem comes as in many minds as 'development' and 'evolution' are both linked with progress, or the idea that things are better than they were before. Thus progress for Hoover in his 1928 US presidential campaign slogan was a 'chicken in every pot and a car in every garage', whereas in modern urban New Zealand it might be 'an overseas holiday every year and two cars outside every house'. However, taking the *Nachhaltigkeit* view of sustainability, the current situation in the developed world is worse than it was 200 years ago since this lifestyle cannot be sustained into the future, so in these terms we have not progressed, even though individually we have more stuff. What is clear is that there has been change but to have an idea of whether or not there has been progress we need to measure what that change has meant. The following quote from George Eliot, written at the height of Victorian industrialization, links these ideas together in a useful way:

> Is all change in the direction of progress? If not, how shall we discern which change is progress and which is not? and thirdly, how far and in what ways can we act upon the course of change so as to promote it where it is beneficial, and divert it where it is injurious?... Change and progress are merged in the idea of development. The laws of development are being discovered, and changes taking place according to them are necessarily progressive; that is to say, if we have any notion of progress or improvement opposed to them, the notion is a mistake... I really can't see how you arrive at that sort of certitude about changes by calling them development... There will still remain the degrees of inevitableness in relation to our own will and acts, and the degrees of wisdom in hastening or retarding; there will still remain the danger of mistaking a tendency which should be resisted for an inevitable law that we must adjust ourselves to ...
>
> (Eliot, 1876/1967: 584–585)

Or in the words of Gomez Davila (2005): 'Doubt in progress is the only progress'. Eliot's idea of questioning what human tendencies should be resisted is not new. Bacon, in his utopian writing of 1627, proposed that scientists should vet their inventions carefully before 'giving' them to human society (Bacon, 1627). This is a long way from the ideas behind the free market where the 'fittest' products will survive and those that do not make the grade will sink without trace. Unfortunately, this does little to suppress items that might have little benefit for long-term human society but that provide distraction in the form of a 'craze' for a short time, as exemplified by the hula hoop toy in the late 1950s which sold some 25 million in a few months from its launch (Townsend, 2011). However, leaving progress to the market means that progress becomes associated with the new and with innovation, not just with abstract qualities like having an equitable society or reducing loneliness. This in turn may have influenced assessment of the sustainable built environment, as in two of the widely used systems, LEED and BREEAM (see Chapter 1), points are gained for innovation but without discussion of how or why innovation might be important for reducing the impact of the built environment on the natural environment. Indeed, traditional vernacular architecture and its reliance on local and renewable materials suggests the value of the opposite of innovation.

The question remains, therefore, as to whether development, and in particular sustainable development (World Commission on Environment and Development, 1987), means in market terms having more, or whether there might be a deeper meaning in sustainable development, which could be defined as changes in the organization of society that, as an essential first step, ensure all humans have access to basic resources and that this access can be sustained for at least a number of generations to come. This is, of course, the basis of the economist Schumacher's *Small is Beautiful* (1973), where he aimed to show that current economics produced both an unsustainable and an inequitable system.

Definitions

Development in history

In contradiction with the popular perception that human development is somehow having more and better than in the current situation, in ecology development is associated with the passage of organisms from the stage of youth to maturity (Odum, 1959), with maturity leading to death and the recycling of organic remains back into the system. Thus, in ecology development is part of a cycle of growth and decay. The difference between the perception of human development as a linear improvement that can be extended indefinitely and its manifestation in ecology creates divergent realities between what can be seen happening about us (every year deciduous trees have new leaves that develop, mature, die and fall off to become leaf mould) and what we expect to have in our own lives. In turn, this dichotomy creates more confusion about what needs to be sustained. The approach of looking at development as synonymous with linear progress, as discussed above, or as a natural process of growth and decay, have both defined ways of understanding change in history that are still in use in the present and that continue to influence the goals of a society. Consequently, it seems worth elaborating on these further.

The linear understanding of history was mainly introduced with the consolidation of monotheism. The Christian idea of history has a clear origin, maturity and an ending (for each individual hopefully a good ending) in the apocalypse. The development of the life of a believer implies a passage through a sequence of epochs that define a progression to God. Therefore development comes to mean a positive progress, so it is not surprising that such attitudes underpin much of Western society. Another way of looking at history suggests that human development is not a continuous upward trend but something that goes in cycles. This view of history has its roots in Ancient Greece where life was considered as a repetition of unaltered and destined events that had no meaning (Lee, 2014). Using the cyclical approach of the Greeks but with a cultural viewpoint, Spengler in his book *The Decline of the West* (1934) and also Toynbee (1934) presented the idea that the unit of analysis of history is not an epoch but a whole culture, a civilization (around 1,000 years) that undergoes developmental change from youth to maturity and decay, like an organism.

These two differing approaches, the linear and the cyclic, have added to the confusion of what sustainability of the human population might mean and might look like. The linear view is that sustainability can be organized to achieve an ideal where human society can always live on the services of the planet's ecosystems. The creation of eco-cities as an ideal sustainable form is linked with this. In the cyclical view, sustainability is linked with the behaviour of natural systems and how much can be extracted for human use with disturbing them too much. In this there will always be good years and bad, plenty and famine. This latter is thus not so far from the description of the subsistence farmer and his or her relationship to local resources and sustainability, as described at the start of this chapter.

Urbanism and progress

The Roman Empire is an example of the cyclical development of a civilization. Life for many people under Rome was a little less brutal and sometimes more settled than before Roman rule. Rome organized trade and the exploitation of resources to achieve this better quality of life but this apparent progress in the human condition came to an end when the cost of supporting the empire surpassed the benefits of its maintenance (Tainter and Taylor, 2014). It was a cycle rather than a progression. Other empires have come and gone in a similar way, such as the Egyptian and the Mayan, incidentally leaving behind tangible, and awe-inspiring, evidence of their achievements in their built environments. Thus development cannot be sustained but can only happen up to the point where resources are exhausted or some other disturbance changes the whole system and that specific path of human development alters radically or disappears. This comes back to the same point that development can only happen up to the point where the available resources can sustain the end point of the development both now and in the foreseeable future. This was what the 1972 book (Meadows *et al.*) commissioned by the Club of Rome was attempting to show, and what Turner (2008) at CSIRO has since shown was an accurate prediction of the collapse of Western civilization around 2050. In his more recent update, the collapse begins in 2015 (Turner, 2012). If such a dramatic change were to happen, the built environment that would be left as testimony to the genius of the current age would be acres of tarmac winding and intersecting across the land and clusters of high towers, mostly of glass. This would be the modern human handiwork left for future generations (hopefully of *homo sapiens*) to admire.

Collapse is a tricky word because people use it regularly in everyday life to describe a crisis or to describe the sudden end of a process (the contractor walked off the job due to a 'collapse' in the relationship with the architect) or thing (the chimney stack collapsed in a high wind and fell through the roof), but collapse can be good as well as bad (the chimney stack was due for removal anyway and it did no damage when it fell ...). Although collapse, which is a facet of resilience, will be discussed later, it is worth considering further here. First, what is really being described is change, but very considerable change, consequently how these changes happen and in what quantity have to be described; second, the definition of collapse has to define what will be lost when a system collapses. The end of the Roman Empire could be described as a collapse, but at the same time the language and the newly espoused Christian religion and the Roman Catholic Church persist to the present. So, what has collapsed in the Roman Empire? The fact that the Romans did not become extinct leaves us with only one option: what has collapsed is the empire, a socio-political formation, not the Romans, a human and natural resource. From this point of view, Tainter (1988) has stated that the collapse of a civilization implies a huge loss of social-political complexity in a short period of time. Tainter refuted the argument that ancient civilizations collapsed due to the depletion of natural resources. Instead he asserted that the depletion of natural resources only exacerbated the marginal returns produced by the maintenance cost of the complexity of a socio-political system. It thus seems that some parts of a complex system, such as human society, will persist even when the society itself undergoes a radical change. This is both a salutary and a hopeful message for the developed world, or what might be termed the overdeveloped world in the way it uses resources in an unsustainable manner. It is salutary because it is very hard to predict what will persist in the face of a general collapse. At the same time it is hopeful because it would be possible to look at Western society and examine all the resource flows through it and which, if any, of these flows might be able to be sustained in the long term. With these established then it would be possible to arrive at a sustainable quality of life.

24 Definitions

This long digression into views of history is necessary for any discussion of 'sustainable' development. This is because, as stated above, development is generally connected with thoughts of progress, and the idea of a linear development in which things get better, not worse. At the same time, getting better has been equated with urbanization, as the city is where economic activity happens (Jacobs, 1969). With industrialization this had led to the rural to urban population shift, as people move to the city in search of money and a perceived better life. This ignores the fact that all urban settlements rely on rural areas for most of their resources (food, water, raw materials). This brings with it the need to move these resources to urban areas and to dispose of the wastes generated there, which in turn requires more resources to feed this transportation. Thus equating development with urbanization implies using more resources rather than less, while the sustainable viewpoint would be to try to arrange life to use fewer resources not more. These ideas will be explored further in the case study of eco-cites.

2.6 Technological development and sustainability

Efficiency

Those who argue that urbanism is essential for the wealth and well-being of humankind (Swaminathan, 2007) point to technological development as the means by which collapse, meaning a dramatic change in the way human societies, especially urban societies, are organized because of a shortage of the resources that currently underpin them, can be avoided. Thus there is support for a new generation of nuclear reactors as the means to supply electricity rather than the certainty that burning coal will lead to climate change (Brand, 2009: 75–76). However, the resources and time to build these new reactors still have to be found very quickly if nuclear electricity is really to reverse the climate changes and pollution that come from burning coal. At the same time, people also have to be cleverer at using energy through the development of techniques, such as well-insulated buildings, to reduce energy use. Efficiency in use of conventional resources is often seen as a win-win situation, as according to Amory Lovins (1997), saving energy makes money rather costing than money. However, past events question this approach. As long ago as 1865, William Jevons noted that making things more efficient tended to increase consumption as production costs were lowered, thus leading to increased wages. This is a common problem in low or very low energy houses where the expected energy savings are not achieved because the reduced bills allow users to maintain higher temperatures in the dwelling. As an example, all seven of the twelve International Energy Agency Task 13 low energy solar houses for which monitored data were available used more energy than predicted. Although some of this increase was due to failures of the technologies included, houses were also kept at higher temperatures than the modelled assumptions, in one instance in Denmark higher by 4°C (Thomsen et al., 2005). Perhaps the classic example of Jevons' paradox is lighting. When light came from candles it was expensive, but light is now so 'cheap' that houses have more lights than in the past and arguably more than are needed (Burgess et al., 2010). So unless there is rationing of resources, being more efficient in using these may not lead to being more sustainable. However, this comes back to the same question of how limits or rations should be established. These are the hard questions in the sustainability debate.

Unforeseen consequences

The other problem with relying on changes in technology is the concept of unintended consequences (Merton, 1936). Although Merton's discussion was considering the outcomes of social action, showing for instance that the Protestant work ethic based on having less and working hard was self-defeating, since it led to the accumulation of possessions through being industrious, he acknowledged that the same concepts applied to technological choices. A curious example of this is two Australian studies of the consequences of adopting a seemingly sensible move of making cycling helmets compulsory, thereby encouraging more cycling in urban areas, which is an often cited sustainability objective (Parkin, 2012). One study suggested the measured drop in the number of head injuries could be the result of having fewer juvenile cyclists, as having to wear a helmet was so unattractive that they stopped cycling (Cameron *et al.*, 1994). A later health-benefit study suggested the reduction in head injuries was counterbalanced by the adverse health effects of the decrease in exercise (De Jong, 2012). So the seemingly sensible move of making cycling helmets mandatory, and therefore making cycling appear more attractive through being 'safer', had the opposite effect. Closer to building, the IEA Task 13 to build low energy solar houses found that the increase in measured energy use compared with what was predicted resulted not just from higher temperatures in the houses but from unforeseen problems and failures with technologies intended to improve the sustainability of the houses.

One other problem of relying on technology is that without agreement as to how environmental impact is measured, innovations may lead to unnecessary resource consumption. Green walls seem at first sight like a sensible move towards sustainability since they provide space for plants without taking up land. However, for plants to grow on walls there has to be some way of holding, feeding and watering their roots. A life-cycle study of alternative green wall systems found that the least resource-intensive way was the very traditional one of self-clinging plants rooted in soil at the base of the wall and growing up over the wall surface (Gerhardt, 2009).

The other modern problem is that technologies which result in products that can be sold tend to be favoured over other strategies, such as behaviour change, when it comes to reducing resource use or using resources more efficiently. Cars are gradually becoming more efficient in terms of the fuel used per passenger kilometre travelled (Volte-Dorta *et al.*, 2013), although creating cities that are easy to cycle and walk through would be a far better strategy for sustainability, but this approach cannot be made into a saleable product.

2.7 Sustainability and economics

The reason developed world societies continue to use more resources is linked to their obsession with economic growth. China is the prime example with a clear link made between its GDP and national energy consumption and the realization that growth in GDP cannot continue in face of energy shortages (Yuan *et al.*, 2008). A move towards sustainability involves substituting the idea of continuous economic growth with an economic system that acknowledges the need to live within the available resources. Thus sustaining economic growth is not the same as economics for a sustainable society. In fact, the former is impossible in any sustainable society. Sustainable economics implies a system of exchange within agreed resource limits. How we agree what these limits are is the big problem. In the 1970s, when the energy crisis first became apparent, Chapman proposed an economic system based on exchange of energy, using a currency called the 'kwat' (Chapman, 1975: 11–16). In this society the price of things was determined by how much energy it took to make them. This was an economic system based on resources, rather than the far more abstract and fluid thing called 'money'. At present, however, it is the views of the economists who believe that technical fixes will enable economic growth to continue that prevail over those who argue for an economics based on available resources, although as Pacey (1983: 68) noted, the former do not have the 'best evidence on their side', a situation which has not changed thirty years later.

What also seems to be happening in modern money-based economics is increasing urbanization with the view that it is the cities that generate wealth, but because urbanization also tends to increase resource use, more wealth has to be created to support this. The spiral only stops when resources run out. However, because sustainability is a holistic concept a sustainable society will have to be underpinned by a sustainable economic system, which will be radically different from the current economic paradigm.

2.8 Sustainable design

Viewed one way, sustainable design is obvious. If we want sustainable buildings we have to have sustainable building design. However, this ignores the fact that the impact of the building depends not just on the design but the users. A sustainable building design is no more than the interface between people and their choice to live in a sustainable way. The building can certainly help people do this, either unconsciously or consciously. If the building has low flush toilets (6 l/flush) then it will use less water than a building with old-fashioned toilets (13.5 l/flush). A building near public transport stops could encourage less resource use by being conveniently placed but users would have to make a conscious decision to use this 'designed' convenience. In contrast, the Shard in London, with its minimal parking spaces, appears to force users to come by public transport, but could just lead to them choosing to park the car somewhere else (Londontown, 2015). Thus the best sustainable design can do is to support sustainable behaviour. The latter depends on a much deeper change related to individual and societal values.

2.9 Happiness: the ultimate goal of sustainability?

What is being questioned here is not only the downsides of having a society based on ever-increasing consumption (given the fact that such consumption is unsustainable) but more importantly, whether a society can measure its progress and well-being in terms of economic growth alone. We know by experience that in order to make the economy of a country grow, a country has to produce more products and motivate people to consume more of these. This pattern of consumption can be stimulated by intrinsic factors, for example, the existential hollow which is only satisfied by, for example, having a house with two bathrooms or a bathroom with two washbasins, rather than having one of each shared between household members, or extrinsic factors, like the pressure to climb the socio-economic ladder and be able to show your friends your two bathrooms and multiple basins.

Whatever the case, having more stuff has become the measure for evaluating our individual progress. This reality has an inevitable impact on our level of satisfaction or frustration about our achievements in life. The paradigm that capitalism has filtered through the society of consumption is that if you have more you will be happier. For a Mr Micawber now spending less than he earns is probably not enough to produce a smile. Therefore if we use the same simplistic logic we can assume that all the rich people in the world must by definition be happy. If this is true, then we can say with precision that 99 per cent of the world's population is not happy; or in other words, we are living in the saddest civilization that has ever existed. Nonetheless, Wilkinson and Pickett (2010) have suggested that people in countries with higher average incomes are not necessarily happier than countries with lower average incomes.

Tatzel (2002) argues that the situation is more complicated than this. In poor societies having money is associated with well-being but once the poverty threshold is passed then money is less important. Societies with more money are associated with individualism, which also produces well-being. What may be more pertinent for thinking about sustainable societies is Tatzel's observation that poorer societies are often collectivist rather than individualistic because this is a way of dealing with resource scarcity. Banding together and being dependent on each other means that needs are more likely to be met. In richer societies each individual has the resources to meet their own needs. The question that naturally arises is the following: can sustainability, and specifically sustainability thinking and living, contribute to moving our society toward a happier state? Given our current obsession with consumption and the collection of stuff, maybe this is a question that only future generations can answer.

2.10 A sustainable society

What is immediately apparent is that for the already developed or overdeveloped world, moving towards a sustainable society will mean a large retrenchment in the use of resources, towards a much simpler and less resource-intensive lifestyle. However, for many other and poorer human communities it will mean guiding development to improve quality of life within the available resources. This is the human tragedy; those who have a good life have too much and are unwilling to release what they do have to allow the less fortunate to develop. Within a family this would seldom happen; possibly within a small community there could be a fairer sharing of resources but between nations this seems at the moment impossible.

Sustainability is not a static concept. Human societies will continue to change, as they always have. Sustainability is not a utopian concept as within something that is always changing there is no ideal state. What it does demand is the ability to measure resources flows and how resources are used by people to ensure that these are achieved without damaging the ecosystems that supply them. Whether these resources are then to be distributed equitably is a different question. Equity is probably something more easily achieved at the small rather than large scale. What sustainability is not is a series of quick fix products that can be bought and applied to existing developed world lifestyles. It is also something that concerns everyone as all actions have resource consequences. Sustainability is the diverse and changing patterns of human living that are possible within available resource limits, wherever the boundary is drawn.

Notes

1 By definition, capital is linked with non-human assets that can be traded in a market and therefore things that someone owns. Consequently, human and natural resources should not be considered capital, unless perhaps dealing with slavery for the former. The latter is more complicated – no-one owns the air or much of the oceans but who owns the land?
2 Appliances have become cheaper, making multiple-ownership possible. In New Zealand the cost of a refrigerator in 1956 equated to seven weeks of average income whereas now it is less than two weeks (Statistics NZ, 2013). Tracking modern conveniences in the home, available at www.stats.govt.nz/tools_and_services/newsletters/price-index-news/apr-13-article-chores.aspx, accessed March 2015; Statistics New Zealand, 2013. Home appliances have come a long way in price and technology, available at www.stats.govt.nz/tools_and_services/media-centre/additional-releases/home-appliances-11-apr-13.aspx, accessed March 2015).

Bibliography

Arndt, H. W. (1983). The "trickle-down" myth. *Economic Development and Cultural Change* 32(1), pp. 1–10.

Bacon, F. (1627). *New Atlantis*, available at www.gutenberg.org/ebooks/2434, accessed 21 March 2015.

Berner, R. A. (2003). The long-term carbon cycle, fossil fuels and atmospheric composition. *Nature* 426, pp. 323–326.

Böhringer, C. and Jochem, P. (2006). Measuring the immeasurable: a survey of sustainability indices. Discussion Paper No. 06-073, Centre for European Economic Research, available at www.econstor.eu/bitstream/10419/24527/1/dp06073.pdf, accessed 12 April 2015.

Bosselmann, K. (2008). *The Principle of Sustainability: Transforming Law and Governance*. Aldershot: Ashgate Publishing.

Brand, S. (1994). *How Buildings Learn*. New York: Viking.

Brand, S. (2009). *Whole Earth Discipline*. New York: Viking.

Buck, P. (1952). *The Coming of the Maori*. Wellington: Whitcombe and Tombs.

Burgess, J., Camilleri, M. and Saville-Smith, M. (2010). Lighting in New Zealand homes – lighting efficiency as a sustainability indicator. *Proceedings of SB10*, available at www.branz.co.nz/cms_show_download.php?id=04e6aad5be81dcf9fe6d844d2bca85ad46cbe3f9, accessed 2 November 2014.

California Energy Commission (2012). Energy story, available at www.energyquest.ca.gov/story/chapter08.html, accessed 14 October 2014.

Cameron, M., Vulcan, A., Finch, C. and Newstead, S. (1994). Mandatory bicycle helmet use following a decade of helmet promotion in Victoria, Australia – an evaluation. *Accident Analysis and Prevention* 26(3), pp. 325–332.

Chapagain, A. K., Hoekstra, A. Y., Savenije, H. H. G. and Gautam, R. (2006). The water footprint of cotton consumption: an assessment of the impact of worldwide consumption of cotton products on the water resources Clements in the cotton producing countries. *Ecological Economics* 60(1), pp. 186–203.

Chapman, P. (1975). *Fuel's Paradise: Energy Options for Britain*. Harmondsworth: Penguin.

Crosby, A. W. (1986). *Ecological Imperialism: the Biological Expansion of Europe, 900–1900*. Cambridge: Cambridge University Press.

Darwin, C. (1859/2009). *The Origin of Species by Means of Natural Selection, or, The preservation of favored races in the struggle for life* (Modern Library pbk edn). New York: Modern Library.

De Jong, P. (2012). The health impact of mandatory bicycle helmet laws (February 24, 2010). Risk analysis. Available at SSRN: http://ssrn.com/abstract=1368064, accessed 29 March 2015.

Dickens, C. (1850). *David Copperfield*. Chapter 12. Liking life no better on my own account I form a great resolution. Available at http://www.gutenberg.org/ebooks/766, accessed 12 April 2015.

EIA (2013). World coal production in tonnage (black) and BTU content (red) 1980–2011. Available at http://en.wikipedia.org/wiki/File:World_Coal_Tonnage_and_BTU.png, accessed 21 October 2014.

Eliot, G. (1876/1967). *Daniel Deronda*. Harmonsworth: Penguin.

Gerhardt, C. H. (2009). Multifunctionality as a strategy to decrease resource use in building envelopes. Thesis, Victoria University of Wellington, available at http://researcharchive.vuw.ac.nz/handle/10063/1223?__utma=1.1520254792.1383513478.1429252663.1429302848.6&__utmb=1.5.10.1429302848&__utmc=1&__utmx=-&__utmz=1.1429245232.4.1.utmcsr=(direct)|utmccn=(direct)|utmcmd=(none)&__utmv=-&__utmk=56897834, accessed 12 April 2015.

Global Footprint Network (GFN). (2015). *Global Footprint Network*, available at www.econstor.eu/bitstream/10419/24527/1/dp06073.pdf, accessed 12 April 2015.

Golley, F. (1993). *A History of the Ecosystem Concept in Ecology: More than the Sum of the Parts*. New Haven, CT: Yale University Press.

Gomez Davila, N. (2005). *Escolios a un texto implicito* (Vol. I). Bogota: Villegas Editores.

Hamilton K. (2000). Genuine savings as a sustainability indicator. World Bank Environment Department, available at https://openknowledge.worldbank.org/bitstream/handle/10986/18301/multi0page.pdf?sequence=1, accessed 5 April 2015.

Intergovernmental Panel on Climate Change (IPCC). (2013). Climate Change 2013: The Physical Science Basis, available at www.climatechange2013.org/, accessed 24 March 2015.

Intergovernmental Panel on Climate Change (IPCC). (2014). Climate Change 2014: Mitigation of Climate Change, Summary for Policy Makers, p. 20, available at http://mitigation2014.org/, accessed 24 March 2015.

Jacobs, J. (1969). *The Economy of Cities*. New York: Random House.

Jevons, W. (1865). *The Coal Question* (Vol. 3). London: Macmillan.

Lee, S. H. (2014). *New Essentials of Unification Thought: Head-Wing Thought*. Tokyo: Kogensha.

Londontown. (2015). Car parks near The Shard, available at www.londontown.com/ParkingInformation/Attractions/The-Shard/f0f7a/, accessed 2 May 2015.

Lovins, A. (1997). Climate: Making Sense and Making Money. Rocky Mountain Institute, available at www.rmi.org/Knowledge-Center/Library/C97-13_ClimateSenseMoney, accessed 24 February 2015.

Meadows, D. H., Meadows, D. L., Randers, J. and Behrens, W. W. (1972). *The Limits to Growth*. New York: Universe Books.

Merton, R. K. (1936). The unintended consequences of purposive social action. *American Sociological Review* 9(6), pp. 894–904.

Odum, E. (1959). *Fundamentals of Ecology*, 2nd edn. Philadelphia, PA: Saunders.

Odum, E. (1997). *Ecology: A Bridge between Science and Society*. Sunderland, MA: Sinauer Associates.

Pacey, A. (1983). *The Culture of Technology*. Cambridge, MA: MIT Press.

Pamungkas, G. (2013). Kampung Naga, Indonesia. In R. Vale and B. Vale (eds), *Living within a Fair Share Ecological Footprint*. Abingdon: Earthscan.

Parkin, J. (ed.). (2012). *Cycling and Sustainability*. Bingley: Emerald Group.

Reynolds, K. M., Thomson, A. J., Khöl, M., Shannon, M. A., Ray, D. and Rennolls, K. (2007). *Sustainable Forestry: from Monitoring and Modelling Management to Knowledge Management and Policy Science*. Wallingford: CAB International.

Rios, C. J. (2015). Environmental assessment of vernacular thatched building traditions in Mexico. Unpublished PhD thesis, Victoria University of Wellington.

Raupach, M. R. *et al.* (2007). Global and regional drivers of accelerating CO₂ emissions. *Proceedings of the National Academy of Sciences of the United States of America* 104(24), 10288–10293.

Robertson, L., Flinders, C. and Godfrey, B. (1976/1981). *Laurel's Kitchen*. Petaluma, CA: Nilgiri Press.

Schumacher, E. F. (1973). *Small is Beautiful: A Study of Economics as if People Mattered.* London: Blond and Briggs.

Spengler, O. (1934). *The Decline of the West*. New York: A. A. Knopf.

Sustainable Life Media. (2013). 13 hot sustainable products to follow in 2013. *Sustainable Brands*, available at www.sustainablebrands.com/news_and_views/blog/13-hot-sustainable-products-follow-2013, accessed 2 March 2015.

Swaminathan, N. (2007). If you can make it there… cities are the greatest generators of innovation and wealth. Scientific American, available at https://www.scientificamerican.com/article/cities-generate-innovation-wealth/, accessed 17 April 2016.

Tainter, J. A. (1988). *The Collapse of Complex Societies*. Cambridge and New York: Cambridge University Press.

Tainter, J. A. and Taylor, T. (2014). Complexity, problem-solving, sustainability and resilience. *Building Research and Information* 42(2), pp. 168–181.

Tatzel, M. (2002). "Money worlds" and well-being: an integration of money dispositions, materialism and price-related behavior. *Journal of Economic Psychology* 23, pp. 103–126.

Thomsen, K. E., Schultz, J. M. and Poel, B. (2005). Measured performance of 12 demonstration projects – IEA Task 13 "advanced solar low energy buildings". *Energy and Buildings* 37(2), pp. 111–119.

Townsend, A. (2011). All-time 100 greatest toys: Hula Hoop. *Time*, 16 February, available at http://content.time.com/time/specials/packages/article/0,28804,2049243_2048654_2049245,00.html, accessed 24 February 2015.

Toynbee, A. (1934). *A Study of History*. London: Oxford University Press.

Turner, G. (2008). A comparison of *The Limits to Growth* with thirty years of reality. Socio-Economics and the Environment in Discussion CSIRO Working Paper Series 2008–09, CSIRO Sustainable Ecosystems, Canberra, Australia, June. Available at www.manicore.com/fichiers/Turner_Meadows_vs_historical_data.pdf, accessed 6 March 2015.

Turner, G. (2012). On the cusp of global collapse? *Gaia* 21(2), pp. 116–124.

United Nations Development Programme (UNDP) (n.d.). Human Development Reports, available at http://hdr.undp.org/en/content/human-development-index-hdi, accessed 5 April 2015.

Vadicheria, T. and Saravanan, D. (2015). Sustainable measures taken by brands, retailers, and manufacturers. In S. S. Muthu (ed.), *Roadmap to Sustainable Textiles and Clothing*. Heidleberg: Springer.

Volte-Dorta, A., Perdiguero, J. and Jimenez, J. L. (2013). Are car manufacturers on the way to reduce CO₂ emissions? A DEA approach. *Energy Economics* 38, pp. 77–86.

Vale, R. and Vale, B. (2009). *Time to Eat the Dog? The Real Guide to Sustainable Living.* London: Thames and Hudson.

Wiersum, K. F. (1995). 200 years of sustainability in forestry: lessons from history. *Journal of Environmental Management* 19(3), pp. 321–329.

Wilkinson, R. and Pickett, K. (2010). *The Spirit Level: Why Equality is Better for Everyone*, rev. edn. London: Penguin.

World Coal Association. (n.d.). Available at www.worldcoal.org/coal/where-is-coal-found/, accessed 21 October 2014.

World Commission on Environment and Development. (1987). *Our Common Future*. Oxford: Oxford University Press.

Yuan, J., Jang, J., Zhao, C. and Hu, Z. (2008). Energy consumption and economic growth: evidence from China at both aggregated and disaggregated levels. *Energy Economics* 30, pp. 3077–3094.

3 Defining resilience

'Ka mura Ka muri.'
['Walking backwards into the future.']

Maori proverb

3.1 Why bother with resilience?

The history of life on Earth is one of change, slow or fast, more or less predictable, desirable or undesirable, cyclical, linear or exponential – everything is about change. Those who dispute the effects on the climate of both burning fossil fuels and modern ruminant-based farming point out that the climate has always been changing (Freedman, 2015). Species also appear and disappear, the dinosaurs being the example everyone knows. The tectonic plates are always on the move, leading to the kind of dramatic changes like earthquakes and volcanoes that building resilience into human settlements is somehow supposed to cope with. The Earth moves, and so the oceans and airstreams move with it. Change is part of living on a moving planet. Nevertheless, we are still trying to explain and to understand change. Why do things change? How do they change? This is not only because we want to know how some things came to be as they are now (history), but also because we want to learn how to deal with change so as to cope with future change. From the moment we became aware that our actions can impact on the physical environment to produce a change in our lives, learning how to buffer and cope with change became a means of survival.

Resilience is about understanding change. This means understanding that change happens globally in systems, which are at best complex and at worst impossible to manage, like the winds and ocean currents created as the Earth moves around the sun. These systems, like ecosystems or cities, are complex because they have many variables, and because they involve different resources and actors in their processes. This complexity also happens because everything is woven together in such a way that it is difficult to predict the outcome of an intervention. At the end of the nineteenth century importing stoats into New Zealand to control the population of previously imported rabbits was considered a good idea. Sadly, the stoats had little effect on controlling rabbit numbers but a devastating one on the native bird population (Peden, 2015).

The human problem is that our situation can suffer change, both natural and manufactured, that is not always desirable. In the face of this continuous change the human aim is to steer it such that we can keep going without radically altering what we want to preserve, such as modern industrialized societies. This is the subject of

32 *Definitions*

resilience. Resilience is focused in trying to understand and explain change, with the ultimate aim of adaptation leading to persistence without mutating into something ⟨illegible⟩ to try to understand resilience because it is linked with improving our ⟨illegible⟩ ping the status quo.

3.2 Why architects, urban and landscape designers should care about resilience

By 2050 more than half of the human population will live on the coast where cities are more exposed to natural hazards, such as floods following storms or sea-level rise triggered by global warming, and more dependent on their capacities to adapt to these events so that they can keep going. Consequently, coastal cities are now habitats where the significant social and economic capital invested is at risk (Tibbetts, 2002). Cities built in the shadow of volcanoes are also vulnerable. One, Pompeii buried in volcanic ash, is a tourist attraction, but five such cities would be a disaster. Contenders might be Naples (Italy), Arequipa (Peru), Legazpi City (Philippines), Shimabara (Japan) and Auckland (New Zealand).

Holling (1973), who first proposed resilience as a property of ecosystems, and with fellow scholar Allen (Allen and Holling, 2010) have suggested two reasons for architects and urban designers to care about resilience: climate change and landscape change. Climate change is linked to sea-level rise, floods and landslides, all natural hazards that threaten the stability of cities. Landscape change is linked with transformation in the land cover and use, which can also threaten stability. A sudden storm can cause flooding because so much of the city surface has been made impervious and storm water systems cannot cope. This happened in Wellington, New Zealand while this chapter was being written, with people unable to get home after brief but heavy rain because of floods and landslips which closed roads and railways. Since the resources of cities come from rural areas and we still need land for conservation of our ecosystem services and for habitat, then changes in land cover can also challenge the growth and expansion of cities. Perhaps we should be designing urban areas with these issues in mind.

3.3 Why bother with the definition of resilience?

When first conceived, the definitions of new concepts like resilience tend to be vague, creating confusion and disagreement between scholars, rather than generating the conditions for advancing knowledge. Ideally definition should be a collective exercise, and a bridge between fields of research, communities and people, something this book is not yet doing. The intention here is to start investigation of resilience within the built environment disciplines. The point of unravelling resilience is connecting people through knowledge. Vague definitions are of little use if we want to apply an idea to the study of real situations, which is where built environment professionals act. The objective of fundamental theory is thus to provide meaning and rationale to practice. Those who have tackled Scottish country dancing will recognize the need to understand the theory (who dances first, numbering couples, who is your opposite corner, etc.) in order the reproduce the intricate patterns of the dance. Only knowing the steps and moves without the theory normally leads to chaos. In other words, using a concept without knowing the meaning is like running to nowhere, when in real life projects have to arrive somewhere.

Architecture, landscape design and urban design demand tangible results, and yet these results emerge from infinite opportunities, which is why students often find design difficult. Why is one solution better than another? Concepts like sustainability and resilience are used as a means to narrow design possibilities, and this use is more important than a deep understanding of what the concepts entail. Using a concept as just a label is a sure path to failure and disappointment. However, by digging into the theory of resilience and questioning its nature, or what we call unravelling, it should be easier to observe and discover the characteristics, limits and potential of both resilience and sustainability: what they are and what they are not.

The aim of this chapter is to produce a 'resilience panorama' for designers interested in using the concept. The chapter is divided into parts to cover the questions. Where did resilience originate? What is and is not resilience? What are the criticisms of the concept? The chapter should act like a map with which to explore the question: how can resilience be useful for architects, landscape architects and urban designers?

3.4 Early definitions

Resilience in engineering

The origin of resilience is related to the mechanics of materials and its meaning here is close to the concept of elasticity. Etymologically, 'resilience' comes from the Latin *resilio*, which means to 'jump back'. So a rubber band or length of elastic has resilience. The Oxford English Dictionary states the word was introduced in the mid-seventeenth century from the Latin verb *resilire*, which means 'to rebound or recoil'. McAslan (2010) suggests the first written use of resilience in English is in the nineteenth-century book *On the Transverse Strength of Timber* by the English engineer Thomas Tredgold (1818). He used the word to describe the property of timber that allows a beam to bend and support heavy loads without breaking. Those familiar with old timber beams will observe that resilience in this sense is different from the piece of elastic as a timber beam under load will bend (deform) but will not spring back to its original shape if the load is removed. This concept was later advanced by the Irish engineer Robert Mallet (1856) who defined the *modulus of resilience*. This is how much energy needs to be applied to something, like a piece of elastic, to prevent it returning to its original shape, or the energy it takes to pull and over-stretch the elastic. Here resilience is not so much to do with springing back or deforming under load but rather with not deforming or collapsing in a catastrophic way, so already the same word means different things. Mallet's concept was used in naval architecture, buildings and finally included in the *Manual of Civil Engineering* in 1867. The concept of resilience as some form of elasticity explains the origin of the term and marked a first wave of resilience thinking that is still persistent, as will be shown later, and that has influenced later definitions derived in the social and natural sciences. Since the 1970s this understanding of resilience has been revised. Contributions from scholars in ecology and psychology have extended the original mechanical understanding of resilience so it can be applied to the analysis of living systems. The introduction of free market economics after the world wars, the appearance of postmodernism and structuralism in philosophy, the oil crisis, the emergence of environmental concerns and an overall

34 *Definitions*

climate of social change together appear to have created a suitable environment for the exploration of resilience in the natural and social sciences, making this the first of resilience outside engineering.

Resilience in psychology

Although Holling (1973) has more than once been mentioned as key to the modern study of resilience (see below), the concept also emerged in the behavioural sciences in the 1970s as the result of a group of psychologists interested in the study of children at risk. This group looked at the effect of the children's biological inheritance and their adverse living environments (Garmezy, 1973), although the term resilience was not explicitly defined. The studies showed a percentage of these children developed with no problems because of their capacity to adapt to and cope with risk (Garmezy and Streitman, 1974). In psychology, therefore, resilience refers to the ability of individuals to cope with adverse situations and adapt to stress and crisis. At present the American Psychological Association (APA, 2015) synthesizes the definition as 'bouncing back from difficult experiences'. This definition has been used in psychology for investigation at the scale of the individual, the family and the community.

Resilience in ecology

In 1973 Holling introduced the concept of resilience in ecology with his groundbreaking article 'Resilience and stability of ecological systems' (Holling, 1973), which questioned the theory of how ecosystems worked by contrasting two behaviours: stability and resilience. Holling realized that the understanding then of the way natural systems worked was mainly inherited from physics, mathematics and the study of materials in engineering. In all these fields, stability meant constancy and invariability. Any departure or variance from pre-established parameters was linked with instability and uncertainty, both factors that put the delivery of expected outcomes at risk. From this point of view, the stability of a system meant a 'consistent non-variable performance' (Holling, 1973). For example, if ecologists applied this view of stability to the management of production of a particular species of fish in a lake, then all actions would be focused on reinforcing the predominance of the desired species to the detriment of the rest. The robustness and homogeneity of the one species would effectively eliminate possible predators and secure a sustained yield. If the lake were to keep on providing the same yield of fish every year, it would be stable, predictable and profitable. But we know that change happens, and situations change, hence the proverbial advice not to 'put all your eggs in one basket'. If the quality of the water changes for any reason, then all the desired stock could be at risk. Holling realized that the challenge in managing an ecological system, like a fish farm in a lake, is to understand that it is subject to external and unexpected changes that will cause it to deviate from a stable condition. He stressed that ecosystems are mostly not found in one stable condition but that they are changing constantly. Such systems tend to vary on a regular basis, and these variations are the normal response of an ecosystem to external or internal disturbances, and are not a prelude to collapse. Contrary to managing ecosystems for non-variable performance and stability, Holling (1973) proposed that it was more important to create 'conditions for persistence' in an ecosystem for its survival, as this acknowledged the fact it is constantly varying. The survival of an ecosystem is also complicated as the system is made up of many different species and other elements like water and air. Persistence for Holling meant establishing conditions to lessen the probability of the extinction of any of the species in an ecosystem. Therefore, in systems that are under a lot of pressure the most important thing to understand is not how far they are from being in a stable state but rather how many chances for survival they have. This way of looking at the behaviour of ecosystems recognizes resilience as a property that can help to create the conditions for persistence when a system is not stable. Taking a simple example, pandas are famed for having a diet that is almost all bamboo (WWF, 2015). As human settlement reduces the available bamboo, and a panda needs to eat 12–48 kg a day, then the panda has two options – migration to somewhere with a supply of bamboo or learn to eat something else. Human settlement has worked against the former and pandas, being not very resilient, have not done the latter and the species is threatened with extinction.

For Holling, the conditions for persistence were associated with the two properties of variability and resilience. This led to defining resilience as something that 'determines the persistence of relationships within a system and is a measure of the ability of these systems to absorb changes of state variables, driving variables, and parameters, and still persist' (Holling, 1973: 17). In the panda example above, a driving variable would be increasing human settlement and loss of bamboo-producing land. A stable variable might be bamboo. In a good year there will be lots of young pandas, but if this is followed by a bad year for bamboo many will not survive. The system adjusts to keep panda numbers relative to their available food source. This is sad for the baby pandas but good for the panda system. Holling developed the concept of resilience as an alternative to the idea of stability in ecosystems. Stability would mean a constant panda population with births replacing deaths; resilience means panda populations fluctuate in line with the availability of bamboo. Contrary to the earlier assumption that stable ecosystems come back to their previous state after a disturbance, Holling proposed that systems rarely exist in a stable condition but are constantly changing. He suggested that ecosystems work like this, even when far from being stable, because adaptation happens, at least for some species if not for pandas.

Due to Holling's questioning of stability in ecosystems, at the present there are two views of resilience: ecological resilience and engineering resilience (Gunderson, 2000). Engineering resilience is related to the time a system takes before coming back to its stability state and is clearly linked with the original definition of resilience in materials mechanics. This position implies systems work around a single equilibrium state that they lose or recover in more or less time. The faster a system recovers the more resilient it is (Pimm, 1984). A new stretched rubber band is very resilient, whereas an old one which has lost some of its 'spring' will be less resilient. Such conditions are important for engineering where stability and a constant performance from the system are required. We need a gun that will recoil and come back to the starting position every time. If it fails to work we will probably die. The faster a system returns to its equilibrium the more stable it seems to be for engineers. However, scholars in ecological resilience (Gunderson, 2000; Holling, 1973, 1987; Peterson *et al.*, 1998) have criticized this idea. They propose that as complex systems with adaptive properties change due to external or internal disturbances, their balance and equilibrium are also affected (Folke *et al.*, 2004). Therefore, after a disturbance, the system readjusts its organization to work within the new context. Foxes in the UK have responded to increasing human settlement by seeing human food waste as a useful change in diet, and the species has survived loss of its original habitat and, unlike pandas, has taken to urban living (Harris, 2013).

Holling proposed that complex systems can survive disturbances because some parts can absorb change without altering the organization or structure of the system. A resilience response to a disturbance is the capacity of the system to maintain its interrelationships while absorbing the change. Changes are absorbed because the system has many scales, is diverse and has redundancy. Therefore, from an ecological point of view, a complex system has the capability to work in a diversity of conditions and to absorb changes without losing its identity (Walker and Meyers, 2004).

3.5 The consolidation of ecological resilience

Complexity, adaptive systems and resilience

For Holling, resilience is a property of an ecosystem that is linked with an alternative understanding of the idea of an equilibrium, and thus is in opposition to the idea of a balanced nature (Gunderson and Holling, 2002). The next challenge was to explain how resilience occurs in ecosystems and to find evidence to support the explanation. To do this Holling used advances in the theory of complex adaptive systems (Levin, 1998), hierarchy theory (Allen and Starr, 1982) and the theory of dissipative structures (Prigogine and Stengers, 1984) to create a model that not only explains how resilience happens but also how ecosystems work. For the latter Holling used a systemic approach, meaning ecosystems are analysed as complex adaptive systems. A system is complex when it has many variables that are linked and tend to create subgroups that generate hierarchies, and that have both a history and non-linear behaviour. Cities are a good example of complex systems because they have many elements and generate subsystems that are equally complex. For example, in a city a household can vary from one person to a group of people, a community is composed of a group of households and a society of different communities. This not a simple pyramidal hierarchy as in military ranks, there will be cross-links, since family members and friends may be part of other households and communities. In ecological resilience, a hierarchy is thus an emergent structure, the result of the interaction between a set of things that occurs at different levels. In the example of the city there may be a pattern of visiting between communities, but if people move the pattern will break, and a new pattern might emerge. There is no central control over the entire system, as with the example of military ranks where everyone knows their place, nor is the structure a predesigned model imposed to create the hierarchy. There are also different scales of interaction between the parts of a system. If you have a disagreement between household members, resolution and reconciliation usually take place fairly quickly as people have to live together, whereas a disagreement between communities can lead to longstanding feuds, as between the Montagues and the Capulets in Shakespeare's *Romeo and Juliet*.

When it comes to ecosystems, processes occur at different scales. For example, all the biophysical processes linked to the fast change in the growth and death of a plant occur at a small scale, while the big scale is linked to the slow processes of change in something like the shift in tectonic plates (Allen and Starr, 1982; Simon, 1962). The underlying idea is that complex systems can adapt because every level has some autonomy. If the feedback paths between what happens at the different scales persist then it is possible to change or even lose some of the elements at each scale and the system will keep functioning. These ideas lie behind understanding ecosystems as complex adaptive systems and were essential for the development of the theory of resilience.

The next challenge was to link these ideas with real case studies. Based on Paine's keystone species hypothesis (Paine *et al.*, 1998), Holling found it was possible to simplify study of the structure of ecosystems by analysing the key processes and how often each changed. This would define the scales of each in space and time. For example, in the boreal forest, the type of forest that occurs in cold temperate regions south of the Arctic where evergreen cone-bearing trees dominate, the spruce budworm is a pest (Natural Resources Canada, 2015) and devastating outbreaks occur in cycles of thirty to forty years. Holling found four cycles of change in such a forest that occur at four different speeds. At the smallest scale (three to five years) the key process is the interaction between the budworms and the foliage. If there is foliage to eat the budworm population will begin to grow. However, the spruce budworm has predators, like various species of warbler. When the trees are small with scarce foliage, the birds can find the budworms easily but when the trees are older their foliage is denser and the birds have more difficulty finding the budworms. So the key process of the next scale (ten to fifteen years) is the relationship between the foliage and the budworms. The timescale is defined by the time it takes the trees to recover their foliage after being eaten. However, there comes a point when the predators cannot find the budworms and the population explodes, denuding the trees which die until, with no food to eat, the budworm population rapidly declines. This scale (thirty-five to forty years) is defined by the rapid spread of budworms and their impact on tree mortality, as at this stage budworms can kill up to 80 percent of trees in the forest. The biggest scale (more than eighty years) is defined by the trees that survive (persist). In this way Holling pictured four different scales in the same system. The system, in this case the forest, can be understood by analysing these few scales. Each scale has a structuring process and a set of variables interacting in such a way that they produce a periodicity of change (number of years). Each scale is defined by a periodicity and an area where the processes happen. In other words, each scale has a time and a space that are related and characterized by a cycle of change.

Panarchy and the adaptive cycle

As research of this type continued, Gunderson and Holling (2002) proposed that ecosystems are hierarchically organized through multiple scales, with key processes driving the rhythm and cycle of change at each scale. They named this dynamic a 'Panarchy' in reference to the Greek god Pan (the god of nature) and the word 'hierarchy'. This is quite confusing since the non-capitalized word panarchy, meaning an all-encompassing form of governance, was first used in the nineteenth century. Confusion often arises when old words are appropriated and given new meanings. However, a Panarchy according to Gunderson and Holling's version is a metaphor to help explain how ecosystems work. In a Panarchy ecosystems are visualized as a nested set of scales. At each scale, changes happen in a cyclical manner. These cycles, called by Holling adaptive cycles, have different phases that are linked with the processes of development and decay, just as the budworm population grows, burgeons and then rapidly decays as the trees die. In the adaptive cycle the first phase (exploitation) is

38 *Definitions*

a period of rapid development. A system in this phase is not very stable but is highly resilient. The second phase (conservation) is characterized by an accumulation of 'capital' to the appearance of mature trees in a forest and complexity gained by a due to its having more components and more connections between these. In the for this might be the attraction of more species of insects and birds because of the presence of mature trees, with insects eating trees and birds eating insects. These phases can also be illustrated by visualizing the emergence of plants following a bushfire. First, there are lots of small plants of many varieties. In the conservation phase some will have grown and others will have disappeared and the biomass accumulated by their growth (the wood in the trees) is the 'capital'. At this stage the system has more stability but also more rigidity; this is a situation that lowers its resilience to the point that small disturbances can cause huge problems. If a bushfire comes, the large trees will burn and the biomass capital will be lost. The system is more fragile and any unpredictable (or even predictable in the case of bushfires) change can make it collapse. The third phase (release) is characterized by an important loss of connectivity and potential in a short period of time (the fire). After the system collapses it either restarts a new cycle, a period of reorganization (new growth) with lots of small plants appearing again, or shifts to a different stability state (becomes a desert) (Gunderson and Holling, 2002: 40–47).

The adaptive cycle can thought of as having two trends: the 'front loop and back loop' (Gunderson and Holling, 2002: 47). The front loop (the black line in Figure 3.1) is the exploitation and conservation phases. In a built environment this could be exemplified by slow incremental growth, and the accumulations of 'capital' in the form of buildings and infrastructure in the city CBD for people to use. It also represents the stability needed for the identity of a place to be consolidated. The back loop (the light grey line in Figure 3.1) is the release to reorganization phases (Gunderson and Holling, 2002), and is when opportunities arise following a crisis (Schumpeter, 1994). To go back to an earlier example, my roof tiles are old and becoming porous and the roof needs stripping off and retiling, but this gives me the opportunity to insulate the roof easily. Importantly, in the adaptive cycle, both loops cannot be maximized at the same time, they occur in sequence. As complexity and stability increase, the same processes make the system more rigid, unstable and unpredictable, reducing its resilience capacity (Holling, 2004). This is the resilience problem. Things are most resilient when they are just starting but we need to live in stable built environments, not on a continuous

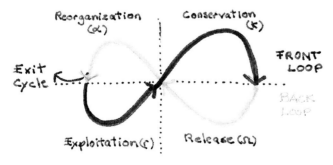

Figure 3.1 Diagram of the adaptive cycle (based on Gunderson and Holling, 2002)

construction site. Resilience in the built environment means finding a balance between the front and back loops, or between persistence and renewal.

The Panarchy helps in thinking about how ecosystems work together, not just in isolation. This is important for the built environment as a house sits in a neighbourhood, which sits in the city, which sits in a landscape, which sits in a hydrological cycle, and so on. The Panarchy sees ecosystems as a dynamic hierarchy where change, and adaptation in the face of change, occur not only within one scale of an adaptive cycle but also across the scales (Figure 3.2) (Gunderson and Holling, 2002: 69–72). At large scales, changes are slow and not so frequent because their processes are mainly managed by slow variables (hills are gradually eroded by wind and rain but often this is too slow for us to see). At small scales, changes occur more often and they happen faster due to the predominance of fast variables (deciduous trees lose their leaves in winter as light levels fall, and then regrow them six months later).

All these interactions produce emergent changes, which help the system to self-organize and apparently 'learn' from experience. In a Panarchy changes across scales happen due to two processes known as *'revolt'* and *'remember'* (Gunderson and Holling, 2002: 75–76). A 'revolt' (light grey line in Figure 3.2) is a bottom-up process that starts at lower scales in the Panarchy with the possibility of cascading up and having an impact at bigger scales, a situation that does not occur frequently. An example would be the Black Death in fourteenth-century Europe, where the original infection in one place in central Asia spread to kill 30–60 per cent of the European population (Herlihy, 1997: 17) with consequent loss of agricultural labourers. In Britain this led to the enclosure of land and the abandonment of whole villages (Beresford, 1954). In contrast is the opposite 'remember' force (dark grey line in Figure 3.2), a top-down process that tries to keep the system stable and is driven by slow variables. An example is the attachment of a community to its vernacular architecture, which is based on

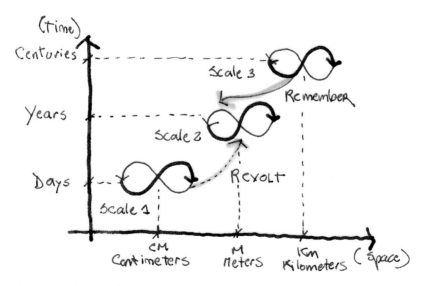

Figure 3.2 A Panarchy (based on Gunderson and Holling, 2002). Units added to x-axis and y-axis illustrate increments in spatial and temporal scales

memories, experiences and stories that provide it with meaning. Systems that do not allow *revolts* (Gunderson and Holling, 2002) can stagnate and become rigid because of a progressive loss of resilience. Systems where restructuring or resetting processes (revolts) are frequent are not stable enough to sustain a development. Consequently, a Panarchy demands a broad understanding of the dynamics of change within and across scales, which means that the general resilience of the whole system is as important as the comprehension of the specific resilience of the system at one scale of interest. It is no good designing a resilient neighbourhood without making the city it sits in resilient, or making a resilient city without making its region resilient.

All these ideas are useful for provoking thinking about how nature works and how ecosystems evolve. For designers, what is more important about the idea of Panarchy is that it could be a way of understanding change in the built environment. At the moment changes in the urban environment in developed, capitalist societies often come about because someone wants to make money from developing a site, or sometimes change happens because of public outcry from the loss of open space or old buildings in the urban landscape that result from such development. The theory of resilience gives designers the chance to observe and think about how the built environment changes with the emphasis on what happens rather than why it happens. There is always a danger in taking a theory developed in one discipline and applying it to another, but this is what this book set out explore, recognizing that people are already talking about urban resilience and ways of increasing this. However, we cannot do the latter without a means of measuring resilience in the built environment (see Part 3). In addition, since Panarchy analyses ecosystems as complex systems, then it should be possible to apply it to the analysis of urban landscapes, because these also have multiple scales (region, city, neighbourhood, block) that influence each other (see Chapter 8).

Heterogeneity and discontinuities

For Holling, the heterogeneity or diversity of a landscape and variety of sizes in the members of ecological communities (from insects to mature trees) were not just something that happened randomly but were linked with the processes of change derived from a Panarchy. Holling was trying to show that the 'discontinuities' in the size of animals in a system (as I write this native birds in my garden are silver eyes, average 11 cm, fantails 16 cm, tuis 30 cm and NZ pigeons 51 cm – with no linear relationship between these numbers) were a product of the discontinuous distribution of resources in nested ecosystems in the Panarchy. Discontinuities can thus be understood as breaks in the continuity of a variable (size in the case of native garden birds). Holling speculates that discontinuities result because of the variability of resources between two scales, which forms the reason behind the absence of species of certain sizes. This was the base for his 'Textural-Discontinuity Hypothesis' (TDH). The TDH (Holling, 1992) implies animal body sizes are related with behavioural choices and availability of landscape resources and foraging scales. The African savannah has herbivores of zebras (450 kg), buffalo (590 kg), wildebeest (250 kg) that form a 'lump' of species of very roughly the same order of magnitude relating to size; and then there are elephants (6,000 kg) as another 'lump'. If landscapes are 'lumpy', their discontinuous resource distribution will tend to cluster animals of similar sizes in lumps, at different scales of space and time. Changes in the availability of resources will produce changes in the composition of the clusters. For this reason, the stability of a landscape interacts with the morphology and functional diversity of its constituent elements. The analysis of size changes and functional diversity, at each scale of the landscape, should reflect the dynamics of adaptation of the communities that inhabit it. An understanding of how a heterogeneous landscape behaves at different scales of space and time thus becomes the key variable for testing the resilience capacity of a landscape in the presence of unpredictable changes (see Chapter 8).

3.6 The expansion of ecological resilience: from ecology to social science

The characterization and bifurcation of resilience

The advances Holling made in observing, defining and explaining how resilience may happen in ecosystems were extended by scholars from ecology and social sciences, but in divergent directions. The research of Scheffer, Carpenter and Kuznetsov (Folke et al., 2010) was focused on describing resilience in a mathematical way using the theory of complex adaptive systems. Resilience has also been applied to global issues arising from the management of natural resources, by merging theories of management from social sciences and ecology (Berkes et al., 1998). To explain this approach in simple terms (that may offend ecologists) we can say the managers of a resource and the people that depend on that resource are part of the social system while the resources being exploited and their related ecosystems are part of the ecological system. Building a timber house is part of the social system but the wood comes from an ecosystem. The social-ecological system as used by the Stockholm Resilience Centre (see Chapter 1) is defined as an ecological system that changes because of interaction with human beings (Lade et al., 2013). Given the prevalence of humanity it would be hard to find an ecosystem on Earth that had not been affected by the presence of people. Adger (2000) neatly links social and ecological systems in the statement 'Ecological and social resilience may be linked through the dependence on ecosystems of communities and their economic activities' or you cannot build timber houses without having some sort of forest. The social-ecological approach thus aims to link the institutional, economic, social and ecological challenges around the exploitation of a resource, while the resilience management of social-ecological systems aims at avoiding moving to undesirable scenarios, like building so many timber houses that there are no forests left.

It is possible to say that the expansion of research into ecological resilience has obliged ecologists to produce a deeper understanding of Holling's theories. The ecological studies by Brian Walker (Walker et al., 2012; Walker and Meyers, 2004; Walker and Salt, 2006), Carl Folke (Folke et al., 1996, 2004), and Carpenter (Carpenter et al., 2001; Carpenter and Brock, 2006) have been particularly influential in advancing the understanding, and therefore, definition of ecological resilience. Holling has also made significant contributions to his previous definitions and the next section looks briefly at all this work and the advances made in the definition of resilience.

Resilience and identity

Walker et al. (2004) define resilience as 'the capacity of a system to absorb disturbance and reorganize while undergoing change so as to still retain essentially the same

42   Definitions

function, structure, identity, and feedbacks'. As in the original definition by Holling (1973), Walker also describes resilience in relationship to persistence. Walker's argument the structure and function of a system could be used to describe its identity, acity to maintain this identity after a shock means avoidance of changing so m.. s to become something else; in other words it loses its identity. The important contribution of Walker for designers is the link between resilience, stability and identity. Urban designers and architects are used to dealing with identity issues, such as the loss of local identity through the universal application of modernist design ideals and globalization (Relph, 1976), but they rarely quantify these. Walker's definition opens opportunities for exploring resilience and identity together.

Resilience and thresholds

Walker, Carpenter and Folke stressed the importance of researching thresholds (Folke *et al.*, 2004; Walker and Meyers, 2004), or tipping points. Within these the system is more or less predictable but if a disturbance moves it up to one or more of these thresholds, then it only takes a small push to move the system across the threshold(s) and make it pass to a different state, where its performance will be more unpredictable. For example, a tenant and a landlord make a contract that stipulates the rent and conditions of tenancy for a house. The relationship is stable until the landlord sells the house and the tenant has to make a new contract with the new landlord. This new contract could raise the rent to the point the tenant cannot afford it. This is the threshold or tipping point. If the tenant agrees to pay more rent so as to be able to keep the house, other sacrifices have to be made. This might mean having less money for savings, which makes the tenant more vulnerable to any unfortunate event. If the tenant decides not to pay the increased rent and to move to a different house then there will be the challenge of a new place with new rules. Nobody knows what may happen but we do know that it will be different after the threshold is passed. In this example the threshold is easy to define because the limitations are clear but in complex systems like cities or ecosystems, the thresholds are not that clear. The conditions of the 'contract' may have changed without our being aware of it and we continue to behave according to the previous rules, leading directly to crossing a threshold without realizing it. Because of this, scholars trying to expand the understanding of resilience have been concerned about the position of a system in relationship to its thresholds (Walker *et al.*, 2004). To do this they suggest studying the history of a system in order to know where the limit was in the past and then to speculate about the future. Defining when and where the system crossed a threshold in this type of study is easier than defining its future state. However, the main aim behind resilience is trying to understand where the system is now, how precarious it is, and what is at stake. It is the past that provides information about the history of a system (this is one of the properties of complex adaptive systems). So the historical performance of a system is a reference point that can be compared to where the system is now, and how far it has moved from the reference point (Golley, 1993). This information is important for defining the margin for action that we have in the present and for obtaining an insight into how far from the tipping point a system might be. However, the past is not the future and this is what makes these studies so complicated. The fact that someone showed a huge resilience in overcoming an episode of depression in the past is not evidence for the person getting through a new period of depression without problems.

General and specific resilience

Walker also differentiated between general and specific or specified resilience (Walker, 2007). Specific resilience is the resilience of a part of a system to a specified threat or shock (Walker and Salt, 2012) and is based on the idea developed by Carpenter *et al.* (2001) that an operational definition of resilience should address the following imperative: the *resilience of what to what* is being analysed? For example, in the case of cities, the concept can be used to analyse the resilience of the built environment to earthquakes. Lately, Walker and Salt (2012: 18) have defined specific resilience as the resilience of part of a system (subsystem) to a particular event or crisis. Even though the specific resilience highlights the relativity of the concept of resilience it also helps to define resilience in proportion to or in comparison with something concrete and quantifiable, the particular event or crisis.

General resilience is what helps a system deal with any kind of shock as opposed to a specific event. The idea of a general resilience is also closely linked with Walker and Salt's resilience thinking (2006). 'Resilience thinking is about understanding and engaging with a changing world. By understanding how and why the system as a whole is changing, we are better placed to build a capacity to work with change, as opposed to being a victim of it' (Walker and Salt, 2006: 14). Resilience thinking is about understanding your system so it is sustainable (Walker and Salt, 2012). Walker's aim was to define the total resilience of a system. For him, resilience and systems thinking are inextricably linked, because in our human-centred world social and ecological systems depend on each other and also because long-term strategies need the holistic approach provided by systems thinking (Walker and Salt, 2006). General resilience acknowledges that a system must develop key properties to have more chance of adapting to a wider range of shocks, in other words making a system more robust in the face of whatever may happen. The key properties according to Walker are diversity, openness, reserves, tightness of feedbacks, modularity, level of assets (capital) and leadership, trust and networks in the social capital (Walker and Salt, 2006). For those interested in resilience and the built environment it is apparent that some of these terms could be measured (reserves, capital) but that others are far more difficult (trust). Table 3.1 shows an example of a framework developed for the assessment of resilience.

This approach is like sustainability indicators which tend to be reduced to what can be measured, with the risk of not taking account of something vital that is very hard to measure, such as a willingness to change lifestyle habits in the case of sustainability. Walker (2014) has highlighted that the assessment of general resilience needs more conceptual rigour and is still vague for practitioners. If it is further developed the concept of general resilience is an opportunity to approach the adaptive capacity of a system in a holistic way. The fact this generalist approach to resilience has influenced institutions in creating their own lists of criteria with which to assess, define and characterize resilience should be seen as a warning. For example, the Stockholm Resilience Centre used Walker's approach to create its own list of general properties for building resilience in social-ecological systems. These do not differ greatly from the original ideas but do not advance the possibilities for developing methods to measurement that can be shared between fields (Table 3.2).

Table 3.2 compares two sets of academic definitions of the properties of general resilience with the principles for building greater resilience in communities. However,

Table 3.1 Walker's framework for the assessment of resilience, based on Walker and Salt (2012)

Walker and Salt (2006) Properties of general resilience	Carpenter et al. (2012) Properties of general resilience	Stockholm Resilience Centre 7 principles for building resilience (n.d.)
Diversity	Diversity	Maintain diversity and redundancy
Modularity	Modularity	
Openness	Openness	
Reserves	Reserves	
Tightness of feedbacks	Feedbacks	Manage slow variables and feedbacks
Level of assets (capital)		
	Nestedness	
Monitoring	Monitoring	Promote polycentric governance
Leadership	Leadership	Foster complex adaptive systems thinking
Trust	Trust	Encourage learning
Networks in social capital		Manage connectivity
		Broaden participation

Table 3.2 Properties of general resilience

1 General resilience

Attribute	Description and criteria	Assessment
Diversity	Different ways of maintaining or performing the same function	Not specified
Openness	Level of difficulty to move in and out of a system ideas, people, species, etc.	Not specified
Reserves	More reserves means more resilience, they can be economic, social or natural	Not specified
Tightness	Weakening of feedbacks	Not specified
Modularity	Loosely connected groups with tight feedbacks between its components	Not specified
Social Capital	Bonding through leadership and bridging through social networks	Change in the numbers of organizations and members
Assets	Amount and quality of capital assets	High debt, income and operating costs, low equity

Specified resilience

Steps	Description	Assessment
Known thresholds	Threshold matrix organized by scales and domains (e.g. economic, social, biophysical)	Not specified
Thresholds of potential concerns	Suspected thresholds	Not specified
Conceptual models	Mental model to describe how the system works and changes	State and transition model
Analytical models	Analytical models of alternate thresholds and their defining thresholds	Mathematical models of linked differential equations. Network models, agent-based models

rather like the checklist approach of the different building rating systems discussed earlier it is possible to see such lists as desirable goals with a roadmap of how to achieve them, or whether there should be priorities in aiming for the various goals.

The key point of the general resilience approach for designers is that the state and performance of a system as a whole are perhaps more important than its ability to resist particular threats (like earthquakes). The problem is the former are potentially much more difficult to measure than the latter. Moreover, misunderstandings may arise when what resilience is expected to deliver is confused with what it is (the property of a system).

Resilience strategies

Walker and his colleagues have also suggested the importance of deciding whether the present situation is desirable or not and how much it would take to move away from or towards the thresholds. This led Walker *et al.* (2004) to define two resilience actions: adaptability and transformability. Adaptability is about making changes in the trajectory of a system so as to increase (if the situation is desirable) or decrease (if undesirable) its proximity to a threshold. This reinforces the earlier point that some changes of state in systems could be desired – an Australian bush fire is both a change in state but desirable because it allows certain plants to regrow. However, when it comes to built environments most changes in state will be undesirable. Transformability is about making massive changes to create new conditions for the whole system (such as slum clearance to create better housing). Adaptability and transformability are potentially useful for designers because they establish a clear link between the situation of a system and the strategy to be taken. In fact, designers are familiar with the situation when renovating old houses. We can put resources in to renew and adapt an old house and make it fit for modern living but there comes a point where it is so bad it is easier to knock it down and start again (transformability).

Resilience, novelty and adaptation

Because the importance of learning from the past has been discussed (see section, Resilience and thresholds) this may lead to the assumption that resilience is mainly reactive instead of proactive or that it is useful for mitigating undesirable changes but not for generating the desirable. Contrary to this, Allen and Holling (2010) suggested there is a close link between novelty, adaptive capacity and resilience and understanding variability is key to learning how novelty enhances the resilience of a system. They studied how variations in the structure of a system, produced by invasion, migration, nomadism or extinction, became opportunities for the creation of novel interactions. They found more variance in the population and diversity of systems that were more successful at adapting and demonstrated that decentralized and diverse structures create opportunities for coping with unpredictable change. Garmestani *et al.* (2006) had previously arrived at similar conclusions when analysing volatility in businesses. They found larger firms that could command more resources were better able to deal with crises and avoid extinction than smaller firms. This is why so many small firms fail unless they can find a niche in the market that no-one else is exploiting. Allen and Holling (2010) demonstrated that migrations and invasions in ecosystems introduce novelty and make the structure of a system more diverse and decentralized. They also

46 *Definitions*

observed that the introduction of novelties in a system could help in avoiding becoming overconnected and losing diversity.

3.7 What resilience is not: misunderstandings

Disciplines researching resilience

Since the 1980s publications dealing with resilience have not only increased but have also used the term without precision (Janssen *et al.*, 2006). Concerns about climate change have also linked the study of resilience with other concepts such as vulnerability (what will happen if there is dramatic climate change) and adaptation (how humanity will have to change to cope with climate change), both discussed below. Institutions trying to assess global environmental change and research into natural hazards, climate change, food security and poverty and inequality have promoted the idea that resilience, vulnerability and adaption have a point of intersection. However, because there was no agreed definition of resilience, this has added to the confusion (Chapter 1). One positive outcome is that opportunities for collaboration between these research interests have emerged (Janssen *et al.*, 2006). Nevertheless, the lack of clarity in fundamental definitions could be an obstacle when it comes to major advances in any of these fields. The aim here, therefore, is to try to unravel the particularities of resilience, vulnerability and adaptation to better understand the former by clarifying how it diverges from the latter two.

Even though resilience has been linked with various research fields from anthropology to psychology, its strongest theoretical background emanates from mathematics (cybernetics), engineering (materials) and ecology. Studies in vulnerability and adaptation are frequently found in the field of mitigation and adaptation to climate change (Janssen *et al.*, 2006), whereas resilience, with a focus on the production of theoretical models to explain processes of change, has been developed in ecology away from the climate change umbrella. The theoretical background of vulnerability and adaptation comes from research in geography, sociology and natural hazards, with a focus on the analysis and comparison of case studies, particularly linked with the effects of climate change (Janssen *et al.*, 2006).

All these observations are helpful to show that resilience has roots in both the scientific approach of mathematics and natural science and in human-centred social science. The latter has produced a new field of research some scholars call social-ecological resilience, which is a mix of adaptation, vulnerability, social and ecological resilience (Wilkinson, 2012). The problem generated by these divergent uses of resilience goes beyond a semantic disagreement about the identity of each field or who has to do what, as the main challenge comes when trying to create and use a definition to define ways of measuring concrete problems. The assumption here is that by understanding the development and differences between definitions it will be possible to infer what is being measured when concepts like vulnerability, resilience and adaptability are used.

Resilience is not the same as vulnerability

As a key for resilience thinking, Walker and Salt (2006: 9–10) stated: '… at the heart of resilience thinking is a very simple notion – things change – and to ignore or resist this change is to increase our vulnerability and forego emerging opportunities. In so doing, we limit our options.' This quote highlights the importance of and linkages between resilience, vulnerability and change. However, the same quote also sets off circular reasoning: if a system is resilient it is not vulnerable and if it is vulnerable it is not resilient, which is not helpful for distinguishing one concept from the other. Therefore it is important to examine the definition of vulnerability, which has also changed according to where it is used.

Mitchell (1989) believed vulnerability is mainly concerned with analysis of a potential loss. Cutter (2003) pointed out that vulnerability is strongly linked with the chances of being exposed to hazards that will produce an undesirable effect. The IPCC, in relation to climate change, has produced a definition of vulnerability that includes concepts like susceptibility to being harmed and ability to deal with adversities (McCarthy et al., 2001). The definitions that emphasize susceptibility to being harmed as a determinant component of vulnerability make Adger's (2006) argument that vulnerability is the opposite of resilience, or at least is something negative (whereas resilience is something positive to be desired), seem reasonable.

Resilience is not the same as adaptation

In terms of climate change, Pelling (2011) sees adaptation as a cheaper and more convenient political and social act than resisting change. He argues that it is too late to make radical changes to the way people live in order to stop climate change, thus making adaptation the only survival strategy. He further draws a difference between conservative and active adaptation. Conservative adaptation is described in terms of what needs to be preserved and what can be lost. For example, conservative adaptation in a capitalistic society could mean the preservation of its economic system as an essential asset and could also suggest that related ecosystems services are expendable. However, from this point of view all conversations about adaptation are useless. It all depends how you define 'what can be lost'. Active adaptation has a different focus. Here efforts are concentrated on thinking about what can be gained or transformed if changes occur. Thus changing to public transport using renewable electricity to mitigate climate change could also produce better cities for low impact walking and cycling because of less pollution and traffic in the streets. These points of view define the two faces of adaptation, as both a backward- and forward-looking process.

Although adaptation is one of the main characteristics of resilience, they are not the same. Resilience can involve adaptation and persistence at the same time. Adapting a city to run on electric rather than fossil fuel transport does not change the persisting identity of the city. As discussed, adaptability and transformability (see section, Resilience strategies) (Walker and Meyers, 2004) are the two main strategies of change for enhancing or decreasing the resilience capacity of a system.

3.8 Critics of the concept of resilience

Vagueness

Resilience has been criticized for being a concept that is vague, blurred and difficult to understand (Strunz, 2012; Sudmeier-Rieux, 2014). Since its appearance in the nineteenth century as a precisely defined term used by engineers, its definition has varied with the research discipline. Variations between definitions are sometimes subtle and for this reason susceptible to being merged, innocently mixed up, or messed up with indifference. Nonetheless, definitions matter because they have huge implications when   to the analysis and measurement of the dynamics of systems. For this reason it is important to try to understand not only the underlying assumptions of each definition but also what is at stake when using one definition rather than another.

Resilience is not difficult to define, it is simply the capacity to adapt and persist. What is very difficult is to say what adaptation and persistence mean and which capacities of the system under examination have to be improved. Both concepts represent ends in themselves that can be rich and that have different meanings in different contexts. In the context of a pedestrian and bike-focused city, electric transport might be good, but for companies that rely on long-distance transport the much lower fuel density of an electric rather than petrol vehicle might mean much more careful planning of journeys, which could be less convenient. Persistence can be both desired and not wanted. The tourist industry in a city will want to keep heritage buildings, whereas businesses in the same city might prefer new, convenient, low energy buildings over the old and would prefer a new identity to emerge from these new buildings. Property developers too will want to pull down the old and build the new because it will make them money. The problem that prevents the understanding of resilience is clearly the relationship between it and the context in which it is used. When resilience is spoken of in an urban context, usually when people talk about resilient cities or resilient neighbourhoods, the first need is to define whose interests are being served by making the city or neighbourhood more resilient. Increasing the resilience of a city will mean investment in the adaptability of a selected part of it to floods, earthquakes or other natural hazards, or the persistence of the main economic activities of a city, which are all good goals, but very different from increasing the resilience of an entire city. This is because activities like the persistence of key economic activities, or shoring up parts of the urban landscape, usually tend to favour a minority over the majority of citizens. A good example of this can be seen in the way that General Motors bought and then closed the electric streetcar (tram) systems in many American cities so that they could replace the clean electric streetcars with polluting diesel buses sold by General Motors (Kunstler, 1993: 91–92). This was good for General Motors, and 'what's good for General Motors is good for America', but it was not necessarily good for the affected cities and their residents.

Although resilience thinking is based on systems thinking, it is not the same as it. Urban designers and architects are familiar with the systems approach as this is how we design. We approach a design problem (a new building) by breaking it down into its sub-systems (numbers and types of spaces, circulation, access, orientation, etc.) and then looking at the relationships between these, some of which may conflict. We then try to come up with a solution that will answer most of the problems and then we reanalyse this solution. We need to 'freeze' the reality and break it into pieces to analyse it. But for understanding resilience dynamics it seems that we need to make the analysis in real time, like designing the building as it is being constructed. This pushes systemic analysis to its limits.

Adaptation to capitalism

Resilience can be criticized for being a theoretical tool serving neo-liberal ideologies (Evans and Reid, 2013; Hornborg, 2009; Joseph, 2013; Walker and Cooper, 2011).

The focus of this critique is the unresolved tension between capitalism and climate change, and the hope that unpleasant results will be temporarily delayed by introducing resilience. The cynical could say that studying the vague topic of resilience is another way of putting off doing anything about climate change. Even taking a more optimistic view, resilience becomes more like poker play, meaning we know we have to adapt to whatever cards are played (climate problems) while also knowing that cards will be played (climate change will happen). Anyone who has played poker will understand. Although the aim is to win money, every play involves the risk of losing it. At the same time the player is always trying to lessen the risk through the cards he or she plays. But the analogy holds only up to a point, if you lose a poker game you can go home, whereas if we lose the game of climate change your home may well be under water.

For Hornborg (2009), the management of resources in ecological resilience is very important, and such management is not possible without a clear understanding of the power relationships that influence how decisions about these resources are made. The interplay of economic and political forces is a significant influence on the use, organization and distribution of natural resources. Acknowledging the political dimension of a culture is essential to avoid the social system being oversimplified, and ultimately, to avoid masking social inequalities.

Philosophical approach and ethics

Part of the philosophy of resilience is simple, being based on the idea that if we have arrived at this point we should be able to carry on. The resilience approach is not about defining the right size, final state or best performance of a system but rather finding a way to keep the system working while maintaining the social and ecological systems intact. Resilience thus links and makes possible the understanding of persistence and adaptation as simultaneous processes. Simplifying this idea, there are many examples of buildings, frequently Modernist buildings, that looked amazing when first finished but which leaked (e.g. Frank Lloyd Wright's Fallingwater) or overheated (Le Corbusier's Cité de Refuge) or were simply uninhabitable (Mies van der Rohe's Farnsworth House). They were not very resilient. There are also buildings like Southwell Minster in England, mostly completed in the twelfth century, that have been used daily for the purpose (worship) they were designed for. There have been changes and adaptations to the building but not so as it make it unrecognizable (its identity is unchanged). It is the latter that demonstrates real resilience and significantly it is not a Modernist building.

There is also a philosophical problem with the ethics of resilience. As a property of something resilience does not necessarily imply having it is either a good or a bad thing. It can either be a good property to be achieved or enhanced or the opposite. Crime, poor health and inequality are all very resilient in many cities but do we want to improve the resilience of crime or try to break it? There is another ethical problem. Resilience represents an almost Machiavellian mechanism, where the ends of adaptation and persistence justify the necessary means. As we said before the emphasis of the definition is not on how you adapt but in adaptation in itself. Therefore, as suggested in the criticism of resilience as a capitalistic tool, it could produce a lot of harm in the name of a supposedly good cause.

3.9 Conclusions

Framing definitions

The main objective of this chapter was to unravel what resilience means before thinking about how we might see if it could be applied to the physical built environment. The final objective is to discover why resilience might be important for designers. Acknowledging that resilience comes from different fields of research, its development in ecology, based on a systemic approach, creates links and opens possibilities for its possible use in understanding and designing the built environment. However, the translation and use of concepts from different fields into another realm always carry the risk of falling into a set of misunderstandings and metaphorical dead ends. So, by defining resilience we are trying to minimize misunderstandings to provoke a better use and flow of interdisciplinary knowledge. The approach we have taken is based on a literature review of the multiple meanings and uses of resilience. This has led to investigation of its origins and its different perceptions depending on the original field of research and the ways it is used.

The relationship between the content and practice of resilience is one of two opposite poles and two tendencies. The two poles are 'scientific' (academic investigation and constructing the theory) and 'social' (applying the theory) resilience, while the two tendencies are definitions with descriptive or metaphorical inclinations. Definitions of resilience tend to be at the intersection of all these categories. Some definitions emphasize a scientific approach with a descriptive inclination, like Holling's (1973) original definition (resilience is a property of all complex systems). Others work as metaphors that allow a variety of interpretations susceptible of being associated with social aims and goals (we need to learn to adapt to climate change). Describing and clarifying the approach taken when using the concept of resilience is fundamental for avoidance of misunderstandings. At the same time, the act of framing definitions might help to minimize misunderstandings by making explicit what is at stake in each case and what will result when using a particular definition of resilience. Designers interested in resilience must realize the definitional position taken will influence how the present and future built environment is analysed and made. Before trying to build resilience into the built environment it is essential to understand both what resilience is and what its limitations are.

What is the importance of resilience for designers of the built environment?

As a species human beings have created an unusual and complex habitat that has its material climax in the built environment of cities. The success of built urban landscapes as the main habitat for our species has both affected how we live and has also placed humanity in a position of needing to find complex solutions to new problems that are themselves getting more and more complex. The effect of this is very clear in the built environment and increases the challenges faced by designers. Cities are becoming more complicated, involving more variables. They have to satisfy more demands for more people, and these demands create more connections and exploit more resources. Such an immense number of players and resources is obviously difficult to manage and the outcome of all these actions is even more difficult to predict. As a result, more complex problems are generated, involving more people dependent on the resolution of these problems. Terrorism, economic crises, violence, poverty and inequity are all problems that have found their climax in cities and that represent major threats to the urban habitat. These problems, and not only the risks posed by natural hazards, should be the subject of designers interested in the resilience of cities.

We know that designers have a small part to play in the solution of urban problems, not least based on the realization that 90 per cent of world architecture is vernacular (Oliver, 2003), but also because many other agents influence why cities are like they are. Even looking at the history of the physical form of cities it seems they have been built little by little and layer by layer, over generations, mainly without architects. The phenomenon of cities designed from *tabula rasa* by architects is quite modern in comparison with the origin of most world cities (see also Chapter 5). Even though the majority of the oldest, still functioning cities in the world have a humble, vernacular origin, they have shown a great capacity to change and to persist. For example, Paris, London and Berlin (among many others) are cities that have exhibited a capacity for resilience in their own processes of development, meaning that in their history these cities have passed through many fires, wars and crises of different types but have kept on functioning. They have survived without collapsing and they have each maintained an individual identity. From this point of view we can argue that cities show a certain capacity of persistence that, of course, has limitations. In the past, many cities and urban settlements have collapsed or were abandoned, such as Tenochtitlan, Angkor Wat and Macchu Picchu, and these now only remain as vestiges of past cities temporarily inhabited by tourists.

The persistence of many of the oldest cities in the world as well as the growth and development of new ones has been possible not only because of their capacity to resist crises but also through their capacities to change and absorb disturbances. They have persisted because they have changed. In this way we can say that they have adapted to the problems generated by their own development as well as to unpredictable disturbances. To repeat, change is inevitable because it is a constant of the evolutionary process, however persistence is just a condition of that change. Even 'historic' and protected places, like Venice, in Italy, or Purmamarca, in Argentina, have inevitably changed in order to persist. So the question here is what is the potential contribution of designers in enhancing the resilience of the built environment if cities inherently already have a resilience capacity that leads to adaptation and persistence?

Designers can create new cities, intervene, change, destroy and transform cities but they cannot generally freeze, undo or move cities (although Ron Herron of the Archigram group in the UK famously proposed a 'walking city' in the 1960s). Moreover, societies do not design new cities every year, not only because it takes time but also because using and improving the infrastructure of the existing ones is usually cheaper and faster than building a whole new one. For this reason we keep living in and transforming the same cities where our parents and grandfathers lived. To be able to keep on building in the same cities after all these years and despite population growth seems like a miracle. If designers cannot move cities, and building new ones is quite expensive, we will have to keep on modifying the existing ones, for which a resilience approach could be helpful, even if up to now cities seem to have managed quite well without deliberately applying such an approach. Even though resilience is not the solution to all urban problems, it may be able to help designers have a better understanding of the dynamics of change in cities, and in this way, provide an awareness of how to adapt the present cities to future challenges, especially to those we know about, such as climate change.

Societies need stability to be able to predict and forecast growth and also to develop a sense of belonging to one place. All these are the benefits gained from the stability of processes and persistence of infrastructure in a landscape. However, designers can learn from a resilience approach that stability is not steadiness and persistence does not mean absence of change. The stability that leads to persistence is an emergent situation of temporary equilibrium in a system. It is not, by itself, an inherent condition or the normal state of a system. Resilience is about all these concerns because it is about understanding adaptation and persistence as being woven together. So designers need a deeper understanding of adaptation and persistence because these lie at the heart of everyday life in cities and are the essence of their survival.

By implementing the theoretical framework of resilience designers can learn how to cope and profit from the capacity that cities have for adaptation and persistence instead of being victims of change, whether predictable or unpredictable. So far, this sounds more like a promise than a reality because so far we have developed resilience as a theory, but even in this case, finding possibilities and opportunities in a concept is a better prospect than not doing so.

What opportunities can designers exploit?

The theory of ecological resilience is based on a set of assumptions about how ecosystems change (for example, Panarchy and adaptive cycles) and could become a first step in new ways of thinking about urban change, not least because it leads us to learn from built environments that have been successful in persisting and adapting.

Most of the concepts used in ecological resilience are not new to social scientists, historians or architects. Designers living and working in cities have been exposed to the kind of changes that adaptation and persistence imply. In architecture, the concept of adaptation has been explored by Brand (1994) and influenced by anthropogolist Rappaport (1977) among others. In history, authors from the Annales School of historiography have discussed the importance of understanding the scales of history (Braudel, 1980) in the same way that Panarchy and the adaptive cycle highlight the value of understanding change within and across scales. Geographers and urban morphologists (Caniggia, 2001; Conzen and Conzen, 2004) have investigated the development of cities and the way they have changed. Some of these ideas were used to establish fruitful comparisons between the ways in which change happens in the built environment and the concept of evolution in biology (Kropf, 2001). Metaphors of evolutionary processes have a long tradition in practice and research in architecture and urban design (Malfroy, 1998). The concept of complexity, which is fundamental in ecological resilience, has also been applied to the study of cities and to the analysis of architecture (Alexander, 1964; Batty, 2010). Urban researchers have carried out research into the complexity (Rapoport and Kantor, 1967) and diversity of cities (Jacobs, 1961/2011) and their dynamics of change (Conzen, 1960) even before resilience was consolidated in ecology. Therefore, many of the key words used by Walker and Salt (2006), as a representative of those interested in the practice of ecological resilience, when defining the general resilience of a system, namely redundancy, complexity, connectivity or diversity, have all been part of the theory and practice of urban designers. So what is new for designers in resilience?

The theoretical approaches developed in ecological resilience offer designers a comprehensive, systemic and methodological way of linking many key concepts that are familiar to architects (complex systems, scales, diversity, connectivity, redundancy) into a cohesive discourse focused on change. The innovation is that resilience is concentrated on explaining the processes of adaptation and persistence as part of a single phenomenon. From this point of view, the concept of resilience could be used as a comprehensive way of thinking about the design of the built environment (Thorén, 2014). The idea of assessing adaptive change in complex systems could be important for understanding the state of social systems, and this might be achieved by analysing the quantity and quality of change observed in landscapes. In the case of cities, for example, the theory could help the analysis and interpretation of changes in the built environment in such a way that the information can be used as evidence to assess the 'performance' and 'health' of the social and ecological systems that produced it. Learning how to amass this kind of information for cities is an important step in advancing the 'science of cities' and explaining the persistence of a social-ecological system.

The idea of understanding the urban landscape of cities as an urban Panarchy could be promising for both managers and designers. The adaptive cycle, Panarchy and the idea of multiple stability states are all theoretical instruments with which to assess the quality and quantity of change of a system. In an era where large databases, online maps and geographic software can facilitate the handling of large quantities of information, a theory that helps to categorize and interpret change will be more than welcomed. The implementation of the resilience theory in urban social-ecological landscapes can give designers an idea of the 'performance' and development of a system using the evidence extracted from the built environment. One of the possibilities that Panarchy and the adaptive cycle offer is a way of understanding where your system is in the cycle and the characteristics of that phase. Moreover, the concept of Panarchy could permit integration and visualization of the behaviour and performance of a system at multiple scales at the same time. This is potentially a big change in the process of urban analysis. This is because it implies understanding change by analysing bottom-up forces that are generated at the micro-scale of the built environment, the architectural scale, while simultaneously acknowledging top-down forces and changes at the large urban scale.

The creation of urban Panarchies, as a theoretical construct for analysing urban landscapes, could give designers an opportunity for taking into account non-linearity and development (the dynamics of change of the built environment) in a pragmatic way. By using the approach described in Panarchy, the future can be considered and understood as an asset and not only as an uncertain zone. Because resilience is also about novelty and the opportunities that emerge when previous conditions change, future transformations, crises or even the collapse of a system can all be understood as favourable circumstances for organizing the capital, suddenly released after a crisis, in an alternative way. For instance, Wren produced a plan for reshaping the city of London that opened up the city with broad boulevards and piazzas, made possible because 90 per cent of the area had been destroyed. Wren was seizing the opportunity to reshape the city of London, even if his plan was never carried out – had it been so, many descriptions of the city found in the novels of Dickens would have been very different. In the end, however much we adopt a resilience approach, most of the future remains unknown, even when we can see the effects of climate change coming ever closer.

The next chapter will summarize the findings so far by comparing the characteristics of sustainability and resilience before moving on to see how useful these concepts are in the description and analysis of three built environment case studies.

Bibliography

Adger, W. N. (2000). Social and ecological resilience: are they related? *Progress in Human Geography* 24(3), pp. 347–364.

Adger, W. N. (2006). Vulnerability. *Global Environmental Change* 16(3), pp. 268–281.

Alexander, C. (1964). *Notes on the Synthesis of Form*. Cambridge, MA: Harvard University Press.

Allen, C. R. and Holling, C. S. (2010). Novelty, adaptive capacity, and resilience. *Ecology and Society* 15(3), p. 15.

Allen, T. F. and Starr, T. (1982). *Hierarchy: Perspectives for Ecological Complexity*. Chicago, IL: University of Chicago Press.

American Psychological Association (APA). (2015). The road to resilience. Available at www.apa.org/helpcenter/road-resilience.aspx, accessed 28 April 2015.

Batty, M. (2010). Towards a new science of cities. *Building Research & Information* 38(1), pp. 123–126.

Beresford, M. (1954). *The Lost Villages of England*. London: Lutterworth Press.

Berkes, F., Folke, C. and Colding, J. (1998). *Linking Social and Ecological Systems: Management Practices and Social Mechanisms for Building Resilience*. Cambridge and New York: Cambridge University Press.

Brand, S. (1994). *How Buildings Learn*. New York: Viking.

Braudel, F. (1980). *On History*. Chicago, IL: University of Chicago Press.

Caniggia, G. (2001). *Architectural Composition and Building Typology: Interpreting Basic Building*. Florence: Alinea.

Carpenter, S., Walker, B., Anderies, J. M. and Abel, N. (2001). From metaphor to measurement: resilience of what to what? *Ecosystems* 4(8), pp. 765–781.

Carpenter, S. R. and Brock, W. A. (2006). Rising variance: a leading indicator of ecological transition. *Ecology Letters* 9(3), pp. 311–318.

Carpenter, S. R., Arrow, K. J., Barrett, S., Biggs, R., Brock, W. A., Crépin, A-S., Engström, G., Folke, C., Hughes, T. P., Kautsky, N., Li, C-Z., McCarney, G., Meng, K., Mäler, K-G., Polasky, S., Scheffer, M., Shogren, J., Sterner, T., Vincent, J. R., Walker, B., Xepapadeas, A. and de Zeeuw, A. (2012). General resilience to cope with extreme events. *Sustainability* 4, pp. 3248–3259.

Conzen, M. R. G. (1960). Alnwick, Northumberland: a study in town-plan analysis. *Transactions and Papers (Institute of British Geographers)* 27, pp. iii–122.

Conzen, M. R. G. and Conzen, M. P. (2004). *Thinking about Urban Form: Papers on Urban Morphology, 1932–1998*. Oxford and New York: Peter Lang.

Cutter, S. L. (2003). The vulnerability of science and the science of vulnerability. *Annals of the Association of American Geographers* 93, pp. 1–12.

Evans, B. and Reid, J. (2013). Dangerously exposed: the life and death of the resilient subject. *Resilience* 1(2), pp. 83–98.

Folke, C., Carpenter, S., Walker, B., Scheffer, M., Chapin, T. and Rockström, J. (2010). Resilience thinking: integrating resilience, adaptability and transformability. *Ecology and Society* 15(4): 20, available at www.ecologyandsociety.org/vol15/iss4/art20/.

Folke, C., Carpenter, S., Walker, B., Scheffer, M., Elmqvist, T., Gunderson, L. and Holling, C. S. (2004). Regime shifts, resilience, and biodiversity in ecosystem management [Review]. *Annual Review of Ecology Evolution and Systematics* 35, pp. 557–581.

Folke, C., Holling, C. S. and Perrings, C. (1996). Biological diversity, ecosystems, and the human scale. *Ecological Applications* 6(4), pp. 1018–1024.

Freedman, A. (2015). Marco Rubio doubts manmade global warming, says 'climate is always changing'. Available at http://mashable.com/2015/04/19/rubio-denies-global-warming/, accessed 10 May 2015.

Garmestani, A., Allen, C., Mittelstaedt, J., Stow, C. and Ward, W. (2006). Firm size diversity, functional richness, and resilience. *Environment and Development Economics* 11(4), pp. 533–551.

Golley, F. (1993). *A History of the Ecosystem Concept in Ecology: More than the Sum of the Parts*. New Haven, CT: Yale University Press.

Garmezy, N. (1973). Competence and adaptation in adult schizophrenic patients and children at risk. In S. R. Dean (ed.), *Schizophrenia: The First Ten Dean Award Lectures*, pp. 163–204. New York: MSS Information Corp.

Garmezy, N. and Streitman, S. (1974). Children at risk: the search for the antecedents of schizophrenia. Part 1. Conceptual models and research methods. *Schizophrenia Bulletin* 8(8), pp. 14–90.

Gunderson, L. H. (2000). Ecological resilience in theory and application. *Annual Review of Ecology and Systematics* 31, p. 425.

Gunderson, L. H. and Holling, C. S. (2002). *Panarchy: Understanding Transformations in Human and Natural Systems*. Washington, DC: Island Press.

Harris, S. (2013). Culling urban foxes just doesn't work. *New Scientist*, available at https://www.newscientist.com/article/mg21729050-200-culling-urban-foxes-just-doesnt-work/ accessed 15 Feb 2017.

Herlihy, D. (1997). *The Black Death and the Transformaiton of the West*. Cambridge, MA: Harvard University Press.

Holling, C. S. (1973). Resilience and stability of ecological systems. *Annual Review of Ecology and Systematics* 4(1), pp. 1–23.

Holling, C. S. (1987). Simplifying the complex: the paradigms of ecological function and structure. *European Journal of Operational Research* 30(2), pp. 139–146.

Holling, C. S. (1992). Cross-scale morphology, geometry, and dynamics of ecosystems. *Ecological Monographs* 62(4), pp. 447–502.

Holling, C. S. (2004). From complex regions to complex worlds. *Ecology and Society* 9(1), p. 11.

Hornborg, A. (2009). Zero-sum world: challenges in conceptualizing environmental load displacement and ecologically unequal exchange in the world-system. *International Journal of Comparative Sociology* 50(3–4), pp. 237–262.

Jacobs, J. (1961/2011). *The Death and Life of Great American Cities* (50th anniversary edn). New York: Modern Library.

Janssen, M., Schoon, M., Ke, W. and Börner, K. (2006). Scholarly networks on resilience, vulnerability and adaptation within the human dimensions of global environmental change. *Global Environmental Change* 16(3), pp. 240–252.

Joseph, J. (2013). Resilience as embedded neoliberalism: a governmentality approach. *Resilience* 1(1), pp. 38–52.

Kropf, K. S. (2001). Conceptions of change in the built environment. *Urban Morphology* 5(1), p. 14.

Kunstler, J. H. (1993). *The Geography of Nowhere: the Rise and Decline of America's Man-Made Landscape*. New York: Touchstone.

Lade, S. J., Tavoni, A., Levin, S. A. and Schlüter, M. (2013). Regime shifts in a social-ecological-system. Working Paper 125, Centre for Climate Change Economics and Policy, available at www.lse.ac.uk/GranthamInstitute/wp-content/uploads/2013/01/WP105-regime-shifts-socio-ecological-system.pdf, accessed 10 May 2016.

Levin, S. (1998). Ecosystems and the biosphere as complex adaptive systems. *Ecosystems* 1(5), pp. 431–436.

Malfroy, S. (1998). On the question of organicist metaphors. *Urban Morphology* 2(1), pp. 47–50.

56 Definitions

Mallet, M. (1856). *On the Physical Conditions involved in the Construction of Artillery: an investigation of the relative and absolute values of the materials principally employed and of some hitherto unexplained causes of the destruction of the canon in service*. London: Longman, Brown, Green, Longmans and Roberts.

McAslan, A. (2010). The concept of resilience: understanding its origins, meaning and utility. Torrens Resilience Institute, Adelaide, available at http://torrensresilience.org/origins-of-the-term, accessed 12 May 2015.

McCarthy, J. J., Canziani, O. F., Leary, N. A., Dokken, D.J. and White, K. S. (eds). (2001). *Climate Change 2001: Impacts, Adaptation, and Vulnerability*. Cambridge: Cambridge University Press.

Mitchell, J. K. (1989). Hazards research. In G. L. Gaile and C. J. Willmott (eds), *Geography in America*, pp. 410–424. Colombus, OH: Merill.

Natural Resources Canada. (2015). Spruce budworm, available at www.nrcan.gc.ca/forests/insects-diseases/13383, accessed 12 May 2015.

Oliver, P. (2003). *Dwellings: The Vernacular House World Wide*. London: Phaidon.

Paine, R. T., Tegner, M. J. and Johnson, E. A. (1998). Compounded perturbations yield ecological surprises. *Ecosystems* 1(6), pp. 535–545.

Peden, R. (2015). Rabbits: using predators for control. *Te Ara, the Encyclopedia of New Zealand*, available at www.TeAra.govt.nz/en/rabbits/page-5, accessed 12 May 2015.

Pelling, M. (2011). *Adaptation to Climate Change: From Resilience to Transformation*. Abingdon: Routledge.

Peterson, G., Allen, C. R. and Holling, C. S. (1998). Ecological resilience, biodiversity, and scale. *Ecosystems* 1(1), pp. 6–18.

Pimm, S. L. (1984). The complexity and stability of ecosystems. *Nature* 307(5949), pp. 321–326.

Prigogine, I. and Stengers, I. (1984). *Order Out of Chaos: Man's New Dialogue with Nature*. Toronto and New York: Bantam Books.

Rapoport, A. and Kantor, R. (1967). Complexity and ambiguity in environmental design. *Journal of the American Institute of Planners* 33(4), pp. 210–221.

Rappaport, R. (1977). Maladaptation in social systems. In J. Friedman and J. Rowlands (eds), *The Evolution of Social Systems: Proceedings of a Meeting of the Research Seminar in Archaeology and Related Subjects held at the Institute of Archaeology, London University*, pp. 49–71. Chicago, IL: Duckworth.

Relph, E. (1976). *Place and Placelessness*. London: Pion.

Schumpeter, J. A. (1994). *Capitalism, Socialism and Democracy*. London: Taylor & Francis.

Simon, H. A. (1962). The architecture of complexity. *Proceedings of the American Philosophical Society* 106(6), pp. 467–482.

Stockholm Resilience Centre. (n.d.). Applying resilience thinking, available at www.stockholmresilience.org/download/18.10119fc11455d3c557d6928/1459560241272/SRC+Applying+Resilience+final.pdf, accessed 10 May 2016.

Strunz, S. (2012). Is conceptual vagueness an asset? Arguments from philosophy of science applied to the concept of resilience. *Ecological Economics* 76, pp. 112–118.

Sudmeier-Rieux, K. (2014). Resilience – an emerging paradigm of danger or of hope? *Disaster Prevention and Management: An International Journal* 23(1), pp. 67–80.

Thorén, H. (2014). Resilience as a unifying concept. *International Studies in the Philosophy of Science* 28(3), pp. 303–324.

Tibbetts, J. (2002). Coastal cities: living on the edge. *Environmental Health Perspectives* 110(11), pp. 674–681.

Tredgold, T. (1818). On the transverse strength of timber. *Philosophical Magazine: a Journal of Theoretical, Experimental and Applied Science*, Chapter XXXXVII. London: Taylor & Francis.

Walker, B. (2007). Module: (1.5) Specified and General Resilience (Document). From Resilience Alliance, available at http://wiki.resalliance.org/index.php/1.5_Specified_and_General_Resilience, accessed 10 May 2016.

Walker, B., Abe, N., Andreoni, F., Cape, J., Murdoch, H. and Norman, C. (2014). General Resilience. A discussion paper based on insights from catchment management area workshop in south Australia, available at www.resalliance.org/files/General_Resilience_paper.pdf, accessed 6 December 2016.

Walker, B., Carpenter, S., Rockstrom, J., Crepin, A. and Peterson, G. (2012). Drivers, "slow" variables, "fast" variables, shocks, and resilience. *Ecology and Society* 17(3), p. 30.

Walker, B., Holling, C. S., Carpenter, S. and Kinzig, A. P. (2004). Resilience, adaptability and transformability in social-ecological systems. *Ecology and Society* 9(2), p. 5.

Walker, B. and Meyers, J. A. (2004). Thresholds in ecological and social-ecological systems: a developing database. *Ecology and Society* 9(2), p. 3.

Walker, B. and Salt, D. (2006). *Resilience Thinking: Sustaining Ecosystems and People in a Changing World*. Washington, DC: Island Press.

Walker, B. H. and Salt, D. (2012). *Resilience Practice Building Capacity to Absorb Disturbance and Maintain Function*. Washington, DC: Island Press.

Walker, J. and Cooper, M. (2011). Genealogies of resilience: from systems ecology to the political economy of crisis adaptation. *Security Dialogue* 42(2), pp. 143–160.

Wilkinson, C. (2012). Social-ecological resilience: insights and issues for planning theory. *Planning Theory* 11(2), pp. 148–169.

WWF. (2015). What do pandas eat?, available at http://wwf.panda.org/what_we_do/endangered_species/giant_panda/panda/what_do_pandas_they_eat/, accessed 9 May 2015.

4   Mapping sustainability and resilience

'A map does not just chart, it unlocks and formulates meaning; it forms bridges between here and there, between disparate ideas that we did not know were previously connected.'

Reif Larsen

4.1 Introduction

The purpose of this chapter is to look first for similarities and then for differences between sustainability and resilience as explored in the two previous chapters. Curiously, the first similarity is that both sustainability and resilience had their origins in the timber industry (first, von Carlowitz's *Nachhaltigkeit* and over 200 years later Holling's interest in budworms and the destruction of Canadian forests). Forestry is rare among human occupations because it is forced to take a long-term view of things, given the years it takes between tree planting and harvest. Long-term thinking like this probably disappeared with the change from monarchy to democratic governments, as most of the latter have a comparatively short turnover, whereas a reigning monarch expected to rule for a lifetime and so would plan for the long term. We also see this in the built environment. When the gothic cathedrals were constructed they were built to last, since they were a permanent symbol of the importance of religion in society at that time. Permanency is apparent in the way that as fashions changed, the new was simply incorporated alongside the old, as seen in the vaulting of the nave of Lincoln Cathedral which changed along its length to incorporate the latest fashion, or the despair of the monks at Canterbury after a fire had destroyed much of the new nave and they had to be persuaded to pull down the old work and start again rather than enjoying the convenience of being able to add on to the existing bits (Clifton-Taylor, 1967: 67–68). Now the old easily gives way to the new as the speed of procuring buildings has accelerated beyond the imagination of our ancestors, who would often have begun construction without the expectation of seeing a completed building within their lifetime. However, the real purpose of this chapter is not to look to history but to map the characteristics and behaviours behind both sustainability and resilience, with the aim of arriving at definitions that will be explored further in the case studies.

4.2 Similarities

Future thinking

Contrary to conceptions of time that value the present over the future, for design and planning the temporal innovation of sustainability and resilience lies in the creation of a notion of time where people have to value the future to take decisions in the present (Moffatt, 2014). There are, however, differences in thinking about the future between sustainability and resilience. The idea of sustainability has come about because the way things are currently done looks as if it might be problematic in the future, because of a perceived lack of resources or even of time. Sustainability is generally currently viewed as being about changing the way something is done at present but without losing the goal of doing it. Thus a switch from petrol cars to hybrid cars reduces crude oil consumption for the same distance travelled, so hybrid cars are seen as a step towards being sustainable. The problem is that it is the current lifestyle in the developed world that is unsustainable, and not just a piece of technology like the car. This means imagining a future world and a future lifestyle that fit within the resources that might be available. This is the real challenge for sustainability.

In the concept of sustainability the future is shaped by specific limits, namely the capacity and availability of resources on the one planet we all inhabit, including the sun's energy. Moffatt (2014) claims sustainability ideas are based on a utopian or static future, although as argued in Chapter 2 sustainability is far from a static situation because the ecosystems on which we depend are far from static. Resilience because it assumes change is also associated with a future that is dynamic because it is changing. However, in resilience what happens is relative to the local situation, not necessarily the global as in sustainability. The future is also not just a repetition or linear extension of the past. At each scale in a Panarchy of nested systems processes occur that follow a cyclical and non-linear path. The only evidence is the past. Consequently, when defining the situation of the system in the adaptive cycle there is a need to look to the past to see what has happened and only then understand where the system is in the present. Not in vain has Ortega y Gasset (1963) suggested that 'I'm I and my circumstance'. This leads to the second point of similarity.

You need to know where you are starting from

The biggest problem with most past discussion of sustainability is the lack of agreement on what the current unsustainable situation is, and hence what needs to be achieved. The Paris climate agreement at least recognizes that global warming is a global problem (and global temperature rise can be measured), but many other areas to do with achieving sustainability, such as redefining economics and a more equitable distribution of resources, remain unexplored. Resilience has the same problem. The first thing is to know where the system is on the adaptive cycle before thinking about what needs to be adjusted to avoid going to the point of unwanted collapse, noting that collapse is not necessarily a bad thing. This leads to another similarity in that approaching both sustainability and resilience is about making choices.

60 *Definitions*

Conscious choice

Attempting to make a city resilient or a building sustainable does not happen without making decisions. Applying the terms to the situation does not suddenly provide the solution. In both cases the decision system will imply identifying what has to be kept, improved or enhanced. As suggested above, you need to know where you are starting from, which implies measuring something, and you need to know where you are going, which implies modelling future possibilities. Thus both sustainability and resilience imply engaging with a problem in a deep and quantitative way that moves beyond ticking a predetermined checklist. This, however, also highlights a difference. The current problem is there is no agreement about the way of measuring resilience, which is viewed as a quality of a system (see Differences, point 6 below).

Change is core

Resilience in ecology is the study of inexorable change and more or less avoidable situations. Sustainability is also about change but here it is human beings deciding how to change the way things are done so that society can survive within the resources available. However, applying the idea of resilience to the built environment also, as suggested above, means making decisions about how things should change, and is about controlling the change. However, although this is a point of similarity it is also a key point of difference as any social-ecological system is going to change with the adaptive cycle whether there is human intervention or not, whereas changing to be more sustainable will not happen without deliberate human intervention.

Invisibility

Resilience and sustainability are untouchable; we cannot hold them in our hands. The ecological footprint of a person as a measure of human impact on the environment is as difficult to see as his or her resilience capacity. However, they are real, as both must be measured if there is to be human intervention to try and control change as discussed above, but they are not tangible. This invisibility has been a huge problem for sustainability and, in a different way, will also be a problem for resilience. The sustainability of a process and the resilience of a system are events that have to be perceived over time, which implies making the invisible visible (see Similarities, point 7). Time and changes are connected and changes are always concrete.

Systems thinking

Resilience and sustainability deal with problems that link people, resources and institutions. Sustainability and resilience study the interrelationship between humans and the physical environment using ecosystem models, as an integrated way of understanding natural processes. Both Commoner (1971) with his idea that everything in nature is connected and Walker and Salt's (2006: 31) statement that 'resilience thinking is systems thinking' clearly highlight the importance of systems theory in both fields. This means it is not possible for true sustainability to talk about 'a sustainable building' unless it is also part of a sustainable society. This will be further discussed in the case study of eco-cities and in Differences, point 1 below.

Persistence

Concern for the well-being of future generations, included in the definition of sustainability provided in the Brundtland Report (World Commission on Environment and Development, 1987), has a parallel in Holling's idea that resilience is about creating the conditions for persistence (Holling, 1973). In both cases survival is a common target, even though there are some differences in the way of using time variables, as explained in points 4 and 5 of the next section.

4.3 Differences

The size of the system under discussion

Resilience applies to a system, since it originated within the study of ecosystems. Resilience theory also posits a Panarchy, or nesting of systems, where effects at one level can have an effect both up and down the scale. Sustainability is usually applied much more loosely and is often attributed to the sustainability of a single thing, such as a building, or a single system, such as the transport system or the financial system. However, whereas a sustainable transport system could be a way of reducing the environmental impact of human travel (although not travelling would be equally, if not more, effective), financial sustainability and environmental sustainability are very different things that are often in conflict (see Chapter 2). This means that whereas in resilience, systems thinking is inherent, something equally true in sustainability, in the latter it is often missing.

In resilience the definition of thresholds is important because they are linked with the scale of a system or problem. In sustainability global thinking is vital since the resource limit is that of the planet.

Perception of the outcome

Moving to sustainability suggests that the outcome will be positive for humanity, since the essential ecosystems on which humanity relies will be preserved. As noted earlier (in Similarities, point 2), within the adaptive cycle collapse may be harmful to humanity or it may be good for humanity. A collapse that wiped out much of the global urban population would be good for humanity as it would lessen human pressure on ecosystems and there would be more resources to go round. It would not, however, be a good collapse for those who did not survive. Given the complexity of the systems that support modern lifestyles, collapse of just some of these might be very good for others. Thus the collapse of the oil industry might help avert temperature rises that would cause catastrophic climate shift. This could be very good for societies of subsistence farmers who already use very little oil. Resilience comes without perception of the outcome as it is simply the property of a system.

Having a goal or being the property of a system

Sustainability has the goal of ensuring human survival in some form but resilience is the property of a system, not a goal in itself. It is like the difference between safety when driving and speeding. Safety is something that everybody wants because the goal is to arrive home alive. However, speed is not positive or negative in itself, it is just an action that is part of getting you home. Sometimes, when you are driving, you might need to speed in order to avoid an accident but without a reason, driving fast will only increase the risk of having accidents (you are more likely to skid on a bend and go off the road) and will increase the damage if you do have an accident. Resilience actions need 'a reason' to be positive or negative but sustainability goals do not need justification.

Controlling or coping with change

To move towards sustainability a society has to decide what the resource limits are and how the available resources are to be distributed within that society. This means making deliberate choices. Conversely, resilience is about change that happens to human systems and how people within these systems react to that change or how they imagine strategies to buffer anticipated change, such as a natural disaster like an earthquake. This is not the same as choosing to make changes, as is implied by moving towards a sustainable society. In sustainability it is necessary to define how much change is needed in a variable but this is not the case in resilience. For sustainability keeping global temperature rise to no more than 2°C (a choice) means that energy supply has to be decarbonized. When it comes to resilience the quantity of change needed to adapt effectively is relative to future (and unknown) conditions. To continue the climate theme, resilience means thinking about how society could adapt to live with future temperatures that might be well above 2°C.

This makes knowing what to change in the built environment to be more resilient much more difficult than knowing what to do to be more sustainable (only depend on renewable energy, ensure recycling of materials, ensure water supply is within local ecosystem services, for example). Sustainability has a defined end-state while resilience has to deal with an uncertain future.

Stability versus multiple stability states

Resilience is more relative than sustainability. To achieve sustainability the maintenance conditions for the equilibrium of a protected system are key. Far from equilibrium, situations increase risk and uncertainty. The sustainability of a project is easier to define than its future resilience, even to a particular threat, noting that as discussed above when it comes to systems, resilience and sustainability are different.

In sustainability, dynamics across scales tend to be assumed to be linear. If more green roofs are created, then the whole city will reduce its urban heat island effect. Therefore if it is good at one scale it might be good for the whole system, although wind energy is an example where this does not apply: large-scale wind generation is very effective, small-scale wind is not (Synergy Files, 2016). In resilience theory different scales can have different and also contrasting dynamics as was shown in the Panarchy. The stability of a big company at a global scale may rely on the variability and constant search for new products in small departments of the company. Failure in just one small part of the company to find a new market/product could bring the whole company down, and equally it could not, again demonstrating the unpredictability of resilience.

Qualitative and quantitative

With few exceptions, sustainability analyses rely on quantitative approaches (even though the output implies a 'quality', that of being less damaging to natural systems) because the key variables to be analysed are very clear. Instead, Holling stressed that resilience is a qualitative property. Walker's determinants of a resilient system (diversity, redundancy, modularity, social capital) are all qualities to be reached rather than defined quantities. This qualitative rather than quantitative property of resilience means that measuring it is difficult, but as discussed above, necessary if you want to make the built environment more resilient. You need to know where you are starting from and you need to be able to measure whether you get there. Therefore, to apply resilience to the built environment it has to move from being just qualitative to also being quantitative.

In resilience, key variables or drivers of a system depend on frequencies of change and scale of impact, and they may therefore change depending on the situation. In resilience quantities are relative, and what matters most is the final quality. However, in applying resilience to the built environment these frequencies of change could be one way of measuring its resilience, and hence the need to look to history (see Differences, point 8 and Part 3 for further discussion of measuring resilience in the built environment).

Regulation versus self-regulation

Since sustainability is more concrete and less relative than resilience, the regulation of the actions and processes needed to achieve certain parameters is a fact. What is not possible in a sustainable approach is to wait until the Earth by itself regulates human excess, at least, this will not be likely to be sustainable in human terms. The sustainable approach is about monitoring and adjusting any variable towards the chosen goal of living within available resources, however this is defined. Resilience is not dissimilar as stability is sometimes desirable, but resilience also includes the possibility that complex systems adapt and learn. Resilience approaches claim that it is important to enhance the capacity of systems to self-organize instead of conserving the status quo, therefore they need the capacity (to a certain extent, of course) to self-organize.

Understanding versus predicting

Sustainable approaches are very helpful for guiding development and making predictions. In simplistic terms, if people pollute more, as a consequence, the environment will be more polluted. With basic mathematical skills everybody can have a more or less detailed idea of what will happen when things change (even though, in thermodynamics, systems far from equilibrium behave in a non-linear way). Sustainability methodologies and measurement are more advanced than the tools of resilience for forecasting but there is a reason for this. The nature of resilience is about understanding change by looking at things that have changed and have persisted. This has only just begun when it comes to the built environment, as the study of urban morphology dates back to Conzen (1960), who studied how built environment changes had occurred and the patterns within them. This may be a first move in understanding how resilience can be applied to human settlements.

64 *Definitions*

Ethics

The idea of sustainability has been largely linked with an ideal of growth management that questions the lack of ethics in narrow economic viewpoints. This is why in sustainability, global equity and social justice are desirable goals that are directly linked with the consumption and distribution of resources. In the case of resilience, that is a property of systems and not an end or goal like sustainability, there is no ethics. Does speed have ethics? Since resilience can be desirable or not depending on the system being analysed, then it cannot have ethics. Stated in a different way, its ethics will be relative to the situation and system in question.

Pro-active versus reactive

Sustainability is a goal that demands engagement and pro-activity of people, institutions and governments. It will not happen naturally (with the exception of a few traditional communities) in most developed and developing countries.

In resilience there is confusion between having resilience and being resilient. Having resilience is not something that can be related to decisions; all complex adaptive systems have resilience. However, building or enhancing resilience is about taking decisions. In the case of resilience, opinions are divided. In the first case, an engineering approach to building resilience will always be more reactive, with a focus on trying to recover and come back to normal as fast as possible. It is concentrated on the threat or hazard that a system has to mitigate. In the ecological view, enhancing resilience will be about reducing vulnerability and risk, or about transforming a system to gain something else. In the first case, decisions need to be taken about what is to be preserved and what is to be lost. Even though something has to be done, the decisions still depend on the threat or disturbance. This can be linked with the resilience of what to what. In the second case, resilience is linked with a strategy to increase the robustness of a system and consequently its adaptive capacity to increase or to transform the potential of a system. This will be associated with the general resilience of a system and will imply taking decisions to retrofit a system and pursue certain goals. It is about gaining something that the system does not yet have. These are approaches that try to practise resilience in order to make a system resilient. Nonetheless, the achievability of that objective, as a final state, contradicts the definition of resilience and is linked with the next point.

Achievability: ideal versus real

Sustainability, as a goal or final aim, is susceptible to being understood as an ideal that is more or less achievable depending on the efforts of society, its governance and the sense of emergency. Resilience, as an inherent property of complex adaptive systems, is a reality. Whether it is robust, or precarious, desirable or undesirable, all complex adaptive systems have a resilience capacity.

The issue then it is not about building resilience but rather increasing the robustness of a system. Adaptation and persistence are the only proof that some resilience was achieved. The resilience of a system in the long term is almost impossible to predict because the future is not a linear extension of the present conditions. We are not saying that it is not possible to take actions to be resilient to something, but what it not possible is to guarantee that this will always be the result.

Governability

The achievability of resilience and sustainability relates to a divergent understanding of governability. The intention of achieving sustainability implies that it might be possible to govern a system, like a society or city, and lead that system in one direction. Conversely, resilience as a mechanism within evolutionary forces stresses the impossibility of governing highly complex systems. As mentioned before, sustainability at small or local scales seems more achievable than global sustainability. This fact can be used as evidence to argue that political interventions to institute or replicate good practices or demand collective actions in order to achieve sustainability are possible and can make a difference. Instead, the evolutionary perspective of resilience (which is not an end, only a property) implies that the direction of slow variables (things/processes that change infrequently but at big scales) depends on the variability and change of fast variables (things that change frequently but at small scales) at lower levels in a system, that are highly unpredictable and volatile. Put it in simpler terms, a system follows the directions that result from the interplay of all the scales in a Panarchy but that direction has no predefined ultimate goal.

4.4 Emergent themes

Table 4.1 compares the themes that have emerged from the discussion of similarities and differences. Table 4.2 looks at the strengths and weaknesses of linking sustainability and resilience together.

Table 4.1 Comparison of themes in sustainability and resilience

Themes	*Sustainability*	*Resilience*
Time	Value the future Probably cyclical Multiple scales (global, local)	Value the future Cyclical Multiple scales
Essence/nature	Goal Objective Concrete outcomes Predictable, linear	Property Relative Abstract Unpredictable, non-linear
Outcome	Persistence within limits Always desirable	Adaptation and persistence Desirable or undesirable
Philosophical approach	Systems thinking Ethics, social justice, equity	Systems thinking No ethics
Governance	Organized, regulated More institutionalized	Self-organized, independent Less institutionalized
Equilibrium	Singular Stable as possible	Multiple Unstable
Boundaries	Concrete limits Predefined	Multiple thresholds Emergent

66 *Definitions*

Table 4.2 Strengths and weaknesses of linking sustainability and resilience

Strengths	Weaknesses
Advance the application and understanding of complex systems.	Sustainability and resilience are being confused and used indistinguishably at the present.
Values, aims and outcomes are partially shared but sometimes complementary.	Values, aims and outcomes are partially shared and sometimes opposite.
Opportunities	Threats, especially to the status quo.
Could provide concrete tools.	
Could provide understanding.	

Discussion

The lists of similarities and differences in the properties of sustainability and resilience above are necessary but perhaps not sufficient when it comes to applying the two ideas to the built environment. Both concepts require an understanding that a built environment, like a city, is not a world of its own but is connected to other cities and to the rural areas it depends on for the resources it needs to survive. This makes the goal of sustainability difficult since everything has to be sustainable for a particular city to be sustainable, however many of its citizens walk to work and however many green roofs and walls it has. The problem seems insurmountable. However, because sustainability (human impact on the environment) is relatively easy to measure then it is possible to move towards sustainability locally by small groups choosing to live in a different way. Examples of this are the Greenest Neighbourhood competitions in places as far apart as Surabaya in Indonesia and the Kapiti Coast in New Zealand (Vale and Vale, 2013). It is, therefore, possible to have local solutions for sustainability within the goal of having a sustainable human society on the whole planet. This leaves aside the issue of equity since the human impact of living in a green neighbourhood in Surabaya is still very much lower than in Kapiti just because what is expected of life is very different. Any local solution should thus still be linked to the idea of resource rationing, raising the question of whether part of the ration of the resource wealthy should be set aside for those who have less, both in the present and in the future. It is not enough, therefore, to insist on local materials and techniques when making sustainable buildings without also avoiding making them larger or grander than they need be. In fact, greater impact reduction will come from making a small building of ordinary materials than from making a large one of the 'sustainable' materials of earth or straw (Vale and Vale, 2009: 129–147).

When it comes to increasing the resilience of a particular place, things become more difficult. Resilience emerged from looking at single ecosystems but in ecology everything is linked to everything else and resilience implies a Panarchy of nested systems where changes in one produce changes up and down the system scales. This suggests that 'local resilience' is impossible. However, since the resilience of a system depends on its resources, this creates a bridge with sustainability thinking. At the level where a household has risen above a hand-to-mouth existence this is easy to understand. Money will be saved as a buffer against future problems (such as illness, job loss or even the car needing a major repair). This is simply ensuring household resilience, since with this buffer the household and the lifestyle of its inhabitants can persist. So if we want to move to a sustainable and a resilient future then our resource use not only has to be within available limits but we also have to set some resources aside against future, unpredictable occurrences. Turning to history, kings were good at this, with grain stored in the royal granary against a bad harvest not just for the royal household but for the citizens, so they would not starve and would be able to plant again the following season (Rios, 2015). This makes moving to sustainability even more difficult since the available resources will have to go further. It is, however, only sensible since the objective of sustainability is the resilience of human social-ecological systems. The two concepts of resilience and sustainability are not interchangeable but nested and both depend on living within the resources available. This implies big changes for human society and its built environment.

How and when we move to becoming sustainable is the issue. As a species we can just carry on as we are and see where things take us, whether to the collapse of modern civilization as we know it as predicted by Meadows *et al.* (1972) or to a future where human ingenuity will win the day and there is a small nuclear reactor in every town. Alternatively, we may arrive at a scenario where a smaller crisis brought about by resource unavailability, for example, a massive failure in the grain harvest, might force those in control to behave differently. Thus in the Second World War, rationing and mass education in cooking and feeding the family in the UK was thought necessary because food was scarce and as a result the health of the whole population was increased because for the first time poorer sections in society had a proper diet. If nothing else, considering resilience and sustainability together raises the question of whether we, as a species, are ready to embrace change in order to keep our identity.

Bibliography

Clifton-Taylor, A. (1967). *The Cathedrals of England*. London: Thames and Hudson.
Commoner, B. (1971). *The Closing Circle: Nature, Man and Technology*. New York: Random House.
Conzen, M. R. G. (1960). Alnwick, Northumberland: a study in town-plan analysis. *Transactions and Papers (Institute of British Geographers)* 27, pp. iii–122.
Holling, C. S. (1973). Resilience and stability of ecological systems. *Annual Review of Ecology and Systematics* 4(1), pp. 1–23.
Meadows, D., Meadows, D., Randers, J. and Behrens, W. W. (1972). *The Limits to Growth: A Report for the Club of Rome's Project on the Predicament of Mankind*. New York: Universe Books.
Moffatt, S. (2014). Resilience and competing temporalities in cities. *Building Research & Information* 42(2), pp. 202–220.
Ortega y Gasset, J. (1963). *Meditations on Quixote*. New York and London: Norton.
Rios, J. C. (2015). Environmental impact assessment of vernacular thatch building tradition in Mexico. Unpublished PhD thesis, Victoria University of Wellington.
Synergy Files. (2016). Small scale vs large scale wind turbines, available at http://synergyfiles.com/2015/04/small-scale-vs-large-scale-wind-turbines/, accessed 11 May 2016.
Vale, R. and Vale, B. (2009). *Time to Eat the Dog? The Real Guide to Sustainable Living*. London: Thames and Hudson.
Vale, R. and Vale, B. (eds). (2013). *Living within a Fair Share Footprint*. London: Routledge.

Walker, B., Cumming, G., LeBel, L., Carpenter, S. R., Peterson, G. D., Anderies, J., Pritchard, R. et al. (2002). Resilience management in social-ecological systems: a working hypothesis for a participatory approach. *Conservation Ecology* 6(1), p. 14.

Walker, B. and Salt, D. (2006). *Resilience Thinking: Sustaining Ecosystems and People in a Changing World*. Washington, DC: Island Press.

World Commission on Environment and Development. (1987). *Our Common Future*. Oxford: Oxford University Press.

Part 2
Case studies

Introduction

The purpose of these case studies is to examine how much three aspects of the built environment – eco-cities, heritage and compaction – are sustainable and resilient (or both or neither). *Eco-cities* studies attempts to build the ideal new sustainable city, *heritage* loosely looks at how and why things persist and resist change (if they do) in the built environment, and *compaction* looks at attempts to make existing built environments more sustainable, for example through reducing travel distances, and the effect this might have on resilience. Obviously there are cross-connections between these aspects, since it might be sensible to design a compact eco-city where everyone walked or cycled to work and school, but where possible each of the three topics is examined as if it were a separate entity. There is also the issue of how heritage is important in a city, since it is associated with its identity, and how heritage might accrue in a new development like an eco-city. For ease of consideration, however, these ideas have been separated into the three case studies.

The case studies also require defining additional aspects in detail. The case study of eco-cities considers what a city is and whether it is possible to build new, ideal cities. In heritage, identity and persistence are first defined and then applied to the built environment. When it comes to compact cities and compaction in the built environment, the issues of density and intensity of use are considered.

5 Eco-cities

'A city is not a tree.'

Christopher Alexander

5.1 Why eco-cities?

Even before Thomas More introduced the idea of utopia in 1516 (More, 1516/1965) or the creation of an ideal place for people to live, the right way to make the built environment had puzzled some of the best minds. Plato considered a city should contain 5,040 households (Gutkind, 1969: 496; Backhouse, 2002: 18). Once this level was reached then a new city colony had to be founded elsewhere. However, the history of most urban development is less to do with this colonization than with city growth. The ideal city is not just the perfect master plan but has to cope with change and an eco-city is no different. As seen below, eco-cities tend to be founded to meet certain goals in terms of greenhouse gas emissions reduction, or a prescribed use of public transport, without thought as to how these targets might be met if the population of the eco-city increases, or if climate change means the renewable water supply systems can no longer cope with demand.

As explained in Chapter 2, the risks of misunderstanding the theory behind sustainability, and particularly its definition, can result in overselling practices, including eco-cities, that are essentially business as usual but a bit 'greener'. Eco-cities were chosen as the main subject of this Part not only because they represent the biggest and most ambitious scale of intervention around the idea of sustainability in the urban built environment, but also because they have yet to show any fully working examples. For instance, Freiburg in southern Germany, which is said to be the country's ecological capital (Bund, 2013) (and which to be fair has never called itself an eco-city), has put in place policies to achieve 20 per cent of its electricity from renewables by 2010 (C40 Cities, 2011). However, improvement is slow with CO_2/capita falling from 10.6 tonnes in 1997 to 8.5 tonnes in 2007. Currently, the average per capita 2011 emissions for Germany were 8.9 tonnes (World Bank, 2015), so Freiburg is still not doing much better than the average. The IPCC (n.d.) gives average current global emissions as 1 tonne carbon/capita, which equates with 3.7 tonnes CO_2/capita. They go on to state that this would have to drop to 1.1 tonnes CO_2/capita to stabilize at 450 ppmv (parts per million by volume) by 2100, or 3.3 tonnes CO_2/capita to stabilize at 650 ppmv. A CO_2 concentration of 450 ppmv is effectively a doubling of pre-industrialization levels (Harvey, 2010: 509), while a more 'realistic' target of 650 ppmv could lead to a rise in temperature greater than 2°C (Egenhofer and van Shaik, 2005: 3). These somewhat daunting statistics are almost as hard to uncover as the targets will be to meet, but they do suggest that to be sustainable in terms of avoiding the consequences of significant climate change will require very stringent targets for all cities, not just for eco-cities. Furthermore, at the 2015 CoP in Paris, 196 countries successfully negotiated the legally binding Paris Climate Agreement with the global goal of holding temperature increase to below 2°C above pre-industrial levels, with the parties agreeing to make efforts to keep it below 1.5°C (Climate Action, 2015). This will require a large reduction in CO_2 emissions for developed societies, and total carbon neutrality in the medium to long term (Rogelj et al., 2016). Given the longevity of the built environment this could be read as meaning at the very least that all new building and infrastructure must be net zero CO_2 emissions from now onwards, or all new building must contribute to making eco-cities. This runs completely counter to the fact that globally most new development is still business-as-usual (Bulkeley and Marvin, 2014: 20).

There are currently over 200 eco-city projects in China alone, both new developments on the outskirts of existing settlements and retrofits of existing cities (Chien, 2013). At the same time, it has been forty years since the creation of the concept of eco-cities but no large-scale projects have yet been completed. (It took only forty years to build Durham Cathedral in the eleventh century and forty-one months to build Brasilia in the 1950s–1960s.) If eco-cities are such a great idea why have none been built? Is it because the net zero emissions targets described above are just too difficult to achieve and, if so, what does that imply for sustainability? Moreover, why are there so many countries still keen to build eco-cities regardless of the fact that previous projects have failed?

What should an eco-city be?

An eco-city, as well as being carbon neutral, could be one that tries to live within the resources of its environment (so the city is part of the local ecosystem), or perhaps one where all the resources come from its ecological region, which also processes all its wastes. Register (1987) defined the concept as a city that was ecologically healthy, and later as a city rebuilt so as to be in 'balance with nature' (Devuyst et al., 2001; Register, 2006). The latest definition is more descriptive, calling for 'urban diversity at close proximity, instead of scattered uniformity… land uses, architecture and a steadily and rapidly growing infrastructure for pedestrians, bicyclists and transit, powered by renewable energy sources and balanced with preservation and restoration of natural and agricultural lands and waters' (Ecocity Builders, 2014). However, this definition fails to deal with what is the purpose of the city, what work will its citizens do, where will their food be grown and how will it be transported, and how will wastes be handled. This is utopia without guts. The World Bank (2010) has suggested a different definition in *Eco2 cities*. The slogan 'ecological cities as economic cities' mixes economics and ecology in a city package so at least the city has a reason for being. Any move towards sustainability is good, but the whole idea of an eco-city suggests a major move towards being sustainable although no-one seems to know how to achieve this.

Cities have been likened to organisms, they absorb food, materials and energy which they use and move around or store in the built environment, and they excrete wastes to water, air and land. In the 1970s a study of Hong Kong measured the rate at which these things happened in the city (Newcombe *et al.*, 1978; Boyden *et al.*, 1981). Any attempt to make an eco-city that lives within its ecosystems has to be based on a quantitative analysis of this type. However, what most such analyses show is that knowing what the flows are does not lead to their reduction. A more recent analysis of Hong Kong (Warren-Rhodes and Koenig, 2001) has shown that per capita consumption of food went up 20 per cent, water 40 per cent and materials 149 per cent from the early 1970s until 1997, with higher increases for most waste products. Given Register's ideas that an eco-city would be compact as this would lower the carbon footprint and given that Hong Kong is already one of the most densely populated urban areas in the world (Information Services Department, Census and Statistics Department, 2015), this suggests that making an eco-city without major change to human behaviour in terms of these flows of materials and wastes is not going to achieve very much. Given the high density of tall buildings in a small space in the occupied part of Hong Kong, we might also say that its resilience has lowered over the same period, since the city has become more rigid with fewer opportunities for change except either at the edges or by demolishing and rebuilding. The latter will also increase rather than reduce resource use.

Should we be building eco-cities?

More than forty years ago Toynbee (1970) defined a city not as a thing of streets and buildings and businesses but simply as a *human settlement whose inhabitants cannot produce, within the city limits, all the food that they need for keeping them alive*. The fact that in developed world nations food is still the largest single component of the ecological footprint, and considerably more in developing nations (Vale and Vale, 2013) (see also Chapter 8, Figure 8.1), raises a key issue about what a sustainable city needs. It is not sufficient to think only in lowering its carbon footprint. Ewing *et al.* (2010: 18) show that in 2007 the carbon footprint was 53 per cent of the total ecological footprint, or the total environmental impact. A city, and particularly an eco-city, ideally needs to be planned within a sustainable region that can at least supply one of its key resources, food. However, not all cities have regions and not all regions have ecosystems where political boundaries align with ecosystem boundaries. Current eco-city projects, which might reasonably be expected to deal with resource planning in terms of where water and food is coming from and where wastes are going to, do not seem to deal with the eco-city in the region, but are rather focused on the idea of designing a normal built environment that runs at least partially on renewable resources and saves energy through efficiency measures (such as compaction to reduce transport distances). For example, Curitiba in Brazil is known for its integrated urban planning, successful public bus ways, priority given to pedestrians in the city, social justice and local waste management and recycling (Soltani and Sharifi, 2012), but among these the public transport system is probably its most well-known achievement. The city, with its share of unplanned unofficial settlements, especially beyond the boundaries of the city, and the fact this development has resulted in the usual urban problems of crime, unemployment, homelessness and traffic congestion, has also attracted its critics (Macedo, 2004). This underlines the fact that any eco-city in

74 *Case studies*

setting and monitoring its targets has to allow for change. It is not possible to design an eco-city and then expect it to work in perpetuity.

       also seems to be a disregard for what happened in the past where cities were   ewable energy (biofuels) and allowed for non-fossil fuel transportation   (water, walking and animals). The real nature of what a modern low environ   tal impact city might look like is, therefore, left unexplored, possibly because we fail to grasp that such a city might be very different from those of the present, but also possibly because building new, ideal cities, even if sustainable, from scratch with short delivery dates, is not a very good idea. Cities may start as ideals but can often develop differently. In the sixteenth century the Spaniards founded the Mexican city of Guanajuato, initially laid out in the classic grid across four barrios or neighbourhoods, but because of the hilly terrain, the river that cut the city in half, and the need to provide access for mining the rich deposits of silver and other ores, many roads and service ways pass under the buildings which in turn are linked by narrow alleys and steps. The ideal gridded city has been warped by what the city is (a place for mining) and its terrain (very hilly).

The ideal city

In his discourse on the villas of Le Corbusier, Benton (1987: 15) wrote:

> we can trace the modulation of one design to another… There is a kind of natural selection, a law of nature at work in the conflict of forces threatening to demolish the integrity of a design. The strong or resilient parts survive, some other parts are proved too brittle to be adapted, and have to be discarded wholesale, while other parts are revealed to be passing fancies, easily shed when the pressure is on.

By now some of these words should be very familiar. Benton is describing the process of evolving ideas about a single building – the villa – a process that, given enough wealthy clients, is possible within the working lifetime of an architect. It would be a lot harder to develop the design for a city in a similar way. Cities are far more complex than single houses and their cost prohibits design improvements through iteration, although this was tried to an extent with the post-war British New Towns. These shifted from the first wave of more conventional neighbourhood-focused expansion of towns like Harlow to the compactness and Italian hill-top town imagery of Cumbernauld (Esher, 1981: 247–249). In terms of success, the former has worn a lot better than the second, suggesting that ideas change but not always for the good. However, the post-war UK New Towns were normally massive expansions of existing settlements, though built to a master plan, an idea that comes into conflict with the theory of resilience, which implies constant change. The problem with the history of city design is that it is all about master planning, ignoring resilience theory, with the underlying unspoken intention of creating the ideal city that never needs to be changed.

Gruen (1965: 9), in writing about the urban crisis as he perceived it then, described the passenger liner *Leonardo da Vinci* as '… a city in itself, one which is carefully planned to the last detail to function and operate in order to offer comfort and convenience'. However, as Toynbee implied, this type of ideal city cannot survive without a support system to supply it with goods and deal with its wastes, just as a large liner cannot function without all the services that supply it in the ports where it docks. It is no use designing a new ideal built environment without also tackling this environment as part of a much wider system. Gruen (1965: 11) also illustrates da Vinci's 1488–9 design for an ideal city which in turn shows the simplification inherent in most town and city master plans. Da Vinci's city has underground tunnels for vehicles and barges, with the land above for colonnaded buildings and walking. All the waste is taken away in the tunnels and in this way da Vinci hoped his city would remain clean, thereby avoiding the spread of disease and plague, as he had witnessed in the dirty streets of Milan. Building a healthy city so that people can live in denser arrangements without the rapid spread of contagious diseases has been at the heart of many ideal city designs. Nor is this necessarily a bad thing, recalling that in 1952 the London smog killed over 12,000 more people between December and March than would die in an ordinary winter, making this Britain's biggest civilian disaster (Davis, 2002). Following the London cholera outbreaks in the middle of the nineteenth century, Sir Benjamin Richardson proposed an ideal city he called Hygeia. Effectively, this zoned unpleasant aspects of city life, such as raising animals and their subsequent slaughter, away from where people lived in a city of 25 persons/acre (Richardson, 1876: 18). Wastes were tucked conveniently underground, as was the railway which ran beneath the main boulevards (not unlike Guanajuato). Water and gas was supplied via these underground tunnels (Richardson, 1876: 27). The influence of this utopian ideal is obvious in the form of many cities in the developed world with their hidden pipes, but whether design alone can ever make a city is questionable. The city is the sum of its citizens, not of its sewerage arrangements.

This is not to say that ideas about planning cities are necessarily bad. The street grid that goes back to the Greeks and that has permeated so much of the colonized world is a very resilient way of setting out a city, as evidenced by its persistence over centuries, not least because of the connectivity it offers (Marshall, 2007). The problems arise when designers think they can do more than just lay out the built environment. The issue with urban master plans is not only that they represent a fixed ideal but also that they are simplifications of a complex and changing situation that is simultaneously rural and urban. Both Ebenezer Howard (1898) and Le Corbusier (1947: 17) realized that the problem of cities was not urban but started with improving rural life. Where Howard aimed to do this by bringing the benefits of the town physically closer to the countryside, Le Corbusier (1947: 70) saw the solution through the mechanization of agriculture and good roads, making the life of the peasant less onerous and less separate from the benefits of the city. When it comes to eco-cities, with their aim of minimizing human impact on the planet, then consideration of how resources will be supplied to the eco-city on a sustainable basis becomes paramount. These ideas will be explored further below.

Even when it comes to designing the built environment of an ideal city problems emerge. Marshall (2007: 26) made a distinction between *planning intention*, *city design* and *urban ordering*. *Planning intention* is how the desired future social and political state is achieved, and for an eco-city this would include creating its sustainable economic basis and agreed quality of life based on the resources available. *City design* is the planning of a city as a single object, like designing a house but a lot bigger. In an eco-city this should mean providing only zero fossil fuel energy buildings

76 *Case studies*

and transport systems, and minimizing the life-cycle impact of the built environment through design and material choices. *Urban ordering* refers to the creation of structure through the relationships between key elements, which for an eco-city means considering street patterns that prioritize pedestrians and cyclists and that also allow at the same time for city growth. Using this analysis, the problem with new eco-cities in China, like Dongtan, is that they seem to fall under the category of city design without considering the aspects of planning intention and urban ordering. Dongtan, near Shanghai, was to be a new car-free city powered by renewable energy and with water recycling, thus dealing with city design and urban ordering, but its development has now been put on hold indefinitely (Alusi *et al.*, 2011). Its planning intention seemed to be to skip industrialization but without a clear definition of what was to replace it.

Earlier eco-city examples, like the Arcologies of Paolo Soleri, also fall into the city design category. The name Arcology alludes to a mix between architecture and ecology. Soleri imagined these as single-building cities built on unoccupied land. The aim was to condense the built environment so as to leave as much unbuilt land as possible, in a process referred to as 'miniaturisation' (Soleri, 1969: 2). Arcosanti was Soleri's most ambitious built project in the desert of Arizona, where his foundation, Cosanti, bought 860 acres. The project was intended to hold 5,000 inhabitants (smaller than Plato's ideal city) in a territory of 25 acres (10 ha). Since 1970 Arcosanti has been a work in progress, but only 2–4 per cent of it has been built. Currently, they have around seventy-five residents plus students and temporary guests. The major source of income has been the sale of souvenir bells produced on site and the 35,000 visitors per year. Arcosanti is also not the single building of the true Arcology. What exists is dispersed and the built and population densities are low, the latter around 7.5 persons/ha, which should be compared with 14.1 persons/ha for the nearby Pheonix metropolitan area based on 2000 census data (Demographia, 2015). The physical layout of Arcosanti is rigid and the semi-circular shapes are complicated to extend and match with other buildings. The production and consumption of energy in Arcosanti is not known, making it impossible to check one of the assumptions of Soleri that an Arcology consumes fewer resources than a conventional suburban development. Despite the lack of outcome, such dreams of isolated, dense cities working in perfect harmony with nature (though quite how is never revealed) live on in such projects as Foster's land-based 450 m high Crystal Island in Moscow (Foster + Partners, 2007) and Callebaut's floating Lilipads (Vincent Callebaut Architecte, 2008). It seems the real resilience (in engineering terms) in eco-cities is the concept, which keeps bouncing back despite a singular lack of built examples.

A discussion of Soleri's ideas is important because it highlights the problem of designing an ideal city, rather than setting up a system that will change, but setting it up in such a way that the changes are the desired ones. Register's systemic approach to cities was achieved by stating they are organisms (Register, 2006: 38). His evolutionary way of building a city was a process of 'Miniplexion', which is a mix between the words miniaturization and complexification. This idea comes directly from Soleri (1983) who described miniaturization (M), complexification (C) and duration (D), or MCD, as the processes that drive the evolution of cities to eventually arrive at '... the channelling of the doings of man into vast rivers of action on a harmoniously preserved and man-organized (agricultural) landscape' (Soleri, 1969: 6). These MCD speculations were inspired by Jesuist philosopher Pierre Teilhard de Chardin

(1955: 257) who described what he called the Omega point as the highest degree of maturity humanity can achieve. This idea of the utmost point can be compared with those of the early ecologists Tansley and Clement (Golley, 1993), who believed in the existence of a perfect equilibrium (an idea challenged by ecological resilience) as an ideal state of a system. For them, the development of ecosystems would thus tend to a steady state of maturity (Golley, 1993). For example in subtropical regions, the maturity and more complex state of a landscape would be the forest. In Tansley's view, every region would have only one possible state of maturity or end. For Soleri and later Register, the ideal state of the city would be its most condensed and compact form, achieved through following a shrinking path instead of a sprawling dispersion. Quite how these compact city gems are to be serviced from their surrounding hinterlands (or ecosystems) remains diagrammatic at best or not discussed at worst. The idea of the Omega point also suggests a final goal and thus runs counter to resilience theory which is about recognizing that everything is constantly changing. From a resilience viewpoint the goal would be to set up the system (the ideal city) so that it can reach a state where it can buffer repeated change and shocks without collapsing and moving to a new state. This is a somewhat different view of the Omega point.

To probe the eco-city concept further it is essential to look at built examples, the first here is an eco-town it the UK and the second an eco-city in China. These examples were selected because they have been visited in person, although obviously developments have continued since the visits in 2014–2015.

5.2 Whitehill and Bordon, Hampshire: a UK eco-town

In 2007 the UK government invited proposals for eco-towns that were to create affordable housing and achieve high standards of sustainable living. Essential requirements included: having 5,000–20,000 new homes of which 30 per cent were to be affordable in a place with an identity and with good links to nearby towns or a city; the development had to be zero carbon; business and leisure facilities were required as well as local shopping and a secondary school; and having some type of organization to oversee the delivery of the eco-town (Department for Communities and Local Government, 2007: 4). In 2008 the former garrison town of Whitehill, Hampshire (sometimes known as Whitehill and Bordon), which was no longer required by the military, was designated for development as a 'green town' as one of four successful bids to the UK Eco-towns initiative (Department for Communities and Local Government, 2009). The eco-towns initiative was seen as creating opportunities to bring together the three spheres of sustainability – economic, social and environmental (Shaw, 2007: 6), which suggests the weak sustainability model where all are given equal importance and where sustainability only happens at the overlap (see Chapter 2).

The most obvious sustainability objective is for the new development in the town to be zero carbon (that is, to emit no CO_2), though the boundaries for measuring this are not clear. Zero carbon could apply to the energy the town uses or could extend to a life-cycle assessment of the materials from which it is made and maintained. This means looking at all the energy that goes into obtaining the raw materials, making the building materials and products, transporting them to the site and making the buildings and disposing of these materials at the end of the buildings' lives. It also includes all the materials used for maintenance during the life of the buildings (Mithraratne

78 *Case studies*

et al., 2007). However, the focus seems to be on energy in use as the government made it clear that the new houses would use energy from the sun, wind and earth, have heat recovery systems and grid linked photovoltaics (PVs).

In the UK definition of zero CO_2, the Fabric Energy Efficiency Standard applies to the overall level of heat loss from the building fabric, with verification based on home energy modelling of the design (using SAP, the UK home energy rating system) (Zero Carbon Hub, 2015a). The Zero Carbon Policy applies to new homes so that all energy for space conditioning, hot water and fixed lighting has to be carbon neutral but 'Emissions resulting from cooking and "plug-in" appliances such as computers and televisions are not being addressed as part of this policy' (Zero Carbon Hub, 2015b). Even with this reduced consideration of household energy demand, zero carbon is not true zero carbon, as emissions are allowed up to the 'Carbon Compliance' levels of: 10 kg $CO_{2(eq)}/m^2$/year for detached houses, 11 kg $CO_{2(eq)}/m^2$/year for attached houses and 14 kg $CO_{2(eq)}/m^2$/year for low-rise apartment blocks (up to four storeys) (Zero Carbon Hub, 2015c). So your zero carbon house might be emitting around a tonne a year, plus whatever comes from your cooking, appliances, fridge, TV and all the rest, which seems a very long way off zero.

In terms of design, houses in these new eco-towns would also be only ten minutes' walk from local services and public transport, which was to be so attractive that car journeys would only be 50 per cent of all motorized trips. Green space, including private gardens, would account for 40 per cent of land use and public buildings and schools would be zero carbon (Department for Communities and Local Government, 2009). This is an attempt to design for climate change and an assumed temperature increase as small areas of green have a local effect in lowering temperature (Gill *et al.*, 2007).

Despite these ambitions, during a visit in the summer of 2015 it was hard to see anything that looked different from the car-dominated settlements of the rest of southern England. Three houses with PVs have been built near the visitors' centre (which was unfortunately shut), together with a further wood-clad house, but these were four among a town of normal houses.

By 2015 the alternative transport plan that was set up with Sir Peter Hall as part of the committee has resulted in a public 'eco-bus' service (Whitehill & Bordon, 2011). This consists of three circular routes using perfectly conventional diesel buses with one running services every two hours throughout the day until 19.00 and the other two running a similar frequency of service until late afternoon. This does not sound likely to tempt 50 per cent of drivers out of their cars and obviously you are not supposed to go out using public transport after dark in an eco-town. All three routes stop at the big supermarket (Tescos) so life still revolves around supermarket shopping, despite the aim of making more use of locally grown food as a result of moving to 'one planet living' (Whitehill & Bordon, 2011). The existing settlement is also split by a main road, the A235, although there are plans for a new bypass to be built to the west of the settlement (Hampshire County Council, n.d.). Unfortunately, this new road cuts off some planned new housing from the large green space of Hogmoor Inclosure although there will be crossings for wild life, pedestrians and cyclists (Figure 5.1).

The dominant impression of the master plans, however, is planning for the car and for car access to housing. This hardly feels like a sustainable settlement; being car-oriented means there will be little incentive to change behaviour patterns when it comes to transport. Nor does the planning seem particularly resilient since despite the

Eco-cities 79

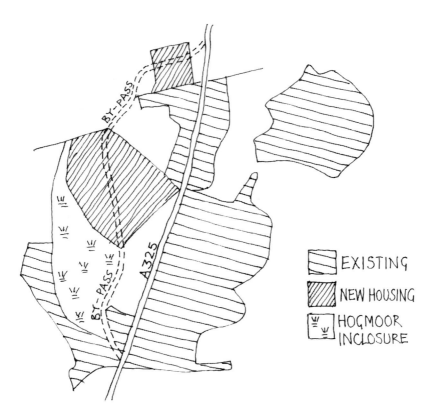

Figure 5.1 Diagram of current master plan (based on http://whitehillbordon.com/home/the-revised-masterplan/)

arguments that to mitigate global warming it is essential to 'leave crude oil in the soil' (Bassey, 2010), the planning revolves around the car. If oil supply really is cut off, a town designed around roads will suddenly have to accommodate very different forms of transport. Because the town was built around housing the military, their withdrawal has meant finding a new economic rationale through the creation of 5,500 local jobs. The latest news from the town states the first 100 developer-led 'zero-carbon' homes are under construction along with the creation of 100 new jobs and low cost accommodation for businesses that are starting up (Whitehill & Bordon.com, 2016). Although creating local jobs is good, to avoid the place becoming a dormitory town this is not rethinking the economic basis to create a sustainable economy but is rather an economy predicated on capitalism with a green tinge.

Obviously it is early days for this eco-town so it is easy to be critical (Rackheath in Norwich, another of the original four, is still farmland on what was once a Second World War US airbase). However, the very slow progress of the eco-town initiative demonstrates the problems of trying to insert something substantial and new into a well-established built environment. For many people this is too much change all at once, resulting in long, drawn-out consultation processes, whereas in terms of moving to sustainability and using resilience jargon, a revolt, or shifting to

80 *Case studies*

a totally new state, is what is required. At present, creating eco-towns is a process of adaptation of the existing. Since the 2007 eco-towns initiative there has also been a change in government, leading to the axing of a number of green policies, including the policy for all new homes to be zero carbon by 2016 (Vaughan and Macalister, 2015), so this removes the pressure on developers at Whitehill and Bordon. Like so many eco-city projects, even this much smaller scale eco-town seems to be heading nowhere fast.

5.3 Tianjin Eco-city, China

In the last twenty years of all countries China has shown the greatest interest in eco-cities (Wu, 2012; Chien, 2013). Globally the most ambitious eco-cities, in terms of size and investment, are in Saudi Arabia and China, at Masdar and Tianjin respectively. Chinese interest in eco-cities makes sense given China's need to move from relying on coal and oil, so an energy-efficient built environment that runs on renewables is an important goal, both for climate change mitigation (sustainability) and fuel security (resilience).

The city of Tianjin is sited on flat land along the Hai River that connects Tianjin with the Bohai Sea. The old city of Tianjin has a rich and complex history. Dating back to the sixth century when the first settlement was established at the intersection of two canals (north and south), the place grew as a trading point for the distribution of resources coming from the south to the north of the country. At the end of the fifteenth century Tianjin became a garrison town to protect the growing city of Beijing and to store imported resources from the south. Its identity shifted during the nineteenth century, with it becoming a key trading point with foreign countries. After the time of the Opium Wars (1839–42 and 1856–60) the city was invaded by both British and French colonists, who left their imprints on the urban landscape. As a result the morphology of the city was a merger of the Chinese traditional core and the Westernized periphery, although this has also been changed recently to accommodate wide roads and high-rise development (Bricoleurbanism, 2010). The core of the city is a clear rectangle as a heritage of its military past, and although once characterized by its many small streets it now resembles most modern Chinese cities, built in the image of Le Corbusier's dream, though with some differences, as discussed below. To the south of the old military centre what has been preserved is the former fringe belt of the old town that was developed by the Japanese, French, German, Russian and British enclaves that settled in Tianjin at the beginning of the twentieth century. This tourist attraction is known as the five great avenues and contains an eclectic mixture of buildings displaying their European heritage (Top China Travel, 2004). There are also moves to preserve more typically Chinese old residential areas in the city (Yu, 2010). The overall result is a mixed urban landscape that is increasingly dominated by the modern Chinese model. Tianjin is now the largest coastal city in the north of China and the fourth largest in the country. Its proximity to Beijing and its constant growth are also pushing the city into a transition phase from being a port to becoming a financial centre. This goal has led to the creation of a new district, the Tianjin Binhai Hi-Tech Industrial Development 40 km from Tianjin and 150 km from Beijing. The aim for this new district was to attract investment and businesses to the region, with the further goal of increasing the population without compromising the infrastructure of Beijing or Tianjin. This, together with the economic development of China, the environmental impact of its urban growth, the importance of Tianjin, the proximity to Beijing and the potential attraction generated by the Tianjin Binhai Hi-Tech Industrial Development led to the siting of the eco-city within the latter (Chang et al., 2016).

The Sino-Singapore-Tianjin Eco-City (SSTEC) (the name stems from collaboration between the governments of Singapore and China, with the support of the World Bank) was started in 2007. The Chinese government had already decided to encourage development of sustainable cities in territories that were not agriculturally productive. This led to the SSTEC being built on non-arable and polluted marshland (SSTECAC, 2009).

The SSTEC was underpinned by three 'harmonies' and three 'abilities'. The harmonies were to create a balance between people, environment and economy, and the abilities were the capacity of the project to be practicable, replicable and scalable (Singapore Government, 2015a). This sounds very much like the weak sustainability model (see Chapter 1, Figure 1.1). Greenhouse gas reduction is also linked to economic development, with a GDP carbon intensity target of 150 tonnes carbon/million (US) dollars (Guo, 2015). The IPPC targets for achieving 450 ppmv by 2100 are 10 tonnes and for 650 ppmv 40 tonnes carbon/million dollars respectively (IPCC, n.d.). Even taking account of the need for China to develop, this suggests the targets for the SSTEC may not be high enough. This carbon indicator is one of the twenty-two indicators that set targets for the SSTEC on the same website, and which include at least 20 per cent use of renewable energy by 2020 (better than Freiburg's target of 20 per cent of only electricity from renewables) and at least 30 per cent 'green travel' by 2013 rising to at least 90 per cent by 2020. The built environment also has a series of targets that include at least 12 m^2/capita green space by 2013, 100 per cent green buildings, free exercise facilities and green space within a 500 m walk of all residential accommodation, and daily water consumption of not more than 120 litres/person. The good thing here is that these targets are all measurable.

By 2020 the city is expected to occupy 30 km^2 and accommodate 350,000 inhabitants (Singapore Government, 2015a) but like Whitehall and Bordon progress is slow. Non-governmental sources suggest that by 2014 only 3 km^2 of the project have been completed, housing 23,000 residents (Kaiman, 2014). If the population density is to be 10,000 people per square kilometre by 2020, the SSCTE will have to attract 55,000 people per year, which is more than fifty times the average growth of the city since 2010. In the meantime the SSCTE remains an urban development with a low population density in a built environment of empty tall buildings.

One of the targets of the project is to establish a 90 per cent public transportation system (Singapore Government, 2015b). Currently, the system that connects Tianjin, Beijing and the SSCTE is light rail with a journey from Tianjin (Railway Station) to the SSTEC (Donghai Road) of an hour (China Travel Guide, 2016).

Perceptions of Tianjin Eco-city

Because the project is not yet complete there will be differing views of its success to date. The designers' intentions of building a 'social place' (Caprotti, 2014: 14) is perhaps questionable, particularly if the city looks unoccupied. Reporters and visitors have highlighted the fact that the city is empty (Kaiman, 2014). Like many modern Chinese cities, to Western eyes the urban landscape looks uniform and standardized

82 Case studies

and the street life is non-existent. Perhaps for this reason, the SSTEC has been described as 'a city which looks remarkably like other cities' (Caprotti, 2014), or 'like a child in its development phase' (Kaiman, 2014).

Even though apartments in the SSTEC are less expensive than similar units in Beijing or Tianjin (Fang.com, 2016), they are not affordable for the people working in the construction of the city. The workers live in the periphery of the city in buildings that do not appear at all 'eco' (Caprotti, 2014). The same situation was observed in Brasilia during the 1960s when the workers built their houses at the periphery, thereby creating the first slums in the city. Paradoxically, all those slums have now become desirable satellite cities where 80 per cent of the population of Brasilia lives and works. Despite moves like making the schools in the SSTEC cheaper than the schools in Beijng to encourage families to move to it (Kaiman, 2014), the SSTEC could follow the same trajectory as Brasilia and its future inhabitants will build the real city on the periphery of the eco-city. However, rather than speculate, it might be fairer to assess the SSTEC on what it will be like when it is finished, rather than its present state.

Tianjin Eco-city built environment

At the centre of the master plan for the SSTEC is the linear park or Eco-valley, through which the light rail runs to link the proposed three high-density centres, with the aim of everyone having easy access to this recreational facility (Weiss, 2014). The city's five districts are based on the neighbourhood concept of Singapore: the basic building block or eco-cell is 400 m x 400 m, as this is considered a good distance for walking, and contains 2,500 dwellings with 8,000 residents. Four of these cells form an eco-community and four such communities are an eco-district (Weiss, 2014) (Figure 5.2).

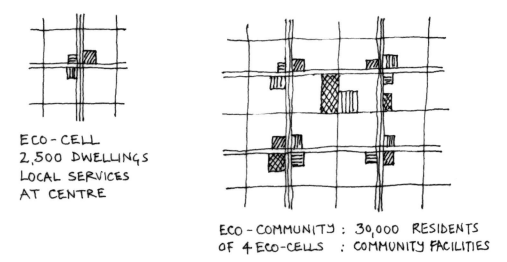

Figure 5.2 Eco-cells and eco-communities (after Government of Singapore, 2012)

In this simple scaling process housing units are grouped into medium and high-density apartments, townhouses and villas within each eco-cell.

This primary element of the SSTEC townscape, the eco-cell, is a version of the modern superblock first used by Le Corbusier in his ideal Ville radieuse (1933) and more recently by Lucio Costa in the design of Brasilia. Le Corbusier's original idea was to create compact habitats (*unités d'habitation*) of medium and high density surrounded by green areas to secure better exposure to sun and daylight than found in the traditional block of European cities. The SSCTE, like most modern Chinese urban developments, follows the same ideals. The size of the eco-blocks responds to the need to create a more walkable built environment, and each is subdivided into four areas separated by pedestrian paths, and within each quarter, buildings are arranged to create green areas in between them. Again, being typically Chinese, these areas are (or will be) beautifully landscaped and well used by the residents. Tall buildings within superblocks are systematically organized on a diagonal grid, thus keeping the same orientation. Because the Chinese Building Code requires two hours of sunlight per day in each apartment, tall buildings cannot shade those less tall. This leads to a more rigid and hierarchical arrangement than in the 'super-quadra' in Brasilia (El-Dahdah, 2005) (incidentally built in only forty-one months rather than the two decades of the unfinished SSTEC), which are more diverse than those of the SSTEC. Accepting that change is always with us, this arrangement poses problems. Introducing new buildings would mean a change in the building code and accepting less or no sunshine in some apartments or it will mean demolition, which is a potential waste of resources. A master plan for an eco-city that does not allow for change is potentially not very sustainable, either in resource or social equity terms (who decides who gets the sunny apartments?). The perimeter of the superblocks, as in all modern developments in China, is exclusively dedicated to wide roads which are hard to cross. However, a tram and cycling/pedestrian routes run through the green spine which links the four eco-districts (Figure 5.3) (Government of Singapore, 2012). Although this provides movement across the whole city, local movements between blocks may be harder to achieve on foot or bicycle.

The absence of life in the streets (which is probably mostly due to the low population) and the rigid design of the superblocks in the SSTEC have produced urban landscapes that mirror the criticized rigidity of le Corbusier's modern city (Vidler, 2000: 35–45). There are playgrounds and open areas within the residential blocks but the streets between the blocks are wide, and life begins above the street because of the enclosed car parks at ground level (Caprotti, 2014).

At the architectural scale, the built environment looks like the standardized, manufactured urban landscape it is. Standardization is not necessarily a problem but it depends on how it is used. The apartment layouts as published on real estate websites (Fang.com, 2016) are organized around vertical circulation serving four to six apartments per floor. The cheapest have structural modules of 2 and 3 m, the former producing rooms more like wide corridors. The buildings seem normal for modern China and lack features that might promote the SSTEC both as an eco-city and a city of the future. It is interesting to observe the differences between the images used in different websites to market the SSTEC (Cliento, 2011) and the pictures taken on site (Suburbana, 2014). The contrast is astonishing.

84 *Case studies*

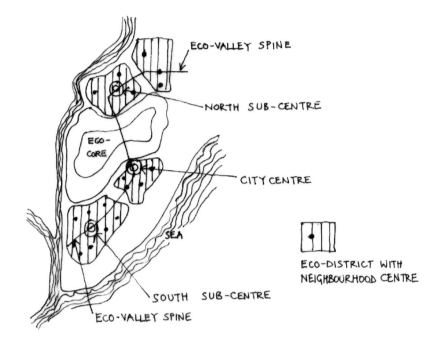

Figure 5.3 Diagram of Tianjin Eco-city master plan (after Government of Singapore, 2012)

Assessment of Tianjin Eco-city

Visiting the SSTEC revealed that although it is far more of a presence than the UK eco-town described above, it is as yet incomplete, so that the fact its documentation is also incomplete and at times confusing is no surprise. Moreover, without quantitative data on how it is performing it is hard to assess what has been achieved.

By following the World Bank idea that eco-cities are economic cities, in the SSTEC sustainability is reduced to the accommodation of people in closely spaced apartment blocks surrounded by green areas, and with provision for public transport. However, whether the SSTEC could even be called a city is questionable. It is highly dependent on monetary support from the government of China, a situation that lessens its resilience capacity to withstand any economic crisis. Moreover, the survival of the SSTEC is closely linked with the functioning of Beijing, Tianjin and the success of the new financial hub which led to the eco-city. Considering that China's economy has started to feel the impact of slowing growth, the fact the SSTEC is not yet economically productive and autonomous could be an issue for its ability to buffer future change; in other words, its resilience to such changes could be low. This may be more of a problem than the fact it has been designed to be energy efficient, which should help it buffer changes such as a future increase in the cost of energy.

The vernacular tradition of old Tianjin, although now sadly depleted, was diverse and rich, but there is no hint of this in the new eco-city. The standardization of the latter, together with a lack of diversity at a morphological (shape of the city) and functional (economics of the city) level could, as mentioned above, be problematic for its resilience, because it makes change more difficult and increases the risk of collapse if one of its standardized elements fails to work as expected. Similar intentions of building ideal cities from scratch without understanding or caring about their past have universally failed. A good example is found in the tourist centres, like Cancun or Ixtapa, created in Mexico during the 1970s. These cities were new developments with the single purpose of exploiting the natural resources of the coast. However, they have not become real cities because they still depend on a workforce coming from other states, on the resources provided by the old cities around the area and on private investment from foreign hotel chains. The urban life of these touristic cities is dead, particularly out of season (Garcia, 2008). Their infrastructure is also expensive to maintain because of the lack of permanent residents and the obsolescence that characterizes the hotel business. The urban landscape of the SSTEC is very similar to these 1970s Mexican urban developments. In both cases the developments were seen as satellites of other cities. Nevertheless, it is important to emphasize the persistence of the tourist hubs in Mexico, which has been possible due to the resilience of the natural resources available for tourist exploitation. For this reason these cities still attract foreign capital, which keeps them going. However the SSTEC, developed in a wasteland with fewer natural attractions, could face a tougher future.

Is Tianjin Eco-city sustainable?

There is no problem with an unfinished city being sustainable, since sustainability is not an ideal state but a goal for measuring human impact on available resources and waste sinks. However, the lack of quantitative data to measure the achievement of SSTEC means it is impossible to discuss its sustainability. It is fair to say that basing its design on the weak sustainability model, together with the importance given to its conventional economy poses problems. In its favour, if it runs totally on renewable energy this is essential for its sustainability. However, without a sustainable economic system in the SSTEC it is hard to see how its sustainability claims will be achieved not least because there will have to be money to replace ageing renewable energy systems. Most PV panels have a twenty-year guarantee but will last longer although possibly with a reduced output. They take energy to make and will need to be disassembled at the end of their life so that valuable elements can be retrieved, which will again take energy (Gerbinet *et al.*, 2014). Large-scale wind generators are designed to have a life of twenty-five years (Renewable Energy Association, 2016). This emphasizes the fact that sustainability is not a goal to be achieved but rather a way of doing things that can be sustained, which will include planning for renewal of the parts that go to make up the system.

In previous projects for other eco-cities in China, environmental impact calculations for the planning were based on the average impact as measured by something like the ecological footprint of existing cites or societies (Yang, 2013). This was never the case in the SSTEC and there is a sense that implementation has also changed some goals. The fact this eco-city had to be economically sustainable, meaning construction costs were covered by sales of real estate, has led the proportion of affordable housing to be reduced from 50 to 20 per cent of total (Chang *et al.*,

86 *Case studies*

2016). This is not only lower than in Tianjin and other Chinese cities but could also have an effect on the social sustainability of the city when complete, and its resilience is discussed below.

Is Tianjin Eco-city resilient?

It is difficult to discuss resilience and the future of the SSTEC when there is little certainty about its present. The infrastructure is being put in place but the other essential resource, human capital, is still scarce and potentially disconnected because of the physical layout of the blocks. Moreover, a slight change in the economic or political conditions could finally provide the excuse the few residents of SSTEC need to move back to Tianjin, with its greater accessibility to work. This will push the adaptive cycle of the SSTEC to shift to a new beginning and renewal process. At least this future exploitation phase will benefit from the capital (buildings and infrastructure) already established. Perhaps there will be a chance to reuse the infrastructure and redirect the development toward a different goal, or maybe something more humble, like starting an ordinary city.

The SSTEC was aimed at being the starting point of a new cycle in the region, with the first move being to change the area from non-arable wasteland to an urban landscape. However, the actions taken have not yet succeeded in producing the desired 'eco' identity (for definition of identity and its relationship to resilience, see Chapter 6). The SSTEC looks more like a European neighbourhood from the 1950s, or a modern Chinese city, than an eco-city for this century. As suggested in Chapter 4, the future thinking encouraged by a resilience view should help in revaluating and considering the paths by which to develop a desirable future but it cannot create a future from nothing. The future of the SSTEC is difficult to forecast because it has as yet no consolidated identity, beyond its label as an eco-city. Another challenge for the SSTEC is whether an instantaneous top-down design can buffer change. If the built environment of the SSTEC is finished and fully occupied, how will it deal with making future changes like allocating housing for unexpected inward migrations of rural populations and the consequent sudden rise in its overall ecological footprint, as has happened in many Asian cities? At least in China this has been recognized as a problem by the government and moves are in place to improve rural housing and facilities to prevent such migrations.

The lack of diversity in types of apartments and apartment buildings, along with a systemic and rigid organization of the blocks, means there is a degree of standardization at these two different scales of the built environment. The danger is that if one element changes, the rest at their different scales will change in a domino effect. As suggested in Chapter 3, a city needs some diversity in its physical form in order to adapt to change without moving to a new state. The apartments, buildings, blocks and streets of the SSTEC have been built at the same time. If one standard apartment does not function properly (whether in terms of satisfying people's physical and psychological needs or to allowing change without impeding its function), the whole building is in trouble, and consequently all the buildings of the block. This high connectedness and homogeneity together create opportunities for small disturbances to affect all the scales of the urban Panarchy.

As Figures 5.2 and 5.3 show, the master plan is not complex and can be represented by simple diagrams. Following the principles of New Urbanism, the urban landscape of the SSTEC is dominated by medium and high-density buildings around a public transport system. Unlike traditional Chinese cities, such as the lost areas of Tianjin, the small plots and narrow streets have been replaced by large blocks with their high-rise developments separated by wide streets designed for cars. The urban landscape has lost the small-scale plot. Where these small plots are all owned by different people, as in traditional cities both in the East and West, many different things can happen along the street in terms of opening businesses and mixing business with residential. In resilience terms this is a more stable situation than having a single block with a few large buildings. In the small plot city area, if one business fails, the rest are not necessarily compromised because the change is contained within one plot. The small plot system thus provides resilience to streets because some units of the landscape can be dysfunctional without interfering with the working of the rest. Because large blocks are easier to develop this should not disguise the effect this might have on the resilience of the built fabric.

The lack of a plot system together with the car parking that forms a barrier between street and apartment also means that the life on the streets could be compromised. The public spaces, within each block, even though well landscaped and well used, are not ideally related to the ground floor of the buildings. However, this is the way modern Chinese cities work, being very much a realization of the ideals of the Ville Radieuse of Le Corbusier. This kind of modern approach to urbanism became a paradigm in European countries after the Second World War and was then used in Africa and South America at giant scale, threatening the persistence of streets as key public spaces and places of social interaction by designing them with the single function of being places for cars. The design of the eco-cells in SSTEC is very similar to the design of the superblocks surrounded by arterial roads with inner pedestrian paths that Le Corbusier proposed in Chandigarh. Sadly, in the SSTEC some of the internal paths have been transformed into streets for the use of cars as car ownership in China increases (Barman, 2015). Although this might be viewed as using an opportunity for change, once the streets are full of cars, as many cities in the developed world have discovered, there is nowhere else to go.

One factor that might help to prevent undesirable changes in the built environment of the SSTEC is the presence of more than one building in a completed block. One building could be demolished and replaced without disturbing the others, although this would still be a more significant change than in built environments made up of very small plots, as discussed above. For resilience, the most important design decision is leaving the green spaces between buildings. If the city experiences an unexpected population increase, green spaces between buildings offer opportunities for making changes in the built environment, whether by allowing illegal occupation or by permitting infill buildings that incorporate new activities to keep the city working. The latter, however, will represent a change in the identity of the city, from being an intended eco-city to becoming an informal city. This happened in Brasilia with the difference that it occurred on the periphery of the city. Such change implies the collapse of the eco-city and the starting point for a new adaptive cycle that might be good or bad depending on the future conditions. Only time will provide the answer. Thus the new city might have resilience but not as an eco-city.

At the apartment level the flexibility is highly compromised by the fact that tall buildings offer fewer chances to add new spaces to apartments without involving high cost. Even though informal interventions in tall buildings do happen, these are

88 *Case studies*

rare and not safe enough to be encouraged. The single vertical circulation core in the SSTEC apartment buildings does provide maximum free perimeter and therefore more chance to change the interior layout without losing ventilation or daylight.

Finally, one threat to the stability of present and future cities in China is corruption. The eco-city project of Dongtan was affected by corruption scandals in Shanghai (Brenhouse, 2010). By partnering with Singapore, the government of China has increased the overlaps in management and in this way they have achieved more control over the development of the SSTEC. However, the system is still vulnerable, as shown by the dramatic events in Tianjin Port in the Binhai new district in August 2015 where a petrochemical plant exploded due to shortcuts taken by the owners to avoid security policies and processes (State Council, People's Republic of China, 2015).

5.4 Conclusions

The reason for using eco-cities as case studies to look for examples of sustainability and resilience in the built environment is because increasing global urbanization must be based on ways of living with much lower resource consumption in urban areas. However, from the two examples considered, this seems difficult to achieve. The present construction of eco-cities is based on a simplistic understanding of what a city is, with the emphasis more on the buildings and infrastructure than the people or citizens, for as Rousseau (1762) asserted, it is the citizens that make the city. People are also vital for sustainability. As argued in Chapter 2, sustainability depends on people's behavioural choices and decisions. A calculation of the ecological footprint of a city cannot be made without measuring how resources are used, a factor that largely depends on people's behaviour. If it is not prescribed and forced, behaviour tends to be the result of mixed actions that are often inequitable and unpredictable, but that also follow patterns, habits and traditions. The future behaviour of people cannot be predicted before the city exists, therefore people's impact and that of the eco-city cannot be measured in a realistic way until the city exists. The resilience of a system such as an eco-city will largely depend on understanding cities as built environment/people systems. Eco-cities, however, tend to be designed on simple ideas, such that energy will come from renewables (but renewables may not be as reliable and controllable as fossil fuel-derived sources, nor as profitable), there will be more green elements and more public transport and that people will therefore walk and cycle rather than use their cars.

There is also a danger in building cities based on the vision of one or even a small group of people. The eco-city completely depends on its designers' views of what a city might and might not be, and how they think people will behave. Resilience, if nothing else, underscores the fact that everything is changing all the time, including the values and aspirations of people. Any design for an eco-city is no more than a starting point for a built environment that will change with time, but presumably in a way that will continue to minimize its non-renewable resource use, and hence the environmental impact of its citizens. The caveat here is Jevons' (1865) paradox. In his book *The Coal Question*, Jevons put forward the paradox that more efficient use of a resource tends to increase its usage. If living in an eco-city is cheaper because less is being spent on energy then the danger is that the 'spare' money will be spent on some other resource. As an example, the people who live at the organic and renewable energy settlement of Findhorn in Scotland fly more than the Scottish national average (Vale and Vale, 2013: 269; Tinsley and George, 2006: 29). The work in China to convert existing settlements to use fewer resources seems far more important than building flagship eco-cities (Chien, 2013).

One criticism of eco-cities is that they are not viewed as open-ended systems but rather as ones where the 'eco-ness' stops at the city boundary. No city exists in isolation as it depends on a hinterland for its survival. In making any settlement more ecological the relationship between the urban and the rural must be considered. A concern is that eco-cities are just another way of selling sustainability rather than grappling with what this really means. Emerson pointed out that a city 'lives by remembering' (Mumford, 1961/1966: 118). Life implies change, constant adaption and discontinuity, while remembering implies continuity. So creating a new eco-city that also has resilience may be very difficult. Before thinking of making an eco-city we have to have a city that works fairly well. Creating cities is not easy, particularly if you try to do it alone. An easier starting point might be to work in existing urban environments and through education help people to see reasons for changing their behaviour to being more sustainable. This, however, is not a design solution, so it is not likely to be popular with designers. It is also not profitable, and so it is also not likely to be popular with developers.

Bibliography

Alusi, A., Eccles, R. G., Edmonston, A. C. and Zuzul, T. (2011). Sustainable cities: oxymoron or the shape of the future? Harvard Business School Working Paper No. 11–062, available at http://papers.ssrn.com/sol3/papers.cfm?abstract_id=1726484, accessed 10 September 2015.
Backhouse, R. (2002). *The Ordinary Business of Life*. Princeton, NJ: Princeton University Press.
Barman, S. (2015). Car ownership reaches record in China, available at www.bbc.com/news/world-asia-31065433, accessed 24 March 2016.
Bassey, N. (2010). I will not dance to your beat, available at http://oilsandstruth.org/i-will-not-dance-your-beat-poem-nnimmo-bassey, accessed 18 April 2016.
Benton, T. (1987). *The Villas of Le Corbusier 1920–1930*. New Haven, CT and London: Yale University Press.
Boyden, S., Millar, S., Newcombe, K. and O'Neill, B. (1981). *The Ecology of a City and its People: the Case of Hong Kong*. Canberra: Australian National University Press.
Brenhouse, H. (2010). Plans shrivel for Chinese eco-city. *The New York Times*, available at www.nytimes.com/2010/06/25/business/energy-environment/25iht-rbogdong.html?_r=0, accessed 18 April 2016.
Bricoleurbanism. (2010). Demolition of Tianjin's old city, available at www.bricoleurbanism.org/china/demolition-of-tianjins-old-city/, accessed 18 April 2016.
Bulkeley, H. and Marvin, S. (2014). Urban governance and eco-citites: dynamics, drivers and emerging lessons. In W. Hofmeister, P. Rueppel and L. L. Fook (eds), *Eco-cities*. Singapore: Konrad-Adeneur Stiftung Ltd and European Union.
Bund. (2013). Freiburg and Environment: Ecological capital – Environmental Capital – Solar City – Sustainable City – Green City?, available at www.bund-rvso.de/freiburg-environment-ecology.html, accessed 10 September 2015.
C40 Cities. (2011). Case study, available at www.c40.org/case_studies/freiburg-an-inspirational-city-powered-by-solar-where-a-third-of-all-journeys-are-by-bike, accessed 10 September 2015.
Caprotti, F. (2014). Critical research on eco-cities? A walk through the Sino-Singapore Tianjin Eco-City, China. *Cities* 36, pp. 10–17.

Chang, I-C., Leitner, H. and Sheppard, E. (2016). A green leap forward? Eco-state restructuring and the Tianjin-Bihai eco-city model. *Regional Studies* 50(6), pp. 929–943.

[...]n, S-S. (2013). Chinese eco-cities: a perspective of land speculation-oriented local entrepreneurism. *China Information* 27(2), pp. 173–196.

[...] Travel Guide. (2016). Tianjin Railway Station–Donghai Road, available at www.[...]velchinaguide.com/cityguides/tianjin/light-rail.htm, accessed 7 December 2016.

C[...], K. (2011). Tianjin Eco-City/Surbana Urban Planning Group, available at www.archdaily.com/102887/tianjin-eco-city-surbana-urban-planning-group, accessed 24 March 2016.

Clim[...]on. (2015). Find out more about COP21, available at wwwcop21paris.org/about/cop21, accessed 24 March 2016.

Davis, D. (2002). The Great Smog. *History Today* 52(12), available at www.historytoday.com/devra-davis/great-smog, accessed 16 June 2015.

Demographia. (2015). USA Urbanised Areas: 2000 Ranked by Population (All Areas), available at www.demographia.com/db-ua2000pop.htm, accessed 24 March 2016.

Department for Communities and Local Government. (2007). *Eco-towns Prospectus*. London: Department for Communities and Local Government.

Department for Communities and Local Government. (2009). John Healey: Green light given on eco-town sites plus tougher standards for future homes, available at http://webarchive.nationalarchives.gov.uk/20120919132719/www.communities.gov.uk/news/corporate/1284621, accessed 15 July 2015.

Devuyst, D., Hens, L. and de Lannoy, W. (eds). (2001). *How Green is the City? Sustainability Assessment and the Management of Urban Environments*. New York: Columbia University Press.

Ecocity Builders. (2014). The solution, available at www.ecocitybuilders.org/why-ecocities/the-solution/, accessed 10 March 2016.

Egenhofer, C. and van Shaik, L. (2005). *Towards a Global Climate Regime: Priority Areas for a Coherent EU Strategy*. Brussels: Centre for European Policy Studies.

El-Dahdah, F. (2005). *CASE: Lucio Costa, Brasilia's Superquadra*. Harvard University, Graduate School of Design, Munich and New York.

Esher, L. (1981). *A Broken Wave*. Harmondsworth: Penguin Books.

Ewing, B., Moore, D., Goldfinger, S., Oursler, A., Reed, A. and Wackernagel, M. (2010). *The Ecological Footprint Atlas 2010*. Oakland, CA: Global Footprint Network.

Fang.com. (2016). Kaaba color county two, available at http://tianfangcaijun.fang.com/, accessed 24 March 2016.

Fook, L. L. and Chen, G. (eds). (2010). *Towards a Livable and Sustainable Urban Environment: Eco-Cities in East Asia*. Singapore and Hackensack, NJ: World Scientific.

Foster + Partners. (2007). Foster + Partners presents a new mixed-use destination for Moscow, available at file:///C:/Users/Brenda/Downloads/Foster_+_Partners_presents_a_new_mixed-use_destination_for_Moscow__Foster_Partners.pdf.pdf, accessed 10 September 2015.

Garcia, E. (2008). Urbanismo y arquitectura para el turismo de masas en las costas mexicanas: Ixtapa, un caso de estudio. Master in Architecture, Universidad Nacional Autonoma de Mexico.

Gerbinet, S., Belboom, S. and Leonard, A. (2014). Life cycle analysis (LCA) of photovoltaic panels: a review. *Renewable and Sustainable Energy Reviews* 38, pp. 747–753.

Gill, S., Handley, J., Ennos, R. and Paulei, S. (2007). Adapting cities for climate change: the role of green infrastructure. *Built Environment* 33(1), pp. 115–133.

Glasson, J. and Marshall, T. (2007). *Regional Planning*. Abingdon: Routledge.

Golley, F. (1993). *A History of the Ecosystem Concept in Ecology: More than the Sum of the Parts*. New Haven, CT: Yale University Press.

Government of Singapore. (2012). Master Plan, available at www.tianjinecocity.gov.sg/bg_masterplan.htm, accessed 10 April 2016.

Gruen, V. (1965). *The Heart of Our Cities*. London: Thames and Hudson.
Guo, Y. (trans.). (2015) Available at www.eco-city.gov.cn/eco/html/zjstc/zbtx.html, accessed 15 July 2015.
Gutkind, E. (1969). *Urban Development in Southern Europe: Italy and Greece*. Toronto: Collier Macmillian.
Hampshire County Council. (n.d.). Whitehill & Bordon Relief Road: Overview and Role of the Relief Road, available at http://documents.hants.gov.uk/transport-consultations/whitehill-bordon/WhitehillBordonExhibitionBoardsFinalWebsiteVersion20140225.pdf, accessed 14 September 2015.
Harvey, D. (2010). *Energy and the New Reality 1: Energy Efficiency and the Demand for Energy Services*. London: Earthscan.
Howard, E. (1898). *Tomorrow a Peaceful Path to Real Reform*. London: Swan Sonnenschein and Co. Ltd.
Information Services Department, Census and Statistics Department (HK). (2015). Hong Kong: the facts, available at www.gov.hk/en/about/abouthk/factsheets/docs/population.pdf, accessed 10 March 2016.
IPCC (Intergovernmental Panel on Climate Change). (n.d.). Working Group III: Mitigation, available at www.ipcc.ch/ipccreports/tar/wg3/index.php?idp=57, accessed 8 October 2015.
Jevons, W. S. (1865). Of the economy of fuel. Chapter 7 in *The Coal Question: An Inquiry Concerning the Progress of the Nation, and the Probable Exhaustion of Our Coalmines*. London: Macmillan and Co.
Kaiman, J. (2014). China's 'eco-cites' empty of hospitals, shopping centres and people. *The Guardian*, 14 April 2014, available at www.theguardian.com/cities/2014/apr/14/china-tianjin-eco-city-empty-hospitals-people, accessed 10 March 2016.
Le Corbusier. (1933). *La ville radieuse*. Boulogne: Editions de l'Architecture d'Aujourd'hui.
Le Corbusier. (1947). *The Four Routes*. London: Dennis Dobson.
Liu, C. (2011). China's city of the future rises on a wasteland. *The New York Times*, available at www.nytimes.com/cwire/2011/09/28/28climatewire-chinas-city-of-the-future-rises-on-a-wastela-76934.html?pagewanted=all, accessed 10 March 2016.
Macedo, J. (2004). City profile: Curitiba. *Cities* 21(6), pp. 537–549.
Marshall, S. (2007). *Cities Design and Evolution*. New York: Routledge.
Mithraratne, N., Vale, B. and Vale, R. (2007). *Sustainable Living: The Role of Whole Life Costs and Values*. London: Butterworth Heinemann.
More, T. (1516/1965). *Utopia*, ed. trans. P. Turner. Harmondsworth: Penguin Books.
Mumford, L. (1961/1966). *The City in History: Its Origins, Its Transformations, and Its Prospects*. Harmondsworth: Penguin Books.
Newcombe, K., Kalma, J. and Aston, A. (1978). The metabolism of a city: the case of Hong Kong. *Ambio* 7, pp. 3–15.
Renewable Energy Association. (2016). The voice of the renewables industry in the UK, available at www.r-e-a.net/renewable-technologies/wind, accessed 10 March 2016.
Register, R. (1987). *Ecocity Berkeley: Building Cities for a Healthy Future*. Berkeley, CA: North Atlantic Books.
Register, R. (2006). *Rebuilding Cities in Balance with Nature*. Gabriola, BC: New Society Publishers.
Richardson, B. (1876). *Hygeia: A City of Health*. London: Macmillan and Co.
Rogelj, J., Schaeffer, M., Friedlingstein, P., Gillett, N. P., van Vuuren, D. P., Riahi, K., Allen, M. and Knutti, R. (2016). Differences between carbon budget estimates unravelled. *Nature Climate Change* 6, pp. 245–252.
Rousseau, J. J. (1762). The Social Contract, available at www.marxists.org/reference/subject/economics/rousseau/social-contract/ch01.htm, accessed 21 May 2016.
Shaw, R. (2007). Eco-towns and the next 60 years of planning. *Town and Country Planning Tomorrow Series Paper 9*, TCPA, London.

Singapore Government. (2015a). Sino-Singapore Tianjin Eco-city, available at www.tianjine-cocity.gov.sg/bg_intro.htm, accessed 11 March 2016.
Singapore Government. (2015b). Sino-Singapore Tianjin Eco-city, available at www.tianjine-cocity.gov.sg/bg_kpis.htm, accessed 11 March 2016.
SSTECAC (Sino-Singapore Tianjin Eco-city Administration Committee). (2009). *Master Plan of Sino-Singapore Tinajin Eco-City 2008–2020*. Tianjin: SSTECAC.
Soleri, P. (1969). *Arcology: the City in the Image of Man*. Cambridge, MA and London: MIT Press.
Soleri, P. (1983). *Arcosanti: An Urban Laboratory?* San Diego, CA: Avant Books and the Cosanti Foundation.
Soltani, A. and Sharifi, E. (2012). A case study of sustainable urban planning principles in Curitiba (Brazil) and their applicability in Shiraz (Iran). *International Journal of Development and Sustainability* 1(2), pp. 120–134.
Suburbana. (2014). Sino-Singapore Tianjin Eco-city, available at www.surbana.com/sino-singapore-tianjin-eco-city/, accessed 24 March 2016.
State Council, People's Republic of China. (2015). Tianjin blast probe suggests Action against 123 people, available at http://english.gov.cn/news/top_news/2016/02/05/content_281475284781471.htm, accessed 24 March 2016.
Teilhard de Chardin, P. (1955). *The Phenomenon of Man*. New York and London: Harper Perennial Modern Thought.
Tinsley, S. and George, H. (2006). Ecological Footprint of the Findhorn Foundation and Community, Sustainable Development Research Centre, Forres, Moray, Scotland.
Top China Travel. (2004). Five Great Avenues, available at www.topchinatravel.com/china-attractions/five-great-avenues.htm, accessed 10 April 2016.
Toynbee, A. (1970). *Cities on the Move*. New York: Oxford University Press.
Vale, R. and Vale, B. (2009). *Time to Eat the Dog?: The Real Guide to Sustainable Living*. London: Thames and Hudson.
Vale, B. and Vale, R. (2013). The Hockerton Housing Project, England. In R. Vale and B. Vale (eds), *Living within a Fair Share Ecological Footprint*. Abingdon: Earthscan, pp. 262–274.
Vaughan, A. and Macalister, T. (2015). The nine green policies killed off by the Tory government. *The Guardian*, 24 July, available at www.theguardian.com/environment/2015/jul/24/the-9-green-policies-killed-off-by-tory-government, accessed 23 September 2015.
Vidler, A. (2000). Photourbanism: planning the city from above and from below. In G. Bridge and S. Watson (eds), *A Companion to the City*. Oxford: Blackwell Publishers.
Vincent Callebaut Architecte. (2008). Lilypad, a floating Ecopolis for climate refugees, available at http://vincent.callebaut.org/page1-img-lilypad.html, accessed 23 September 2015.
Warren-Rhodes, K. and Koenig, A. (2001). Escalating trends in the urban metabolism of Hong Kong: 1971–1997. *Ambio* 30(7), pp. 429–438.
Weiss, L. (2014). Tianjin, Eco-City, China: Urban NEXUS case study 05, available at www2.giz.de/wbf/4tDx9kw63gma/05_UrbanNEXUS_CaseStudy_Tianjin.pdf, accessed 11 March 2016.
Whitehill & Bordon. (2011). Town bus, available at www.whitehillbordon.com/transport/public-transport/travelling-by-bus/, accessed 7 July 2015.
Whitehill & Bordon.com. (2016). Minister visits Whitehill & Bordon to see construciton of first homes start, available at http://whitehillbordon.com/2016/02/12/minister-visits-whitehill-bordon-to-see-construction-of-first-homes-start/, accessed 14 April 2016.
World Bank. (2010). Eco2 Cities: Ecological Cities as Economic Cities, Synopsis, available at http://siteresources.worldbank.org/INTURBANDEVELOPMENT/Resources/336387-1270074782769/Eco2Cities_synopsis.pdf, accessed 10 March 2016.
World Bank. (2015). CO_2 emissions (metric tons per capita), available at http://data.worldbank.org/indicator/EN.ATM.CO2E.PC, accessed 6 October 2015.
Wu, F. (2012). China's eco-cities. *Geoforum* 43(2), pp. 169–171, https://doi.org/http://dx.doi.org/10.1016/j.geoforum.2011.08.001.

Yang, Z. (2013). *Eco-cities: A Planning Guide*. Boca Raton, FL and London: Taylor & Francis.
Yu, D. (2010). The 'Tianjin Model': a view from the grass roots, trans. D. Sanderson. *Chinese Heritage Quarterly* 21, available at www.chinaheritagequarterly.org/features.php?searchterm=021_duyu.inc&issue=021, accessed 11 April 2016.
Zero Carbon Hub. (2015a). Fabric Energy Efficiency Standard, available at www.zerocarbonhub.org/zero-carbon-policy/fabric-energy-efficiency-standard, accessed 7 July 2015.
Zero Carbon Hub. (2015b). Zero Carbon Policy, available at www.zerocarbonhub.org/zero-carbon-policy/zero-carbon-policy, accessed 7 July 2015.
Zero Carbon Hub. (2015c). Carbon Compliance Targets, available at www.zerocarbonhub.org/zero-carbon-policy/carbon-compliance-target, accessed 7 July 2015.

6   Heritage

'Memory is life's clock.'

Spanish proverb

Most cities are composed of parts which were built in different eras, or at the same time by different people. When a new building appears in an established city it usually means another has been destroyed, meaning some buildings persist while others perish. Heritage is usually related to preserving or maintaining meaningful buildings or monuments, or iconic urban or architectural features. The heritage of the built environment usually tends to be considered within UNESCO's definition of cultural heritage as buildings, monuments and groups of buildings that have 'Outstanding Universal Value from the point of view of history, art or science' (UNESCO, 2015: 10). However, the approach taken in this chapter is different. This chapter deals with what might be termed modest heritage, as the aim is to consider what has persisted and what has changed or been transformed in the structure of the built environment and its urban landscape. The first step is then to define persistence and its relationship to both resilience and sustainability. This leads to the definition of identity.

6.1 Persistence

When applied to ecological systems persistence is used to mean being in a stable state (Connell and Sousa, 1983). Connell and Sousa were interested in the evidence needed to see if an ecosystem was stable or persistent. They pointed out the need to understand two different ways of defining persistence. The first is the stability of the populations of organisms within the ecosystem (Holling, 1973). To arrive at a conclusion it is necessary to count the number of organisms over time to see whether populations are remaining relatively stable. The other view is to look for the presence or absence of populations of organisms, which Holling (1973: 1) expressed as the 'the persistence of the relationships' within the system. In applying this to the built environment a useful example is Robert Browning's poem (1888) *The Pied Piper of Hamelin*. Hamelin was a town that experienced change that made conditions intolerable. The first change in Hamelin was a huge increase in the population of rats, and then further change when the town was depleted first of rats and then, when the town failed to pay the piper, it lost all its children. There was no change in the built environment but the town was not the same place as the intergenerational relationship also changed with the loss of the children, as without this generation who would look after their parents as they aged? Persistence in resilience, therefore, suggests a system can buffer external pressures without changing to a different state. Persistence is not a term usually applied to sustainability. When it is, it tends to be linked to being persistent in trying to move towards sustainability (Swift, 2011) or ensuring the ecosystems we depend on persist (Fontaine *et al.*, 2005). Persistence has a link with heritage because the latter suggests that some parts of the built environment have been deliberately preserved because they are valued. This leads on to the idea of why they are valued and to a definition of identity.

6.2 Identity

Identity lets us differentiate one thing (or person) from another and is also used to relate things that might be different but belong to the same group. Thus an apple looks and tastes different from a pear but both are tree fruit. When someone says that he or she feels identified with a place, a community or a nation, it means that they share the same values or feelings about that place. Relph (1976) proposed that identity is what links things that we can see (material) with those we cannot see but feel (immaterial). For example, the identity of a group allows the people in it to share the same things (wanting to save the whales) without losing what makes them different (gender, nationality, age), and thus without losing their own personal identities. This type of group could be thought of as a system with shared values and individual components. The ways in which some common qualities are linked, whether by groups, individuals or both, and how others become disconnected to produce differences also can become part of the same identity. Annually the group of people who want to save the whales may not consist of the same number of individuals, but as long as there are enough individuals contributing towards the same goal the group survives. However, a new, passionate member may want the group also to save sharks and this could lead to the group embracing both goals, and thus changing the identity of the group, or splitting into two groups and thus preserving the identity of the 'save the whale' group.

From this point of view, the identity of a system permits us to analyse and understand how sameness and differences coexist. Cars, for example, can be seen as a subsystem within the system of vehicles. They have an identity that makes them different from other groups of vehicles, like motorcycles or trams. How is it possible that after all the years since the creation of the Ford-A in 1903 cars have seen little development in terms of their basic structure and components, and thus their identities as cars? Whether we are aware of the specific reasons that have kept cars working or not, it is clear that they have shown some resilience to other technological advances in transport matters. For example, the first electric cars appeared in the 1890s and had an equal share with petrol in the overall market for cars (Schiffer, 1994: 49), but it has taken the threat of peak oil and climate change for car manufacturers again to begin to make electric cars in competition with petrol ones, and they still look like cars. Given this, how might it be possible to understand the point at which the resilience of a system has been broken? How much does a car have to change before losing its identity as a car? In what moment will a car stop being a car? The sad story of the Sinclair C5 (Anon, 2009) shows how something that was meant as a car substitute was never accepted as belonging to the group called 'cars'. It had lost its identity or 'carness'.

Every place and subsystem of a built environment is unique because it has an identity, whether we perceive its character or not. Therefore, the buildings that are deliberately preserved as part of the heritage of a particular built environment only represent

96 *Case studies*

one dimension of the identity of a place, and one that may not be necessary for the resilience and persistence of a built environment. New York without the Twin Towers is still New York, and from this point of view, its identity has shown a huge resilience to a terrorist attack. In this way identity can be linked with resilience.

Using identity to understand resilience

Based on the definition of ecological resilience (see Chapter 3), it seems possible that when the identity of a system has survived over time, it has exhibited a resilience capacity to whatever has happened during this period. This means the evidence for the resilience of a system can be seen only after a crisis or event has happened, not before. Earthquake codes for building construction, even though they exist, usually become more stringent after an earthquake event. This happened after the two big Christchurch earthquakes in New Zealand. The upgraded earthquake code has led to many buildings being strengthened in Wellington, even though it was not the site of the large earthquake. Although the earlier earthquake codes were developed by modelling what might happen, the real evidence of the resilience of a system (the built environment of Christchurch) only emerges after the crisis (the earthquakes).

This idea can be explored using the earlier example of cars. To understand the resilience of cars to changes in motoring technology it is necessary to analyse how changes have happened in the structure of cars, and thus in their identities. Cars still have internal combustion engines, but the way these are constructed and controlled has changed (engines are no longer fired by turning a starting handle and the manual choke on the carburettor has been replaced by a computer-controlled air/fuel mixture and fuel injection to the engine). Because these changes are effectively hidden from most car users, all they perceive is a vehicle with the same identity (a car) that is faster and easier to drive. A basic understanding of the history of a system can thus be used to show what it has inherited from the past (in the case of the car this is the basic arrangement of four wheels, one at each corner – apart from occasional three-wheelers which have never really been accepted – and an engine), and thus what has persisted and what has changed. In this approach history becomes an essential tool in understanding resilience because it can help to reveal whether the identity of a system has persisted or has collapsed; in other words, whether the system is still the same or has moved to a new state. This requires thinking about heritage not just as preserved buildings, green spaces and neighbourhoods (which are all elements of a built environment) but as what has been inherited from the past that persists and is part of the identity of a place. This idea is explored below in the case study of the city of San Miguel de Tucuman in Argentina.

One problem with the application of resilience thinking to the study of built environments is that cities are much, much more complicated than an object like a car. This is even more problematic for cities with a relatively short history, like the colonial cities of Auckland, Sydney or Wellington. With a short history it could be more difficult to find references that can be used to detect clear changes in their identities, since these are still developing. However, what has been inherited from the past is present in the current built environment, even where this might not be obvious (see Chapter 9).

The history of a system is less important for sustainability. Rather than looking to the past, what is needed for sustainability is analysis of the present state of a system and the relative impact of its components. It you want to make a house more energy efficient, knowing the history of its previous owners is not necessary. However, knowing how much energy it uses through looking at very recent fuel bills is useful as a check or known quantity for modelling of the house's future energy use if changes are made, such as insulating the ceiling, or installing a heat pump rather than an electric resistance heater. This leads on to considering whether heritage has a part in sustainability thinking.

6.3 Why link heritage and sustainability

Heritage is also important for sustainability since the built environment represents an inherited capital in the form of material resources and human labour. However, the perception of the value of that capital means that large buildings are often favoured over the small, whatever their architectural merit. Thus the large medieval cathedrals that have survived crises such as warfare and religious schisms are retained and maintained, whereas smaller church buildings of equal merit are lost, with this often happening over many centuries. As an example, in the city of Lincoln in the UK, which has the third largest cathedral building footprint in England, some forty medieval churches have disappeared as well as a number of monastic buildings (My Maps, 2015). In contrast, favouring the other capital – land – can produce the opposite effect where large buildings disappear to create opportunities for constructing even larger buildings. For example, New Scotland Yard in London, with its iconic revolving triangular metal sign, is to be demolished to make way for an even taller apartment complex (Bury, 2016).

In sustainability terms, therefore, heritage is pulling in two directions, the first being the desire to keep the resources in the built environment and the second to use existing urban land (brown field) rather than new land (green field) for development to avoid loss of agricultural capital. Inevitably, using brown field land means old buildings have to make way for new ones. The other sustainability aspect to consider is whether the cost in both money and resources of repair and maintenance exceeds the costs of demolition and rebuilding. Johnstone (1994) found that the economic life of a house in New Zealand was around ninety years even though the Building Code assumes a fifty-year life for components like the structure that are not renewed during the life of a house. That said, many buildings are demolished before the end of their resource life, such as the early demolition of the 1950s Pruitt-Igoe housing development in St Louis after just over twenty years, which leads to a waste of resources.

6.4 Why link heritage and resilience?

In defining identity it emerged that in a built environment what is inherited from the past and what persists become part of the identity of the place. This is a different view of heritage from buildings and places of significance that meet UNESCO's definition above. As discussed in Chapters 3 and 4, resilience is not a goal, like sustainability. From the resilience point of view the UNESCO view of heritage is not necessary for the continuing life of the city, unless perhaps that city relies only on tourism for its economic basis. The destruction of a very historic building on the corner of your Paris street would not stop you from buying a baguette for breakfast. However, the total

98   *Case studies*

bombing of your city means the loss of its identity, unless as in Dresden or Freiburg it is rebuilt in the image of the old city.

The heritage of a city can influence its identity (Graham and Howard, 2008), this is another link between heritage and resilience. The definition of ecological resilience states that when a system moves to a new state it is not the same system anymore, or in other words it has lost its identity. When this happens, the disturbance that threatened the system in question has transformed it into something else and the resilience of the original system was not sufficient to prevent that transformation. This suggests that by understanding the built heritage of a city in terms of what has been inherited from the past that has become part of the city's identity, we could learn something about what has been adapted to change and what has been transformed by change. In terms of buildings rather than cities, an old industrial mill that has become a museum or gallery is an adaptation whereas a building where only the original facade remains with a new structure behind this is a transformation, since effectively it is a new building – if the facade is removed the building still works. In resilience it is important to analyse what is persisting and what is changing in order to differentiate forms of change. This is important for heritage, with the implication that we want to keep buildings and infrastructure that are important for identity.

6.5 The built heritage is more than old buildings

The heritage of a city reflects the persistence of both traditions and past and present innovations, the new and the old. What is built it is just a fraction of the entire heritage of a culture. The Tuareg live a nomadic life in the Sahara desert. Even though theirs is a society that has not been 'built' in a single place, their culture and traditions have been kept alive for centuries. Rapoport (1969) showed how what was built, in his study of the house, was a response to both culture and the environment. Conversely, the built environment of cities can help us to learn who we are and even to define our preferences in terms of what kind of present and future habitat we want. People are an essential part of this urban system. This is different from the perception of urban heritage as the conservation of iconic old buildings. Angkor Wat is a beautiful and astonishing legacy of more than one culture and generation but since no-one lives there permanently it has become a monumental ruin visited by tourists instead of a city. It is frozen in time. Unlike ruins, inhabited cities cannot resist the passage of time because they are based on a living cultural process. Cities have no other option than to deal with the flow of change imposed by a culture in motion. A resilience perspective can thus offer a way of looking at heritage as a framework for understanding change and ways of exploring the identity of systems.

A designer's perspective

What a designer may want to know is what elements and relationships will tolerate more or less change without causing a massive transformation in the whole system. In others words, what are the elements and feedback loops between elements that have to persist and that are less susceptible to being changed without causing an impact on the whole system, and which ones might be more flexible to being changed. If a truck going along a highway loses one of its multiple wheels, it might be able to keep on working. If a truck loses its load it might be still able to keep on going. However, if the truck loses its engine it will no longer be able to move under its own power. All the parts are important but a few are more important and critical than others. However, these drivers of change are not easily recognizable in the built environment where money, politics, social dynamics and environmental conditions, just to mention a few variables, are changing and affecting each other simultaneously and continuously. By analysing the inheritance of changes in a system, it might become possible to dig deeper into the dynamics of change of a system. It is not only about what has to be kept and what has to be lost but also about how much room can be found or generated to deal with change.

One issue for designers is that the architectural scale is linked with a very specific and small-scale history that is not necessarily always contemplated in the grand history of a country or city. How many times do we come to grips with the history of a neighbourhood, street or a block when designing a new building? The historical events of a city may not necessarily be linked with the development of the morphology of its built environment. Changes in the economy of a country may not have any impact on the shape of one street or block in a small neighbourhood of a small city. The theoretical framework of resilience suggests investigating the history of a built environment by using timelines to see the effect of big (and possibly small) events on the shape of the city, and in this way identify which parts have been transformed and which have persisted. As an example, the small city of Napier in New Zealand was destroyed by an earthquake in 1931. This would be considered a breaking point in the timeline of the city. The buildings changed character, being rebuilt in the latest art deco style, but the existing street layout remained virtually unchanged. Additionally, some art deco buildings contain Maori motifs (Art Deco Trust, n.d.). This points to another break in the timeline of the city when the white missionaries arrived in the area in the 1830s and the previous Maori settlement became colonized (Napier City Council, 2016).

Timelines also help to position events and processes at different scales. Walker and Salt (2012) suggest that a resilience analysis should include multiple scales and then be related with social, economic, ecological or political factors. As designers of the built environment, we will have to add regional, urban and architectural scales to the analysis. However, designers are not historians and they often use very restricted elements when re-creating the development of an urban landscape – maps, drawings, occasionally old pictures, and possibly a record of changes in the ownership and shape of plots. Studies that deal with specific types and styles of buildings or architects may be useful but may not be available for small cities whose heritage may not yet be recognized as important for the identity of the place. Even books that clearly define political, economic or social phases in the history of a country or city are sometimes difficult to find. The information available for designers is (to use resilience terminology) lumpy and dispersed when it comes to organizing a timeline and knowing what events and processes have to be placed at what scales in an analysis.

6.6 Braudel and Waisman

The French historian Fernand Braudel (1902–85) believed it was necessary to take a long-term and comprehensive view of social events to understand history (Harsgor, 1978). The work of Braudel (1969, 1977, 1980) is potentially important for finding a set of principles to frame events and processes at different scales, and this in turn

100 *Case studies*

could be helpful in defining the frequencies of change in a built environment. For Braudel, the history of what you want to know is the unit of analysis instead of a physical one. He proposed three scales based on the duration of historical processes: *longue* (long), *moyenne* (intermediate) and *courte* (short) *durée* (duration). These speeds are related with three conceptions of time: a 'geographical time, a social time, and an individual time' (Braudel, 1980: 4). The geographical time tells the history of humanity and its relationships with its environment. It is a history of slow changes that take place in cycles, where physical structures are produced (changes in land formation through erosion or upheavals) as well as trends beyond the control of human beings, such as long-term variations in climate. In urban studies this scale could be linked with slow processes of large transformations at the level of landscapes and regions. Its measurement could be expressed in thousands of years and thousands of kilometres. The social time is the history of *social realities*, which is constituted by 'all major forms of collective life' (Braudel, 1980: 11) like economies, societies and demographic changes that follow cycles of ten, twenty-five or at the limit fifty years. This scale can be approached in urban studies by measuring its processes in decades or longer (Wegener *et al.*, 1986). Finally, the history of events is the history of individuals which could be measured in days, weeks or years (Wegener *et al.*, 1986). Obviously within this framework things are not as clear cut as this. Wellington in New Zealand experiences frequent, small earthquakes but only some relatively far apart have transformed the shape of the land, so it has both a long history and a short history when it comes to the effect of earthquakes on the local environment.

Basically, this approach defines three scales of time that represent three histories that are independent and interconnected. The idea of breaking a history into multiple scales and dimensions could be helpful in establishing a historical context for finding the size and duration of forms in the urban landscape. These ideas of Braudel could be important when it comes to applying the concept of Panarchy to the analysis of urban landscapes, since Panarchy implies a dynamic hierarchy where things change differently according to the scales that frame them.

The Argentinean architect Marina Waisman (1920–97) founded the Interuniversity Institute of History of Architecture (Liernur and Aliata, 2004) and later the Institute for the Study of History and Heritage Preservation. In her research into Latin American architecture she expanded the approach of Braudel to make it more appropriate for understanding the development of relatively young cities, like those of Latin America. Her philosophical approach can be synthesized in the idea of 'looking at our own reality though our own eyes'. She argued that the approach of Braudel was comprehensive for European cities where the development and the differences between scales were less dramatic than in young cities. In the latter, the development of the built environment is argued to have changed rapidly in medium and short historical times. Young cities inevitably tend to change at the pace of the short and medium scale, which makes the built environment less stable than in European cities, where the relationship across the scales has been more moderated. The identity of young cities like those of Latin America comes both from short-term inheritance and from the fact that they are still changing in a relatively rapid way. This is the complexity of what Waisman (1994) called 'urban time'. In this time the heritage has to be read across scales. However, similar relationships can be seen in older European and Asian cities where the economic imperative to make money can lead to destruction of inherited patterns of the built environment and the effective emergence of a new city. In all cases monumental or heritage architecture, which is usually protected by laws or by being awarded a special status, coexists with a modern context and with something Waisman called 'humble heritage'. This is characterized by a modest set of old buildings, clustered or dispersed, that were once common elements of the urban (and sometimes rural) built environment. This humble heritage is rarely protected by laws because these buildings are the ones sacrificed to provide the opportunities for changes to occur in the city. However, they are as important for the perception of the character and the identity of a built environment as the monuments. The humble heritage of London lies in its terraced low-rise housing, enough of which survives to give an identity to the city despite its more recent high-rise developments, whereas what is normally thought of as heritage are the large buildings such as the Tower of London and Houses of Parliament. London is the sum of both of these ideas. However, these historic parts have no meaning if isolated from the rest of the city, because they are still part of the same present.

6.7 Case study: the inheritance of San Miguel de Tucuman in Argentina

The Argentine city of San Miguel de Tucuman (SMdT) is the capital of the state of Tucuman and is home to almost 750,000 people with a high density of 5,285 people/km^2 (Municipalidad de San Miguel de Tucuman, 2016). Tucuman is a state in northwest Argentina of 1,800,000 people, making it the fifth most populated province and at the same time one of the smallest in the country. Historically it has been the political, economic and cultural centre of the north of Argentina. The city of SMdT rose to importance in colonial times, being a strategic stop on the route that linked the silver mines of Potosi, in Bolivia, with the port of Buenos Aires, the capital of Argentina. The city benefits from a subtropical climate with a dry season in winter. This climate defines the way in which the city functions. People work from 8 am to 1 pm, stop until 5 pm (siesta) and then everybody comes back to work until 9 pm. Supermarkets close at midnight. It is not unusual to see children outside on the streets with their parents or in playgrounds at 1 am during the weekends.

A resilience approach is used here to understand persistence in the built environment of SMdT, and in particular its humble heritage of the '*casa chorizo*' (sausage house). According to the definition of resilience, a system (the built environment and the humble heritage of SMdT) has to be able to keep on working without losing its identity. This historical analysis will attempt to expose the inheritance from phase to phase in the adaptive cycle of Tucuman. The approach of Braudel and Waisman is used to differentiate historical phases at different scales. This should make it possible to build an urban Panarchy to read the information within and across scales and define the key drivers of change that influence the resilience capacity of this built environment.

Large-scale and long duration: the grid and the city centre

San Miguel de Tucuman, originally founded in 1565 and moved to its present position in 1685, developed along an east–west axis linking the base of the hill of San Javier in the west with the Sali River in the east, with the oldest part of the city more or less in the middle of this axis. It was planned using the grid pattern prescribed by the Spanish Leyes de Indias (Indian Laws). The layout comprised nine blocks by nine blocks with a square in the centre around which the main institutions were built (Zamora, 2000).

102 *Case studies*

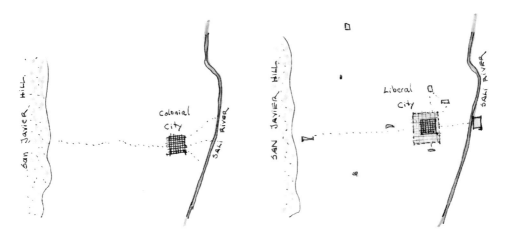

Figure 6.1 Early development of San Miguel de Tucuman

Four avenues defined the limits of the city and outside these the land was cultivated. Since that time, on average blocks have been 152 m by 152 m, though the length of each block can vary from 140 m to 155 m (Municipalidad de San Miguel de Tucuman, 2016). Originally the most important houses were close to the main square. Houses were not very open to the narrow streets, which were 10 m in width including sidewalks. In general, the image of the urban landscape was unfinished because not all the blocks were occupied and the buildings were low and of humble construction, using the materials available in the region. In this period, the identity of the system matches the description of the exploitation phase of the adaptive cycle, where a dispersed capital (land and buildings) starts to be connected to create a more stable and complex system (Figure 6.1).

Between 1825 and 1930, the city was consolidated because its centre and limits were defined. The urban landscape of the city was completed by the extension of some blocks following the grid. The width of the new streets was increased to 13 m with sidewalks and trees in the boulevards. The consolidation of the city as an agro-industrial pole of the north enhanced the development of new infrastructure and transportation systems. With the coming of the railway, workers came to Tucuman from the entire region. From colonial times, the population increased from 17,000 to 100,000 by the end of the nineteenth century (Bomba *et al.*, 2007). The sausage houses appeared in this period (the phases of these are described in detail in the section, Middle scale and duration: the sausage houses and their plots). The identity of this period matches the description of the conservation phase of the adaptive cycle, where the capital has been increased (people, land, buildings) and has been connected to form a more complex structure (Figure 6.2).

From the 1930s to the present the city has faced a time of rapid population and urban growth that has been threatened by economic and political instabilities. All these have left their marks in the urban landscape. The city has continued to grow in two ways: following the concentric pattern around the city centre and in a linear manner toward the west. By the 1950s the city had grown to three times its original size,

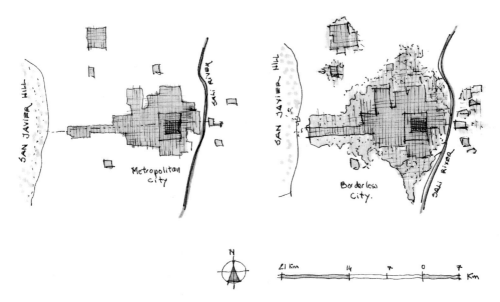

Figure 6.2 Development of San Miguel de Tucuman

always broadly following the grid. The peripheral neighbourhoods took shape and single-family housing was consolidated while the sausage houses declined in popularity and number. Because SMdT experienced an economic crisis during the 1960s, putting the sugar cane factories that were important for its economic success into bankruptcy, it is possible to think of the 1950s as the highest point of development of the inherited colonial city. From this point of view, the identity of this period aligns with the highest point of complexity of the conservation phase of the adaptive cycle. It could also be seen as the end of one cycle that started with the colonial city and the beginning of a new one. During the 1960s the city experienced its lowest population growth (Bomba *et al.*, 2007). While a number of new developments extended the city still based on the grid, informal settlements had started to appear by the 1980s, occupying land in between planned developments (Figure 6.2).

Since the 1980s the city has expanded without any planning, becoming known as the 'borderless city' (Bomba *et al.*, 2007) (Figure 6.2). In contrast to the defined boundaries of the colonial city, the present city continues to grow through creating new residential enclaves for the wealthy along with the occupation of the remaining marginal areas by poor people. The architect Di Lullo has suggested (*La Gaceta*, 2007) that cities cannot grow without direction without also experiencing consequences. The borderless city period has brought heavy environmental impacts because the city has suddenly occupied areas that were previously used for waste management, to produce food or left untouched to avoid erosion. The city is now in a transition period and in the exploitation phase of a new adaptive cycle. The identity is a hybrid, because the city has two realities: one a hard core and consolidated centre whose grid has virtually not changed in centuries, and the other a volatile periphery with soft boundaries that are unstable.

104 *Case studies*

Middle scale and duration: the sausage houses and their plots

In the long duration, the most persistent element inherited by the urban landscape of SMdT has been its grid. The grid has defined the persistence of the square blocks and the connectivity of the street system, qualities that have not seen much change since their initial designs. However, what has changed at a different pace is the content of the blocks, namely, the shape of the plots and how the blocks are occupied.

In colonial times, blocks were subdivided into four quarters (solares). Only some were occupied by colonial houses that were organized around two patios with all the rooms facing into and enclosing each patio. At the end of the colonial times land had become more expensive and there was more competition for living closer to the main square (Zamora, 2000). As a result, quarters were progressively subdivided, producing long, narrow plots. Inside these plots chorizo or sausage houses emerged as a bottom-up local response to the prescriptions of Spanish planning (Figure 6.3).

The sausage house was not unique to SMdT. This popular Argentinean house type originated in Buenos Aires and then spread to other parts of the country from the mid-nineteenth to the first decades of the twentieth century (Liernur and Aliata, 2004: 29).

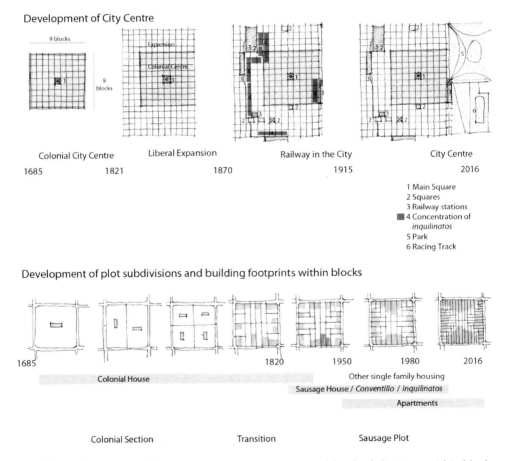

Figure 6.3 Pattern of development of the city centre and land subdivisions within blocks

These houses were basic assemblages of rooms that were aligned and developed on long, narrow plots. A party wall (the *medianera*) separated the plots and a long, thin patio was formed between the party wall and the built line of rooms for ventilation and to allow daylight into the rooms. The length of the plots also led to long, open spaces at the back. The sum of all these green and brown areas, at a larger scale, generated a green core for the entire block. So blocks had a hard edge and a soft core. This green core was consolidated in the next decades when it was mandatory for all owners to leave a portion of the length of the plot as a contribution to the 'lung of the block'.

In their first phases sausage houses were very humble, with a few rooms, a kitchen and a bathroom. Eventually more bedrooms might be built at the front and back of the house or the social areas enlarged. The bathroom and kitchen were at the back of the line of rooms for health reasons. The last part of the plot was dedicated to fruit trees, vegetables and domestic animals. The plot length allowed for progressive infill and extension of the house without destroying the organizing structure (Figure 6.4). The circulation inside the house could be directly between rooms or via a paved passage (Liernur and Aliata, 2004). Some rooms had folding screens or '*biombos*' to separate public circulation from the private sleeping areas. Parents and children slept in the same room. The lack of a defined function improved the adaptability of these rooms and this versatility was a key driver for the diffusion and popularity of the sausage house (Cuezzo, 2011).

The opportunities that the sausage houses offered in the urban landscape were subsequently used for land speculation and to overcrowd families into small plots. These families were mainly immigrants and poor people with temporary or seasonal jobs. This subtype of the sausage house was called '*conventillo*'. The overcrowded and unhealthy *conventillos* differ from the sausage houses in the number and size of the rooms as well as in the ratio of people to the available service areas (Liernur and Aliata, 2004: 167). Another subtype was the '*inquilinato*' house (Natera Rivas, 1996) (Figure 6.5). This accommodated fewer families than *conventillos* and offered better quality accommodation due to the organization of rooms along a linear patio. *Conventillos* and *inquilinatos* were clustered around the city's railway stations where the workers used to be dropped off. Another type derived was the '*casa de vecindad*', a better equipped and more modern version of the *inquilinatos*, which was an early attempt at creating a form of apartments (Figure 6.5). In the first half of the last century the overcrowding of all types of rental houses in STdM reached its peak, with around 3,000 rooms accommodating more than 10,000 people, which is probably an underestimate considering that the census was done when the workers were out collecting sugar cane (Natera Rivas, 1996). From 1930 to 1960 SMdT benefited from the success of the sugar cane industry. This is when the main institutions were built and the economic stability and the need for workers trapped the poor within the city boundaries, thus prolonging the life of the *inquilinatos* (Paterlini de Koch, 1984).

The waning popularity of the sausage house and all its subtypes was linked with changes at institutional, social and economic levels that impacted at the domestic scale. For instance, changes in the condition of women, higher standards of hygiene and the aspiration to live a modern life, including rooms having designated functions, were drivers that changed the perception and use of sausage houses (Sala and Aldonate, 2011). Modernity also brought new housing types, like apartment buildings (Liernur, 2006). The persistence of the sausage house has been challenged by the pressure of the market to satisfy the demand for a greater built density from apartments.

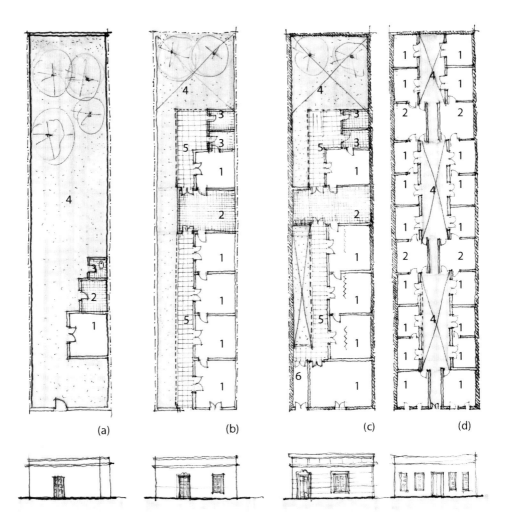

1 Bedroom for 1 family
2 Kitchen
3 Bathroom
4 Patio
5 Gallery
6 Zaguan

Figure 6.4 Development of the sausage house in Buenos Aires. The diagrams show four phases from the single living room (a) to a sausage house (b, c) and finally a *conventillo* (d)

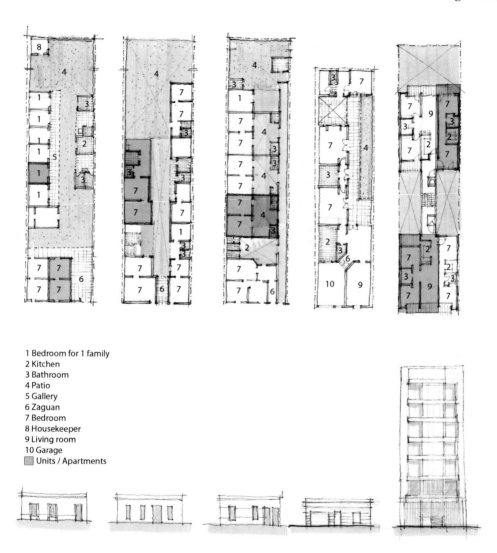

Figure 6.5 Development from *inquilinatos* to apartments units in SMdT. *Inquilinatos* could have more than one shape. They could be like small hostels, with one family per room (a), or with fewer families (b). A subtype was the *casa de vecindad* (c) with more rooms and privacy for families, (d) renovated sausage house for a single family (e) and modern apartment building with two apartments per floor

During the 1990s it was still possible to find *inquilinatos* in SMdT. These still housed the relatively poor, now mostly elderly (Natera Rivas, 1996). Some *inquilinatos* were rented to students with limited money, such as those coming from other states in Argentina, and even from Bolivia or Peru. On the other hand, some chorizo houses were refurbished and occupied by young families from the middle classes. In this case, Waisman's concept of 'perceived time' could be interpreted as the sausage house not being associated with poverty but with the possibility of living comfortably in the city

108 *Case studies*

centre for those families with more money. Similar patterns can be observed in UK cities where nineteenth-century workers' housing has been taken over by the middle

[...] e sausage houses were a common architectural type in the urban landscape of Argentinean cities it is fair to consider them as structural elements that have enhanced the adaptive capacity of the thin plots into which the blocks were divided.

Short duration, big and small scales

The interplay between the dense and intense occupation of the block by the sausage houses and their associated plots within the Spanish grid has been driving the rate of change of the built environment at the medium scale. What has been changing at a faster pace is the perception of the built environment and its functions. From the foundation of the city until modern times, the ability of the traditional plot to accommodate change has provided some resilience in the built environment. In modern times, the pressure (whether from users or from developers is uncertain) for greater density and the consequent increase in the height of what has been built to satisfy these demands (apartments) has made the contents of the plots more stable and rigid. These changes will now prevent short-term alterations to the built environment (such as adding an extra room to a traditional sausage house) and therefore the capacity for change of the entire system. In the city centre the urban fabric resulting from the interplay between the new average building heights of around nine floors with the narrow streets have intensified urban life with more people in the same physical area and this has changed the look of the city.

One factor that affects the perception at the small scale is the change in architectural styles. The facades of the sausage houses were commonly designed and built by Italian workers and were modulated in three sections according to their openings. The modulation of the façades along streets where they were frequent provided unity to the urban environment without being repetitive or uniform. This structure of the facades has persisted in a few streets in SMdT even though the aesthetics and styles of some have changed.

Understanding the heritage of Tucuman through its Panarchy

What we do know about cities is that they change. A resilience analysis reveals that this change is not uniform, but despite this a sense of unity remains in cities via their identities.

One reason for the endurance of the grid in SMdT is that its urban impact was a mix between rules that were rigid and prescriptive and the production of spaces that allowed progressive change in multiple directions. This has contributed to allowing change without disturbing the city centre.

In terms of change, while the city has had more than one cycle, the blocks and the sausage plots are still in the same cycle, meaning that they are strong elements of the urban heritage (Figure 6.6).

The breaks between the long, medium and short scales are not as clear as they are supposed to be in Braudel's approach. This reinforces the ideas of Waisman. More accurate and quantitative analysis of changes in the morphology of the urban landscape should provide a more precise understanding of the implications of the changes

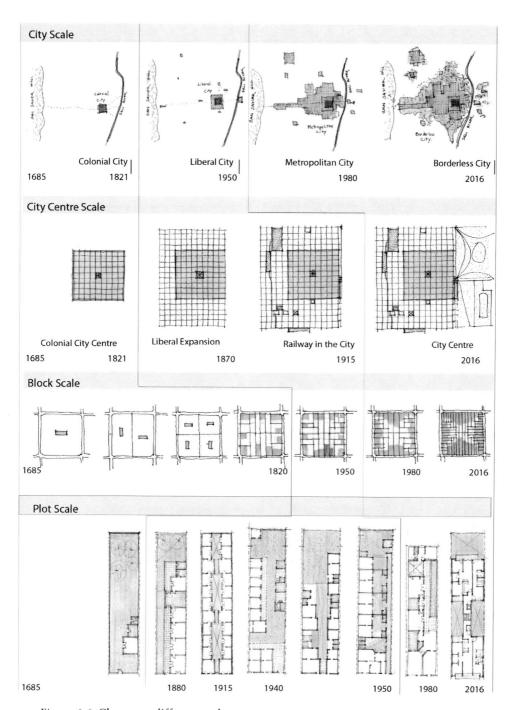

Figure 6.6 Change at different scales

110 *Case studies*

for the resilience of the system, because if speeds of change are similar at different scales, there is less room to buffer disturbances, and therefore a crisis will produce more than one scale. In SMdT, the levels of persistence of the elements of landscape can be defined in relationship with their distances to the main square. Therefore, buildings and functions around the main square have more chance to persist than elements at the periphery of the city. In the urban landscape many identities coexist in the inherited built environment. Some of them keep on changing while others disappear.

6.8 Humble heritage: the tube houses of Hanoi

Cities in other parts of the world have a similar persistence in the inheritance of urban form. For instance, the two- or three-storey terraced shop house, with shops at street level behind an arcade called the 'five-foot way' and accommodation over, is a type that persists in many parts of the world from Europe to Asia (Davis, 2012: 12–85). The mixed-use of business and residential accommodation with direct contact with the street makes for cities with lively street life and means that facilities are often within easy walking distance. Stemming from tax regimes related to the width of the street frontage, this type of building tends to have a narrow public front and then extends behind, often incorporating courtyards to bring in daylight. The street is defined by the row of shop house façades, and each individual shop front and the rooms above together offer opportunities for demonstration of status. Rapoport (2007) suggests that as cultural components like identity and status have become more varied and dynamic, what the house says about the person who lives there has become more important, with each person struggling to be recognized as an individual. This, he suggests, is why people are abandoning courtyard housing forms for detached houses, with their greater visibility from the street. However, the shop house is also a place of business, which is maybe the reason behind the persistence of the type. The fact they are long and thin (as are the plots of the sausage houses of SMdT) may also be a reason for their survival, in many cities, including in a particular area of Hanoi.

In Hanoi, in 1975 after the end of the Vietnam war, overcrowding, coupled with the lack of resources going into housing, meant that the average living space per person was as low as 5 m^2 and the long, thin shop houses in the '36 streets' area of the city were often inhabited by many families as a result (Yeung, 2007). Other sources suggest space in the '36 streets' was as low as 1.5 m^2/person (Hiebert, 1991). Perhaps living overcrowded but side by side in a long, thin tube house, as in a railway carriage, feels better than living in an overcrowded square building – maybe everyone needs a wall behind them?

Before Doi Moi (policies introduced in 1986 to bring economic improvement), tube houses formed one of three types of residential accommodation in Hanoi, the others being large villas in the French Quarter that have been divided up for multiple occupancy and state housing, usually apartment blocks, built under the socialist regime with communal kitchens and toilets (Gough and Anh Tran, 2009). The form of the tube house is obvious from its description but there is no official definition. Normally it is a building that is at least five times as long as it is wide and preferably with a length ten times the width (Kien, 2008a). In the feudal regime, the width of a house reflected the social status of its owner, and tax was also charged on the width of frontage. Therefore residential plots for regular citizens were narrow (2–4 m). Moreover, civilian houses could not be higher than around one to one and a half storeys as when the king was being carried in his palanquin no-one was supposed to see his face. Consequently, these houses were forced to develop in length (20–60 m), thus creating the form of the traditional tube house in Hanoi.

The oldest tube house is 47 Hang Bac; it was built around 1840 and is the home of approximately twenty-five people in five households (Kien, 2008b). Framed in ironwood, this house once had three two-storey structures with open spaces between to let in light and air, and also gave an opportunity to harvest rainwater for washing and cooking. The rear section was rebuilt in concrete in 1981 because of the rotten condition of the wooden structure and additional accommodation was built in the open yards later in the same decade. There is even parking for bicycles and a motorbike behind one of the yards. This has led to far from desirable living conditions (Kien, 2008b). What was once an ideal form by allowing for compact urban living but still giving access to light and air has become, in resilience terms, too rigid because of infilling and roofing the courtyards to accommodate more people. Problems also occur when tube houses are changed by adding additional storeys, as the courtyards become deep, light wells that limit natural ventilation and daylight access (Cities Alliance; World Bank, 2011: 120; Hiebert, 1991; Kien, 2008a). This did not happen with the Argentinean sausage houses which for many years remained single-storey. However, although some tube houses have been cleared to make way for new developments in other places, a new type of tube house has been inserted into the urban fabric.

Traditional tube house and neo-tube house (outside the ancient quarter)

The traditional tube house interwove mass and void to let natural wind and light go through the spaces. Voids (inner yards) inside the traditional houses are shaded by their surroundings, and these spaces thus have a much lower temperature compared to the heat of the outdoor streets. This results in a pressure difference between the inside and the outside, leading to natural ventilation of the rooms. Moreover, these inner yards have no roof, so that light can easily reach the inner spaces. Since 1986 the tube house has taken a new form, which Kein (2008a) calls the neo-tube house. The tube layout is maintained in that the house is both longer and higher than the street frontage. Plot sizes are now 4.5 x 20 m compared with the 3.5 x 35 m of the traditional tube house and most neo-tube houses are three to five storeys, often with no inner courtyards (Kein, 2008a), since the new house is much shorter than the old. Consequently a stair core normally combined with a glass roof and ventilation fan above now replaces the inner courtyard as the lung of the house. The toilet, bathroom and kitchen were considered trivial spaces in traditional tube houses as these spaces were usually dirty and smelly. Accordingly, they were put at the rear of the house – far from major spaces like living room or bedrooms. In the neo-tube house the kitchen is regarded as an important space, and in many cases the kitchen is put next to the living room to ensure a warm welcome for visitors. Some bedrooms even contain private bathrooms to meet rising expectations of living standards.

112 *Case studies*

Learning from the tube houses

What this brief description of the changes to the tube houses of Hanoi demonstrates is how the inheritance of the tube house, which forms at least part of the identity of this area of Hanoi, has both persisted and changed, demonstrating, like the sausage plot form of SMdT, characteristics of resilience in the urban form. The recognition of this inheritance from the past and its re-use to accommodate different ways of modern living in the neo-tube house again both show the importance of not buildings, but plot and block form in urban built form heritage.

6.9 Conclusions

The built heritage of a city is a process of change that is imprinted on the urban landscape. The encounters between people and buildings that happen in the act of inhabiting the city create a complex relationship between persistence and change. The relationship between persistence and change, which can be seen in humble heritage like the sausage house, suggests that the built environment does behave like a complex system that follows the adaptive cycle found in ecological resilience.

The Panarchy can be used to understand the inheritance in the urban landscape of SMdT. The proportion of the plots, characterized by fairly narrow frontages and long depths, form the persistent element at one scale, with the grid doing the same thing at another scale. It is the sausage plot and not the sausage house that is the most persistent element. The relationships formed by the boundaries of the plot and its use as a support and also a constraint for the building are a key element, and the arrangement of the plots within the block forms another element.

It seems that the sausage plot in SMdT remains an important asset because it continues to offer opportunities for containing existing and encouraging new types of buildings. It offers the possibility to think in terms of alternative scenarios. However, not all these scenarios will lead to the persistence of the present identity of the city. The sausage plots in the big blocks can easily be amalgamated to accommodate tower-type buildings that need a free perimeter. However, these new types challenge the present infrastructure. All too easily such apartment buildings could lead to a change in the narrow street pattern, and could therefore precipitate another stage in the development of the city. For instance, this type of development could open up the private green core of the block to the public spaces of the city, if the tower positions are regulated to allow this to happen. In this scenario the identity will change, but not necessarily for the bad. However, if the plot system stays and the towers are allowed to be built without regulation, the landscape will be crowded with buildings competing for sunlight and ventilation, which could be an unhealthy situation.

The recognition of heritage as inheritance provides an important foundation for the continuing development of the city. In this way heritage is not only useful for protecting built form and thereby promoting tourism, but is also is part of analysing, planning and designing the urban landscape. Using the idea of the Panarchy permits an understanding of the elements and their relationships. In the case of SMdT, this is the role of the humble heritage, whose persistence relies on being able to accommodate change. This is different from the view of heritage as the stability of the monument. The links between plot, street, grid, block and traditional core, together with centrality and associated density, define the main inheritance of SMdT and therefore the drivers of its identity, which are still imprinted in the urban landscape. This invisible identity of the built environment is what makes you feel that even though there are not many sausage houses left when you arrive in STdM, and even though sausage houses are found elsewhere in Argentina, you are definitely in STdM and nowhere else.

This historical analysis questions the possibility of building resilience. The sausage and tube houses look like resilient urban forms as both are designed to change but both reach a point where change is no longer possible and they move on to a new and different state. In SMdT, instead of single-storey houses along the street, the visitor is in a new land of seven-storey apartment blocks. However, these forms now have the property of reduced resilience because the urban system is now at a stage of greater rigidity in the adaptive cycle. There is also no point in being theoretically resilient (in engineering terms) if your system still collapses after an earthquake that did not behave as modelled, something all too familiar to the citizens of Christchurch, given New Zealand already had an earthquake code. We can recognize where the opportunities for change might be in a built environment without having certainty over what is going to happen. We can build opportunities, not resilience. A plan to enhance the resilience of a city will not prove that the city is resilient. However, through understanding the history, inheritance and identity of a system, it might be possible to achieve two objectives: first, to understand what has been changing and what has been persisting; second, using that knowledge, to infer that the elements or relationships that have not changed are probably at the core of the identity of the system, and therefore, if they are modified they might drive changes in the whole system, even to a state of loss of identity. However, it is essential to remember that it is necessary to have some room in the structure of a system to allow change, otherwise systems stagnate and their identities get rigid and vulnerable to collapse in the face of even a small crisis. This problem will be discussed further in the case study of the compaction of urban form.

Bibliography

Anon. (2009). Sinclair C5 (original TV advert), available at www.youtube.com/watch?v=0EQetm_qWDg, accessed 10 March 2016.

Art Deco Trust. (n.d.). *Maori Art Deco in Napier*, information leaflet, Art Deco Trust, Napier.

Bomba, H., Caminos, R., Casares, M. and Di Lullo, R. (2007). Perspectivas del medio ambiente urbano. GEO San Miguel de Tucuman. In *PNUMA* (Braudel, 1969) (Ed.), Naciones Unidas, Facultad de Arquitectura de la Universidad Nacional de Tucuman, Municipalidad de San Miguel de Tucuman, Oficina de Gestion para el desarrollo Local, Tucuman, Argentina.

Braudel, F. (1969). *Écrits sur l'histoire*. Paris: Flammarion.

Braudel, F. (1977). *La Méditerranée: l'espace et l'histoire*. Paris: Arts et métiers graphiques.

Braudel, F. (1980). *On History*. Chicago, IL: University of Chicago Press.

Browning, R. (1888). *The Pied Piper of Hamelin*. London: Frederick Warne and Co. Ltd, available at www.indiana.edu/~librcsd/etext/piper/, accessed 7 April 2016.

Bury, R. (2016). Green light to demolish New Scotland Yard to make way for flats. *The Telegraph*, 24 February, available at www.telegraph.co.uk/business/2016/02/24/green-light-to-demolish-new-scotland-yard-to-make-way-for-flats/, accessed 17 March 2016.

Cities Alliance; World Bank. (2011). Vietnamese Urbanisation Review: technical assistance report, available at www.urbanknowledge.org/ur/docs/Vietnam_Report.pdf, accessed 20 May 2016.

Connell, J. H. and Sousa, W. P. (1983). On the evidence needed to judge ecological stability or persistence. *The American Naturalist* 121(6), pp. 789–824.

Cuezzo, M. (2011). La casa tipo chorizo en San Miguel de Tucuman. Pasado y presente. *CAT La Revista* 3, pp. 26–29.

, H. (2012). *Living Over the Store: Architecture and Local Urban Life*. London: Routledge.

, C., Dajoz, I., Meriguet, J. and Loreau, M. (2005). Functional diversity of plant- interaction webs enhances the persistence of plant communities. *PLoS Biology* , p. e1.

, K. V. and Anh Tran, Hoai. (2009). Changing housing policy in Vietnam: emerging inequalities in a residential area of Hanoi. *Cities* 26, pp. 175–186.

Graham, B. J. and Howard, P. (eds). (2008). *The Ashgate Research Companion to Heritage and Identity*. Burlington, VT: Ashgate Publishing Co.

Harsgor, M. (1978). Total history: the Annales School. *Journal of Contemporary History* 13(1), pp. 1–13.

Hiebert, M. (1991). Going down the tubes: will new money destroy the buildings the bombers spared? *Far Eastern Economic Review*, 8 August, p. 44.

Holling, C. S. (1973). Resilience and stability of ecological systems. *Annual Review of Ecology and Systematics* 4(1), pp. 1–23.

Johnstone, I. M. (1994). The mortality of New Zealand housing stock. *Architectural Science Review* 7, pp. 181–188.

Kien, T. (2008a). 'Tube house' and 'neo tube house' in Hanoi: a comparative study on identity and typology. *Journal of Asian Architecture and Building Engineering* 7(2), pp. 255–262.

Kien, T. (2008b). Conservation pressing task and new documentation of old tube houses in Hanoi Old Quarter through the case of no. 47 Hang Bac street house. *Journal of Architecture, Planning and Environmental Engineering* 73(624), pp. 457–463.

La Gaceta. (2007). Una ciudad no crece para cualquier lado. *La Gaceta*, available at www.lagaceta.com.ar/nota/190621/informacion-general/ciudad-no-crece-para-cualquier-lado.html, accessed 19 April 2016.

Liernur, J. F. and Aliata, F. (2004). *Diccionario de arquitectura en la Argentina: C–D* (Vol. 2). Buenos Aires, Argentina: Diario de Arquitectura de Clarín.

Liernur, J. F. (2006). AAADueno. 2amb. Va.Urq. chiche. 4522.4789. Consideraciones sobre la constitucion de la casa como mercancia en la Argentina. 1870–1950. In J. Sarquis (Ed.), *Arquitectura y modos de habitar* (pp. 51–64). Buenos Aires: Nobuko.

My Maps (based on City of Lincoln Council's Heritage Database). (2015). Lincoln's lost medieval churches and religious houses, available at www.google.com/maps/d/viewer?mid=zwqut6EIvalg.knJv7lXnFAoA&hl=en, accessed 30 November 2015.

Municipalidad de San Miguel de Tucuman. (2016). La Ciudad. Infraestructura, available at www.sanmigueldetucuman.gov.ar/ciudad_1.php, accessed 19 April 2016.

Napier City Council. (2016). About Napier, available at www.napier.govt.nz/napier/about/history/early-napier/, accessed 2 May 2016.

Natera Rivas, J. J. (1996). Viviendas colectivas para sectores de poblacion de bajos recursos. Los inquilinatos de San Miguel de Tucuman (Argentina) de principios del siglo XX. *Baetica:Estudios de arte, geografia e historia* 18, pp. 223–242.

Paterlini de Koch, O. (1984). Ingenios azucareros de Tucuman: condiciones de vida y estructuracion del habitat. In CLACSO (Ed.), *Sectores populares y vida urbana* (Vol. 7, pp. 123–136). Buenos Aires: CLACSO.

Rapoport, A. (1969). *House Form and Culture* (Vol. Foundations of cultural geography series). Englewood Cliffs, NJ: Prentice-Hall.

Rapoport, A. (2007). The nature of the courtyard house: a conceptual analysis. *Traditional Dwellings and Settlements Review* 18(2), pp. 57–72.

Relph, E. C. (1976). *Place and Placelessness*. London: Pion.

Sala, J. and Aldonate, S. (2011). Una casa chorizo recuperada. *CAT La Revista* 3, pp. 34–37.

Schiffer, M. B. (1994). *Taking Charge: The Electric Automobile in America*. Washington, DC: Smithsonian Institute Press.

Swift, J. M. (2011). Persistence is the key to promoting and implementing sustainability. *Healthcare Design* 11(4), pp. 24–26.

UNESCO. (2015). *Operational Guidelines for the Implementation of the World Heritage Convention*. Paris: UNESCO World Heritage Centre.

Waisman, M. (1994). El Patrimonio en el tiempo. *Boletín del Instituto Andaluz del Patrimonio Histórico* 6, pp. 10–14.

Walker, B. H. and Salt, D. (2012). *Resilience Practice Building Capacity to Absorb Disturbance and Maintain Function*. Washington, DC: Island Press.

Wegener, M., Gnad, F. and Vannahme, M. (1986). The time scale of urban change. In B. Hutchinson and M. Batty (eds), *Advances in Urban System Modelling* (pp. 175–197). Amsterdam: North Holland.

Yeung, Yue-man. (2007). Vietnam: two decades of urban development. *Eurasian Geography and Economics* 48(3), pp. 269–288.

Zamora, R. (2000). La ciudad de S.M. de Tucuman en la segunda mitad del siglo XVIII. *Clio: History and History Teaching*, available at http://clio.rediris.es/articulos/tucuman/tucuman.htm, accessed 20 May 2016.

7 Compact cities

'Just think of the millions, from all over the globe, who yearned to be on that island, in those towers, in those narrow streets!'

Tom Wolfe

7.1 Introduction

Cities have always attracted people to them and compact cities are all about producing ways of attractive urban living that are more sustainable. It is clear that the climate change problem comes from growth, both of the world population and the demand for a higher standard of living. Around 70 per cent of global CO_2 emissions come from fuel combustion, and there has been an increase in emissions from the energy supply sector of more than 1.5 per cent per year from 1990 to 2005 (IPCC, 2007: 4.2.2). Emissions from agriculture have also grown. The US EPA (2015a) state that in 2013 agricultural emissions formed 9 per cent of all US emissions, and this was a 17 per cent increase compared with the 1990 agricultural emissions. Although there are ways of reducing these emissions it seems that this is not happening as much as might be desirable (Smith *et al.*, 2008). It is not just that there are more people; for example, global meat consumption rose threefold from 1980 to 2002 and is expected to continue to increase along with dairy consumption (NZ Agricultural Greenhouse Gas Research Centre, 2012). The problem with the ruminants whose meat and milk we increasingly like to eat is they emit methane, which is a greenhouse gas with around a twenty-five times greater global warming potential than CO_2 over a 100-year period (EPA, 2015b). At first sight there seems no connection between emissions from fossil fuels and those from agriculture but both revolve around the increased urbanization of the world. Cities are seen as the generators of wealth and to do this, energy is vital, with most of the world's energy still (in 2014) coming from the fossil fuels of oil, coal and gas in that order, with hydroelectricity providing only 6.8 per cent of global energy consumption, nuclear about 4 per cent and renewables 2.5 per cent (BP, 2015: 42).

With wealth comes an increased standard of living and this normally means a Westernized way of life, with its dietary emphasis on meat and dairy products. As outlined in the case study of eco-cities, continuing urbanization raises issues of urban resilience, since energy and food supplies for cities are reliant not on local but on global sources, and moreover many cities are in competition for these resources. One way of trying to reduce this reliance, at least for energy, is to reduce energy use through the way the built environment is organized, and this has led to the idea of having a compact city in place of suburban sprawl, especially given the fact that the latter often occupies good quality agricultural land around the periphery of the original city before its industrial growth. Auckland is a good example here with industry strung out to the south on very fertile agricultural soils (Hunt, 1959) and to the north on the Rosebank Peninsula that was formerly a market garden area (Bush, 1971: 383).

Newman and Kenworthy (1989) collected data on transport use, infrastructure and population and job density for thirty-two cities. Plotting this information showed that as population density increased there was better provision of public transport infrastructure and more use was made of public transport, with the converse that low densities led to higher car usage. This is the argument for compaction of the built environment and it led to the development of ideas like *The Pedestrian Pocket Book* (Kelbaugh, 1989). This envisaged developments where housing, offices and retail space were clustered within a fifteen-minute walk of a 'public transport node' or perhaps, as in the English eco-town of Whitehill and Bordon, just a bus stop. Like Howard's Garden City, this proposal for a new type of suburban development was an urban form clustered around a public transport system and surrounded by agricultural land, where food would be grown. Calthorpe, who had led a team in the workshop that produced the design material for *The Pedestrian Pocket Book*, wrote a further book (1993) proposing a similar transport linked suburban form where the term used was Transport Orientated Developments (TODs). Here development is concentrated along a rail or other public transport corridor, thus reinventing what happened to many cities with the introduction of trams in the late nineteenth and early twentieth centuries, when development happened in spider fashion, with concentration along the often radial tram routes. Christchurch, New Zealand, developed in this way, with suburbs first appearing along the tramlines and then spreading to fill the gaps between (Wilson, 2014). However, as the example of Christchurch shows, such development need not be dense, as Christchurch was then a city of single-family detached homes which functioned because the city was small and walking distances to catch the tram were never too great.

When it comes to the modern compact city and TOD the aim is to increase density around the transport node to reduce the need for travel by private car. Compaction also suggests more intensive use of the built environment by having more people in the same place, which in turn is more tightly constructed. A study of the compaction of the built environment, therefore, has to begin by defining the two terms density and intensity.

7.2 Density

Density is a slippery subject, not least because a city is in a process of flux so that how many people are living in what area of built environment is difficult to assess and statistics are always about what happened, often a few years ago, and not about what is happening right now. Where the boundaries are drawn is also a problem when measuring density. Cheng (2010: 3) gives the example of this in Hong Kong which at the time she was writing had an overall population density of 6,300 people/km^2. However, because only 24 per cent of the total area of Hong Kong is built up, the population density in the urban fabric was 25,900 people/km^2.

118 *Case studies*

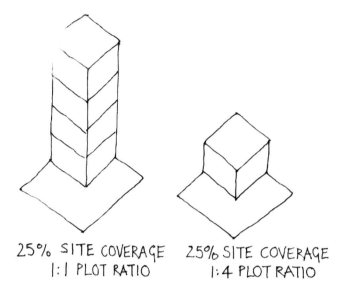

Figure 7.1 Site coverage and plot ratios

Density can also be measured in terms of buildings rather than people, either as a plot ratio, which is the ratio of the total floor area to the building site area, or as site coverage, which is the ratio of the building footprint to the site area. The problem with building density is that the same site coverage could result in very different building forms, single-storey or multi-storey, and hence plot ratio (Figure 7.1). Another complication is that buildings have different forms so that floor to floor distance may vary, leading to the situation where two buildings with the same plot ratio and the same height could still have different numbers of storeys, and hence different floor areas (Figure 7.2). This is a particular challenge when it comes to assessing the built density of a plot from a map because information about the number of levels a building has is more difficult to find and time-consuming to assess visually from the exterior of the building.

These problems are not new and the consideration of what to measure in urban density has been going on a long time. Early in the twentieth century Unwin (1912) discussed the idea of building around the perimeter of the site to reduce the length of roads and increase the open area as part of his discussion of the fact that money would not be lost building at lower densities because savings could be made by having less length of roads and infrastructure. Berghauser Pont and Haupt (2005) also argue that a discussion of urban form and density is incomplete without including the space given to roads, footpaths and open spaces. Thus any discussion of making compact cities needs to be clear both about what is being compacted and also why.

The problem with creating compact cities is, therefore, to know whether what is being discussed is housing more people in the same area of land or inserting into it more buildings or making bigger buildings, which may or may not accommodate more people. Buildings are also occupied differently at different times of the day, with offices and other workplaces mostly occupied during daylight hours and dwellings

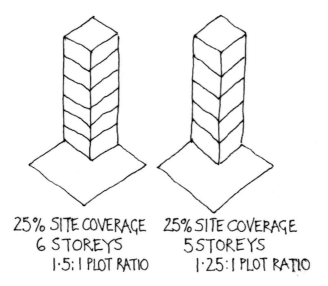

Figure 7.2 Site coverage and plot ratios

mostly occupied at night, although time is seldom mentioned in discussions of urban compaction. Buildings are also not occupied consistently, with office occupancy varying with time of day (Duarte *et al.*, 2013) and school building occupancy varying with the season (empty in the holidays versus full in school terms). Schools in the developed world also have an effect on traffic as the congestion caused by children arriving at school by car suddenly disappears in the holidays (UK Government, 2001).

One further problem is the issue of perceived density, which is to do with how users feel about their urban environment (Cheng, 2010: 12–13). At one extreme, crowding produces a negative response (stress, panic) to an urban environment where there are too many people or other factors, like cars, in a space. At the other extreme, too few people in an urban area can lead to a sense of fear. However, cultural and social factors will influence perception, as in some societies, for instance in some Asian cities, what might be perceived as crowding by someone from Europe is acceptable, whereas being alone on the street for a police officer on the beat in a European city at night is all part of the job. This makes the need to define precisely what is being compacted very important. The issue of perceived density also affects the process of compaction, since without the support of the people living there, imposing compaction could affect the value of properties and hence the perceived identity of the place. Gentrification is blamed for forcing the less well-off to move further out of the city to where prices are cheaper, but equally compaction can have the opposite effect, as seen in the cities of the industrial revolution where the poor lived in highly compact inner-city situations so they could walk to work while the wealthy retreated to the more salubrious, and less dense, suburbs beyond the mass of workers' housing. However, as shown below in the example of Melbourne, compaction can also raise property values, but it all depends where the compaction occurs within the city and its infrastructure.

7.3 Intensity

In the urban design literature related to compact cities, intensity is often used as a synonym or alternative for density (Auckland Council, 2013). However, Shelton *et al.*'s study of Hong Kong defines intensity as the combination of the interaction of several urban qualities, emphasizing *concentration*, *complexity* and *verticality* (Shelton *et al.*, 2011: 7) which implies that intensity is not the same as density (Chung, 2013). However, Shelton *et al.*'s definition sees intensity as a positive quality and as an implied dynamic way of seeing density (more people walking on the streets increasing their intensity of use implies more people living nearby). A similar group of definitions of urban intensity is linked with the sense of vitality offered by places or streets (because they are full of people walking or sitting around the edges) and with the social perception of that vitality (Chung, 2013). In this case, the idea of intensity is closer to the widely used concept of liveability. Partners for Liveable Communities Australia (2010) define liveability as 'the sum of the aspects that add up to the quality of life of a place, including its economy, amenity, environmental sustainability, health and wellbeing, equity, education and learning, and leadership', which is so comprehensive a definition that it probably means nothing. Ex-Prime Minister of the UK Tony Blair saw 'liveability' as having streets which were clean and safe to walk and cycle along, and well-maintained parks and green space within easy walking distance of home (Office of the Deputy Prime Minister, 2003: 7). Being able to walk to nearby facilities has also become equated with the idea of compaction or living closer together. Rather than a city having to provide more parks, or at least some green space within walking distance of low-density developments – and low density also means more streets which have to be maintained and monitored so as to be clean and safe – a high density and more intensely used environment means that more people can live within walking distance of fewer parks and other facilities, so from an economic viewpoint 'liveability' is easier to achieve. As stated before, there are cultural issues at play here as well, as the intensity of use of some streets in Asian cities might be unacceptable to Western sensibilities, and thus not liveable. Moreover, even when the concentration, complexity and verticality suggested by Shelton *et al.* are achieved through generations of a compact built environment, this could also create the perfect opportunity for intensifying not only the desired liveability but also undesirable activities like vandalism or crime (Newman, 1972).

7.4 Compactness

It is impossible to compact all the different physical elements of the built environment (plots, blocks, streets) at the same time. As an example, consider a city block with four buildings each of the same footprint distributed equally within it. The block is divided into four plots with a density d1 (total building footprint divided by the total area). Each building is in the centre of one of the four plots and surrounded by streets. As an exercise in making more compacted buildings, the buildings are moved towards each other until two touch and the four external walls of the original buildings are now three. As a result of this compaction of the buildings there are fences, not streets, now separating the adjacent plots. Then these pairs of buildings are moved to the centre of the block to become a single building with fewer external walls, even more fences and even fewer streets. The density in each case is always the same. However, the different

Compact cities 121

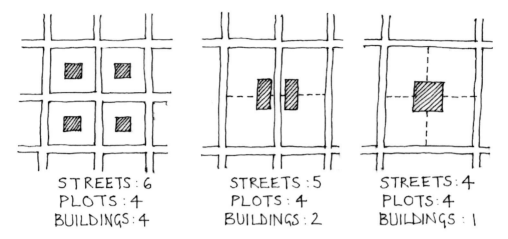

Figure 7.3 Changes in buildings, plots and streets

positions of the buildings and reduction in number of streets imply different levels of compactness of the different physical elements.

As the buildings become more compact on the four plots, going from four separate small buildings to one large one, the number of streets is reduced. When it comes to the streets, Figure 7.3 shows that as the building footprints combine, the number of streets falls, so the connectedness also drops as there are fewer routes across the block as the individual small buildings are compacted into one large building. If the four plots were also combined to give two buildings on two plots in the second diagram and one building on one plot in the third, this would change the concentration of plots. This is just an exercise that shows the process of compaction of building footprints, as might happen if a developer buys up all the small buildings, and the effect it can have. This suggests that compactness depends on the element that is being considered and may not necessarily be applied to all the elements of the city at the same time. Figure 7.3 is about compacting the buildings, which does not change the density, it is not about putting more buildings on the same plot, although it might be about 'compacting' the ownership of the buildings. The most compact building in Figure 7.3 is likely to appeal to a developer because building one larger building is cheaper than building four smaller ones with the same amount of accommodation. It will also appeal to the city authorities because the compact building reduces the number of streets they have to provide. But from the perspective of the residents of the city, larger buildings and fewer streets may reduce the sense of liveliness, intensity and liveability in their city. This reveals some of the complexity present in cities: different elements respond to change in different ways.

A complex understanding of the history of building footprints, plots and streets is necessary to attempt to quantify the relationships between densities, intensities and compactness in the form of a city (Figure 7.4). Small blocks and many streets allow for easier subdivision, whereas large blocks attract larger buildings. This will influence the character of what is built, as the large blocks are more suitable for high-rise buildings (Hong Kong admittedly has tall buildings on small plots but this has now been

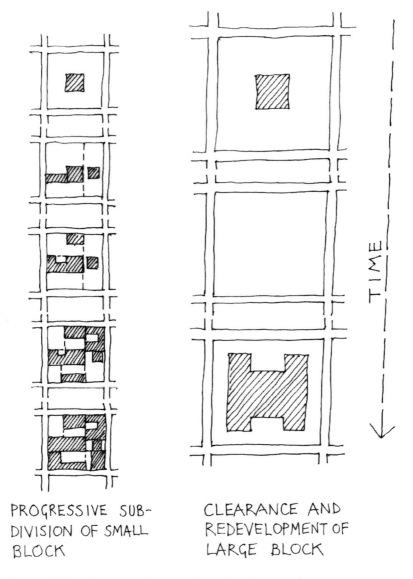

Figure 7.4 Development of large and small blocks over time

seen as a problem when it comes to natural ventilation, leading to a change in housing policies; Ng, 2009). However, at periods of clearance in the cycle of redevelopment at the large block scale, the intensity of use of the land is very low (zero during the clearing and reconstruction period). Although buildings will be demolished to make way for new ones in the same way in small blocks, the intensity of use of the land is more continuous because the scale of the demolition is smaller, leaving most of the activity in the block to carry on. The key point is that the relationship between different elements in a context will affect the final design outcome (small blocks tend to lead to small buildings and vice versa).

The physical form of the city is not the only factor to think about. Intensity, for example, has also been defined not in terms of land use but rather by the activities happening along the street edge (Sevtsuk et al., 2013). The frequency of the appearance of physical elements (cafés on sidewalks) or human behaviours (café culture) in an area is used as a measure of intensity. This is not restricted to particular building forms but rather to having activities at ground level, something that is perhaps easier to achieve in a network of small streets and plots than an area full of high-rise buildings with their wider streets and setbacks. Another example of intensity is seen in street markets. Market stalls are often set up in front of shops but allowing for circulation in front of both shops and stalls, thus potentially doubling the activities along the street front. The distance between sellers, the products and the buyers is small, producing an environment where everything is reachable.

However, it is important to recognize that proximity (having everything easily reachable as in the street market example), having a high density of people in one place (compactness), and intensity are different qualities. Someone living in a sprawling suburb in Melbourne can work intensively online on a project with someone living in a compact built environment in San Jose de Costa Rica, but here there is no close connection (they are not easily reachable). Intensity is created by the interaction of functions and behaviours and particular arrangements of the elements discussed above, of which density (number of people in an area) is only one. Therefore, a compact and dense built environment will not necessarily be an intense built environment in terms of the activities it contains. A city of high-rise developments set back from the road could house a lot of people per square metre but it could have few street-level activities. In fact density acknowledges only one aspect of the compactness of the city form, the relationship between built and non-built landscape or the height and population (number of users) of a building and therefore the number of buildings and people in the same place. Thus density only measures the compactness of building footprints and their associated plot ratios.

Defining the compact city

Compact cities are usually defined as the opposite of sprawling cities such as Melbourne, Los Angeles or Auckland. Sprawl also has a negative connotation making such built environments undesirable. Negative factors include the loss of agricultural land that gets built on to make the suburbs and the increased travel that results from building low-density suburban areas with few local facilities. In English, the word 'compact' has two meanings: the first is linked with size and the idea that a lot can be fitted into a small space, such as a compact camera. The second is related with the quality of a texture as being closely fitted together, such as when soil is compacted in foundations. Taking both definitions as starting points, a compact city would be a city with a lot packed into a small area (people, shops, workplaces, recreation opportunities) and where its substance (buildings, roads, green space) is closely fitted together. If you visit a city like Bangkok, most of which is very low rise, you experience having many functions packed together, or juxtaposed, and the scattering of green areas between the closely packed but low-rise buildings. The Bangkok experience, with workshops, offices, living, shopping all mixed together, is a long way from the tidiness of movements like New Urbanism, which is about living in one place and being near transport to go to work in a different place, with the claim 'Neighbourhoods should be compact, pedestrian friendly, and mixed-use' (Congress for the New Urbanism, 2015). The challenge, therefore, is not only to define what is the substance that cities have to compact (bricks and mortar? people? cars?), but also to determine the limit for the tightness – how much can be fitted into the available space and what space standards are being used to determine this? Thus a compact city is more complicated than a dense city (in terms of floor area to land ratio).

The word 'compact' is used both as a verb that defines the action and the processes that generate a compact city, and as an adjective that describes the quality of the city. If the process is seen as the final goal, this implies that you can keep on increasing the compactness of cities without doing any assessment of the consequences. However, processes of compaction in different cities might lead to different results. Thus the environment of Hong Kong with its compaction of high-rise buildings has led to problems with air movement and air quality, such that new regulations were developed for leaving greater gaps between buildings (Ng, 2009). In New Zealand compaction through introducing more medium-density housing into the suburbs without first addressing the issue of public transport brings the risk of more cars on the roads and more congestion (Sharbin, 2006: 22). This suggests that the quality of being compact might be neither infinite nor positive.

Confusion also arises because the compact city has been linked with other fashionable urban concepts like walkable cities, velo-cities and lately, smart cities. Looking at each of these, walkable cities are often ranked on the basis of a survey of public spaces which is both qualitative (assessment of the pedestrian realm) and quantitative (counts of people and activities) (Matan and Newman, 2012). This concept is thus more to do with intensity than compactness, and also only applies to the public spaces, not the whole city. The velo-city was conceived as the insertion of infrastructure for cycling into existing cities to form '… a network of elevated bikeways that connect distant parts of the city. Each direction of travel in Velo-city has a separate bikeway tube with three lanes of traffic for slow, medium and fast travel' (Hardwicke, 2006: 40). Rather than compacting the urban form, this idea is about making cities safe for cycling by separating the bicycles from the cars. The definition of a smart city has also changed, starting with the idea of information and communications technology being used to connect everyone in the city together (Caragliu *et al.*, 2015), which would make for a more economically successful city. Later the smart city became more associated with sustainability and the 'smart' use of resources, especially energy in terms of installing 'smart grids' (Clastres, 2011). However, being connected virtually with IT is not the same as being connected physically because if you live in a neighbourhood with a network of small streets and plots this means you inevitably have the chance to meet people as you go about your business. So the IT-connected smart city has little to do with the idea of the compact city. These ideas have also been developed, usually by Western consultants, for application to developed world cities. What is of more use is to consider what happens in urban areas that are already physically compact. Many of the world's urban poor already live in compact 'walkable' conditions, but this is not the goal of those currently espousing compaction. Contrary to the Victorian perception that many people living in the same urban area leads to overcrowding and the propagation of unhealthy and risky situations (Chadwick, 1842), the compact cities' physical model is not the overcrowding of the slums but the hopefully healthy development of higher-density development around transport nodes and local facilities that provide everything needed for daily life. This could equally well be conceived as the suburban neighbourhood with its schools, shops and local services linked to the rest of the city by a frequent and affordable public transport service, such as could be found in many UK cities before the advent of mass car ownership. The compact city is only going to work well if the car disappears. It also stands more chance of succeeding if the economic base of the city, which leads to people sleeping in one place and working in another, changes to bring work and home close together.

However, perhaps the concepts of being compact and being a liveable city are incompatible. Melbourne, currently judged the world's most liveable city (Economist Group, 2015), is also a sprawling city, leading to financial stress for those forced to live in the outer suburbs, making them dependent on cars, while the wealthy who can afford to live in the inner suburbs served by the tram network are much less reliant on driving (Milman, 2015). In Melbourne, therefore, the compact part of the city is the most expensive, so what guarantee is there that compaction will not lead to displacement of the less wealthy to the city fringes? Without numbers it is difficult to know how compact is compact in terms of population, income, occupancy, use, perception and built density (or how much land is covered by some impermeable material like concrete).

In order to explain the idea of compact cities, what is often depicted is an image of buildings that are relatively low rise but close together with higher rise at the centre, clustered around a transport node. This suggests that compaction is not just dense, but also intense in terms of the arrangement of the built form. Density could be achieved via the modernist towers in the park of Le Corbusier and his many followers, but these do not look 'compact' and nor do they offer the experience of intensity (street life around the building edges) as discussed above.

Compaction and change

Imagine the process of compaction happening in an area of suburban sprawl which has two possible futures. It can remain a spread-out area or it can turn into a more compact area. In comparison with the sprawl the process of compaction provides fewer opportunities for incremental change. What tends to happen in an already compact environment in terms of building coverage is wholesale clearance and rebuilding, with consequent loss of resources. Warfare and particularly bombing are very good at achieving this by clearing compact areas of cities and allowing rebuilding in a different form, as seen in Coventry in the UK where the compact (in terms of the number of small buildings per hectare) medieval centre was replaced after German bombing with a modernist vision of larger buildings spaced further apart. The compaction process is linear, less adaptable and irreversible without starting again, while sprawling or low-density landscapes are more adaptable since their processes are reversible. 'Sprawl' is always used by designers as a term of abuse, but whether by transforming dispersed urban landscapes into more dense built areas, by lowering density further through removing or relocating buildings or by changing the land use (using open areas to grow food), these low-density landscapes can be changed much more readily than already compact ones.

A compact city results from a process of change that tends to concentrate capital (buildings, people) through forming increasingly tight connections (like businesses wanting to be part of the same CBD). This capital is anything a system relies on to be productive, to grow and develop. It can be social, economic, historical or ecological capital or a mix of them. For example, business firms are part of an economic capital and communities are part of a social capital and green spaces are part of ecological capital, although each also relates to other capitals, for example, business and parks are also social. The criteria and priorities that a society chooses will define what capital needs to be compact, what will be ignored and what others will be affected as a consequence. For example, losing urban green space to more buildings (Mensah, 2014) will have a negative effect on ecological and social capital but could be good for economic capital. The current urban situation in most of the developed and developing world is that economic capital has been favoured and concentrated in the CBD of cities, leading to problems for ecological and social capitals, not least because of the resultant commuting.

When cities are made more compact through concentration of a capital (people, buildings) in a designated area of land, the expectation is that the connections set up between the different types of capital will be stable and not immediately dismantled again, as happens in something like a folk festival. Such an event brings people close together through the setting up of temporary camps for a weekend gathering but this intensity of land use disappears as soon as everyone goes home. However, a compact city is about achieving a stable arrangement even when changes occur. If an area is compacted by mixing socio-economic levels to the point that people no longer like it and those who can afford to move leave, the compaction has failed. This suggests that for compaction to be successful more effort has to be put into building a systemic understanding of urban landscapes. These also need to be more equitable by allowing collective decision-making around what needs to be connected with what. Without this approach, the connectivity promoted in the compaction process may be meaningless for the majority of urban residents.

Compaction and tightness

The very idea of compaction suggests that buildings (and their occupants) will be closer together and living in a more tightly knit way, not unlike the tightly knit fishing and mining villages of the past where shared occupations and common problems bound people together. When people have mobility because they have cars they are not forced to share everything with their immediate neighbours. However, putting buildings closer together will not automatically engender acceptable 'tight' communities. Dharavi is a slum in Mumbai, India that is both home to a million people and on the tourist circuit (Reality Tours and Travels, n.d.). It is an overcrowded area where buildings are close together because people are poor. New York may have a higher built density (ratio of floor area to building footprint) because of the tall buildings, but the fact that far fewer people inhabit the New York buildings (many of which are almost empty at night) means the intensity experienced in Dhavari is higher than in New York. The streets of Hanoi are another example of an intense built environment, where people literally live a big part of their day outside on the sidewalks. They cook, trade, walk, manufacture, repair and rest in this public space. You can find everything on the streets, from fresh frogs to karaoke. Dense urban landscapes where tall buildings prevail tend to have spaces between these buildings, something that it is not compulsory in low urban landscapes simply because low buildings do not require so much free perimeter. Therefore the balance in the compact city is to be sufficiently tight to feel intense but not so tight as to turn into a slum.

It would be possible to intensify the use of office buildings in total life-cycle energy terms not by increasing the density of workers in them, but by changing the pattern of the working day by extending working hours and giving people flexibility in when they choose to work. This means using existing buildings more intensely, with the added benefits of reducing peak electricity loads by having longer and more staggered working hours and easier commuting, although 'giving people flexibility' is the key point; if your boss makes you come in early or work late this idea may not seem so attractive. Having less intensive use of existing office buildings by adopting a nine-day fortnight or allowing workers to work at home one day a week would also reduce greenhouse gas emissions, even accounting for the resources needed to set up a home office for the days worked at home (Jurasovic, 2003). No buildings have changed in these examples but using buildings for longer hours of the day could increase the sense of intensity of use of the urban fabric. These examples demonstrate that changing processes can affect capitals (social and ecological) as much, if not more, than the current obsession with changing physical urban form through compaction. Another example is the intermittent use of tourist hotels in coastal cities in Mexico that were developed only for tourism. For many months of the year hotels in these places are not intensively used. Even the best hotels only have a 70 per cent annual occupancy rate (Garcia, 2008). This example represents a lack of intensity in the use of a built capital. The consideration of which capital is to be prioritized could thus result in a different urban landscape and city form. The important point here is to highlight that the relationship between capital densities is broader than the simplistic idea of a compact city based on dense and tall buildings served by public transport. Despite the common compact city idea of mixed use, residential, retail and office development around a transport node, the concept usually seems wedded to the idea that residents need the transport link to get to work – they are still commuters, whereas in the streets of Hanoi, work for many is very close to home (see also Chapter 6).

7.5 The example of Auckland

Auckland is a city on an isthmus between two harbours and if you climb one of the extinct volcanoes in the city it is possible to look at the Pacific Ocean in one direction and the Tasman Sea in the other. As a place to put a city the isthmus is fabulous for making harbours but not good in terms of growing room since the city can only spread in two ways – north and south. Despite growing up round a network of trams which were removed in the 1950s, meaning that like Christchurch development first happened along the tram routes and then spread to fill in the gaps between them, Auckland, which houses a quarter of the population of New Zealand, is a sprawling city. Even trying to pin down how big it is illustrates the complexity of trying to understand how cities work. Table 7.1 gives four acceptable definitions of the area and population of Auckland from the 2006 census (Auckland Council, 2011). The divergence, particularly in area and density, comes not just because of the suburban nature of much of Auckland but also because of the rural nature of the city periphery.

In 2006 true urban centres like the nation-state of Singapore and special territory of Hong Kong had population densities of 6,342 and 6,531 persons per km^2 (World Bank, 2015). Since the 1950s and the loss of the trams, the growth of Auckland

128 *Case studies*

Table 7.1 Definitions of Auckland, New Zealand

Area Definitions (2006)	Population (2006 Census)	Area (km^2)	Density (population per km^2)
Auckland region	1,303,068	4,998.9	261
Metropolitan area	1,160,751	559.2	2,076
Statistical urban area	1,208,163	1,102.9	1,095
Urbanized area	1,156,623	482.9	2,395

outwards rather than upwards has been the result of the state funding of motorways (which like the trams encourage development along them), a lack of investment in public transport and financial support for housing on green-field sites (Fookes, 2000: 266). Auckland has since become a 'super city' with one elected local body covering an area of almost 500,000 hectares (5,000 km^2), of which more than 70 per cent (384,000 ha) is designated as rural rather than urban. This new super city corresponds to the old Auckland region in Table 7.1, which in 2011 had an estimated population of almost 1.5 million (Auckland Council, 2013).

As early as 1958 there was an exhibition in Auckland called 'Homes without sprawl' organized by the Wellington-based Architecture Centre. In the face of a rising population the aim at that time was to preserve farmland, then as now the basis of the national economy. The intention was to show that houses could still be built with gardens but at higher densities: 'The essential elements of the garden suburb – your own plot of land, independence, privacy, sun, a pleasant outlook – are plentifully supplied… And yet on a 19-acre site which would accommodate only 170 people using present methods of development, 470 people can be housed' (Anon, 1958). (Modern equivalents are 22 persons/ha and 62 persons/hectare, still very low, but nearly three times what was there before.)

One objective of the current Auckland unitary plan is to increase housing density around existing urban centres to strengthen their role, and in places with frequent public transport (a service of at least fifteen minutes between 7 am and 7 pm) to provide access to public transport for as many houses as possible (Auckland Council, 2013). There are also rules for subdividing existing house plots and ensuring dwellings have useable open space. The aim is to restrict parking for higher-density residential developments with their improved access to public transport. Park and ride facilities are also part of the plan. This sounds like a sensible approach to trying to reduce urban sprawl. However, it depends what you choose to measure in terms of the success of compaction. The emphasis in the unitary plan is on reducing the use of the car to commute into and across the city but this is only one aspect of compactness as there is no ruling about car ownership, but rather the hope that providing the infrastructure for public transport might encourage less car use. However, research shows that increasing population without control of the car leads to more traffic and more parking on the roads, even if off-road parking is provided (Dupuis and Dixon, 2002; Dixon and Dupuis, 2003). More traffic and more parking in the road as a result of infill housing are perceived as leading to a greater chance of road-related accidents (Vallance *et al.*, 2005). Moreover, the car is only one aspect of housing. A study of the environmental impact of suburban living in Auckland by Ghosh *et al.* found that typical Auckland detached houses on plots of 500 m^2 had the lowest cumulative environmental impact when solar energy harvesting, carbon sequestration, modest food growing, waste and commuting to work by car were quantified.

> The initial results from the study suggest that lower-density residential developments may have more potential to be sustainable because of the ability of residents to grow food and to make use of on-site renewable energy technologies, which may require behaviour changes among the residents... On the other hand, higher-density residential blocks, despite being closer to the CBD, appear to have a lower potential to be sustainable.
>
> (Ghosh *et al.*, 2007: 355)

Ghosh *et al.*'s study is based on the idea of change and being aware that land use may have to differ in the future. Moriarty, in an investigation of Australian cities, also suggests that householders doing more sustainable actions, like composting waste, recycling grey water and growing fruit and vegetables, may be easier at lower densities (Moriarty, 2002). This links the problems that might arise with compaction not just with not being able to behave more sustainably in the future but also with resilience, in terms of having a form of human settlement that is able to buffer such needs without dramatic, or even catastrophic, change. As it stands, the sprawling nature of Auckland and its looseness may be the very factors that make it a very resilient city. Nor are rural environments necessarily less sustainable than compact urban ones, as discussed below.

7.6 Sustainability and a compact built environment

The arguments for having a more compact built environment, or for having compact cities, have often been based on the professed goal of living sustainably, which means a sustainable situation for people and as much biodiversity as they care to support, since all the people, plants and animals have to live within the resources of one planet. This immediately raises the question of equity, since even assuming that 'one planet living' or living within a fair share ecological footprint could be achieved, some people will have more and some less (see also Chapter 8). Cities are generally great examples of equity, or rather inequity, in built form. The classic example is how the richer suburbs in UK cities are usually found in the southwest, as the prevailing southwesterly winds would ensure they received a lot less smoke and wind-blown pollution from factories. Here are found the employers' large houses in their large and leafy gardens, while the smaller terraced houses and backyards of the workers are to the east and north of the city. However, as factories have moved out of urban areas and smoke and pollution are no longer an issue, other changes come into play. Because the earlier terraced housing for the workers was often close to the city centre, and hence to work, this is seen as desirable and the process known as gentrification can change both the perception and raise the value of such properties. This forces those who can no longer afford such housing to move out of the city to where housing is cheaper, even if the cost of commuting into work has to be added to this (as in the example of Melbourne above). The built form still reflects the financial status of people in society. Extreme examples of this are found in London where what were once service areas at the back of houses have become desirable and expensive 'mews developments'. (A mews is a row of stables and carriage houses with living accommodation for the staff above, the garages of a horse-drawn world.) The 'haves and have nots' are as clear in the built form of the city as they are in the ecological footprints of nations, where it is the city dwellers th... nd to have the larger average footprints (see Chapter 2).

One problem in assessing compact cities is that, like their residents, not all cities are equal and nor are all neighbourhoods within a city. One reason people give for not wanting compaction in their area is the effect it might have on the perception of their neighbourhood, leading to the creation of the 'slums of the future' (Vallance *et al.*, 2005). Nor are all rural areas equal. In the developing countries of the world, rural populations have a very low environmental impact because their food and fuel resources are local (Pamungkas, 2013: 215) and they tend not to travel long distances by car or use much fossil fuel for their subsistence farming, unlike farming in the developed world. However, in developing countries the low impact of rural living changes when people move to the cities and start consuming fossil fuels, whether directly or indirectly through the goods and food they now have to buy. The rise in the national average ecological footprint is noticeable as China urbanizes (Guo, 2013: 185). In cities and rural areas in developed countries the difference may not be so clear cut. Two 2001 studies of ecological footprint (EF) in Wales found a resident of urban Cardiff had an EF of 5.6 gha (WWF Cymru *et al.*, 2005: 3), whilst in rural Gwynedd the average EF was 5.3 gha (Farrer and Nason, 2005: 6). This runs against the earlier evidence (1985/6) that those living in large urban areas use more public transport and travel less than their rural counterparts (Barrett, 1996: 173). However, this is because the measure is EF rather than distance travelled. Those in rural areas may indeed travel farther but their overall use of fuel is less because the car is more efficient as it is driving longer distances but in a 'warmed up' state (Vale and Vale, 2013: 68–69). However, in developed countries one argument for making cities compact is that making people live closer together will reduce EF by encouraging transport modes with a lower impact, such as walking and cycling, and by reducing distances travelled. Certainly if living closer together was accompanied by taking away the car there would be a change in transport modes, and a consequent reduction in resource use for mobility, but examples of such a rigorous approach to densification are hard to find. The Shard office tower, as mentioned previously, has very few parking spaces and these are mostly for the disabled. Getting rid of parking spaces does not guarantee use of public transport, however, as workers in the Shard may just park locally, or make up their commute by driving to where they can park and then taking public transport for the last leg. Similarly residents in compact urban areas may travel less on work days but compensate by travelling more in their leisure time (Williams *et al.*, 2000; Holden and Linnerud, 2011).

Another claimed benefit of the compact city is linked with the relationship between population density and the use of local facilities, with the assumption these are reached on foot. This approach underpins New Urbanism where streets designed for pedestrians are intended to lead to local facilities, though without again restricting car ownership local facilities are always in competition with out of town mega-stores on cheap land (and hence with cheaper prices). High-density cities in Asia, like Hanoi, have a bustling street life because houses are very small and people live above the shop, so the diversity of facilities nearby is vast. Unfortunately, Western compaction is more linked with commuting by public transport than living over the shop. In fact in Auckland the rules are restrictive as to how many people can work from the same house (Auckland Council, 2013). The sustainability equation here is that the concentration of activities in a place uses less land and will save, free or preserve more land for alternative uses. However, the confusion is that the building footprint of a plot is not the ecological footprint of a building and having buildings closer together will not automatically reduce the overall EF of a household. Other measures are needed to change human behaviour in this situation.

Other arguments for compact cities include energy saving through people living in apartments rather than single-family houses, as more surfaces are shared, thereby reducing heat loss especially given some houses use 20 per cent more energy per person than flats (Holden and Norland, 2005). However, as houses have become more energy efficient this reason is becoming less important. The building energy use issue is complex as if buildings are very low or zero energy then reducing surface area through more compact design might be beneficial. However, if buildings still use energy for heating and cooling, compaction can lead to an increased urban heat island effect (Giridharan *et al.*, 2004). Higher densities also make it more difficult to use building roofs as energy collectors unless there is careful design to avoid overshadowing (Ghosh and Vale, 2006). There can also be competition between using roofs as energy collectors and using then as green space in very dense situations. Attaching greenery to buildings as a solution to this is also problematic, and modern green walls systems have additional capital as well as maintenance costs, the latter often being implicated in their failure (Wood *et al.*, 2014: 201).

Compact densities also mean the energy collection/use balance cannot be achieved on a single building basis, so the infrastructure has to bring in energy generated off-site. In ecological footprint terms this means the compact city may use less land but it makes up for this by having off-site land dedicated to the functions that keep it going. For instance, the ultimate compact city, Hong Kong, which houses seven million people in 1,076 square kilometres of which 75 per cent is open space, has to import almost all its energy and food. If the energy used in Hong Kong were generated from large-scale wind farms an additional area of 8,100 square kilometres would be needed (Vale and Vale, 2010). When it comes to the food for the city an additional 105,000 square kilometres is required (Vale and Vale, 2010). The city may be compact but it still has to draw on land somewhere else, land which could also be occupied by rural populations at lower densities.

Compaction is also claimed to have social advantages as it offers more opportunities for people to meet but the immediate counter argument to this is that taller buildings discourage community life and can lead to isolation (Chen *et al.*, 2008). The social benefits of the compact city have been explained through the concepts of liveability. As an example, assume it is Friday night and people on the sidewalk of a pedestrian or shared street are drinking at tables that belong to a bistro pub (assume also that it is not cold and it is not raining). This establishment is in the ground floor of a building where numerous young professionals have their apartments. The people are in groups, they laugh, the street is busy, well lit and nobody has to drive back home (so everybody can keep on drinking). The idea is that the increase of population density in a small area will encourage the generation of more such activities in the streets, which in turn will make the city perceived as busy and compact (particularly for tourists). This is the aspirational picture indirectly promoted by the urban marketing of compact cities and that has been encouraged in the rankings of the most liveable cities. Auckland is amongst the ten most liveable cities of the world but as shown above it is also one of the most sprawling and sprawling Melbourne is the most liveable. This

132 *Case studies*

suggests the definition and use of the concepts of liveability, intensity and density in relationship with the paradigm of compact cities is confused. Street life only happens if people want to come together and share activities, making the idea of social sustainability as much a matter of human behaviour as urban design. Moreover, as shown in the example above it is the inner-city-living wealthy people in these sprawling cities who can come together to enjoy the street life generated by compaction in these developed world cities while the poor watch TV in the outer suburbs.

7.7 Compaction and resilience

Historically, the idea of higher concentrations of people in denser built environments has not necessarily been viewed favourably in urban studies, as with Unwin's arguments for garden city densities discussed above. The architectural and urban revolution that started at the end of the nineteenth century was partially encouraged by the fact cities had become overcrowded and unhealthy places, leading to the interest in making lower-density developments and restricting their growth, as suggested by Howard in his Garden City model. Later Jane Jacobs also questioned whether urban concentrations were either negative or positive. More importantly, she developed her critique by analysing which compact and dense developments could have positive or negative impacts in the city (Jacobs, 1961/2011). She rejected modernist high densities achieved by putting people in high-rise and slab blocks as this divorced people from social life at street level, and was as damaging for the sense of community as putting people in low-density dormitory suburbs.

A resilience approach to cities accepts that they have to be analysed as complex systems that have to cope with change in order to adapt to more or less predictable events. This implies the relationships between intensities and densities in the compaction process can be criticized from a different angle, as having opportunities for change is desirable in a resilient urban form, but as discussed above, the more compact the form, the less chance there is it can change without being flattened and starting again (moving to a new state in terms of the adaptive cycle). Tall buildings are hard to demolish so that materials can be salvaged and even harder to move. This is a point at which sustainability and resilience in the built environment converge, as low buildings offer more opportunities for small changes as long as the compaction is not so severe that there is nowhere left to go apart from starting again. If we really want urban compaction then maybe an increase in connections is the goal so that people need to travel less far for what they want in terms of daily physical and social needs. As Figure 7.5 shows, connectedness tends to be enhanced when building plots are small and numerous and it is compromised as building plots are amalgamated to accommodate larger building footprints. However, in the current economic paradigm it is the latter which is preferred for making money.

Compact cities can be seen as a threat or as an opportunity depending on the approach taken to connect their social and natural resources. They can veer towards rigidity if their physical capitals (infrastructure, built and non-built environment) are connected so tightly that options for change are reduced. In Figure 7.5 the process of compaction of the urban landscape is represented by the four blocks with different textures. Blocks A and C have the same built areas and densities but different plot subdivisions, while blocks B and D also have the same built areas and densities but different distributions of their building footprints and plots. Block A is more homogeneous

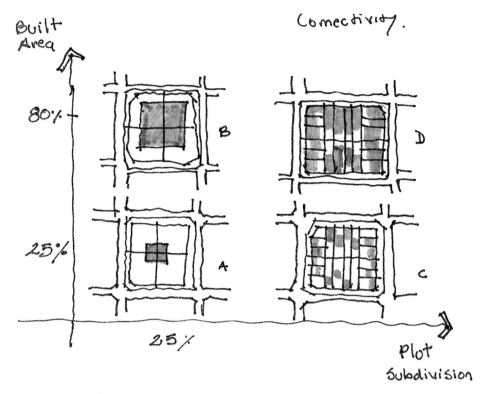

Figure 7.5 Development of compaction in terms of incremental plot subdivisions and an increase in built area

(there is only one element of one size) than block C, where the size of the buildings is more diverse and their distribution uneven. One key difference in terms of the texture of the landscape produced in blocks A and C is linked with heterogeneity. The open spaces in block A are more continuous (you can walk without stopping around the central building) and homogeneous (a section through the block in any direction looks the same) than the open spaces in block C. These are more discontinuous and heterogeneous. The textures of the landscapes in both cases create different environments and spaces based on the occupation of the land. In the resilience theory developed by Holling and Gunderson they have suggested that lumpy landscapes (heterogeneous and discontinuous) tend to be more complex and to have more resilience than homogeneous and continuous landscapes. The level of plot subdivision is higher in block C than in block A and this generates the complexity and texture. The opportunities offered by blocks A and C are still high since the built density is low. What varies is that the distribution of plots in blocks C and D (although still a grid) creates more opportunity for contact between families, either in the street or adjacent plots. More plots also mean more redundancy. For example, if four owners decide to convert their properties into carparks, the overall residential identity of block C is maintained but if the same thing happens in block A, the whole block becomes a car park, abruptly changing the entire land use. The situation is different when the plot subdivisions are

134 *Case studies*

maintained and the building footprint infills are increased, as in block D compared to C. The main difference is in the opportunities that blocks C and D offer for change without transforming the identity of the system. It is not easy to create more buildings in Block D because it is tight and densely built while block C still has room for enlarging buildings or back-land development. The adaptive cycle of plot C can start a new cycle in the same stability state (by keeping on infilling plots) or shift to a new one (by clearing plots). Block D still has room for some change but if it reaches a point where no more buildings can be inserted it has two options: to resist change for as long as possible or start a process of demolition and rebuilding.

When options for change are reduced, redundancy will be low and even though the system may look stable, the situation is probably the opposite as one small change can trigger big transformations. The domino effect is the perfect example of this, where the first domino to fall causes the rest to follow. This would probably happen if someone decides to remove one of the six-floor (or even higher) self-constructed buildings that are so popular in parts of the built environment of Hanoi. The buildings are so tightly connected by a precarious technology that if one falls, all will feel the impact. However, compactness can also give stability to the whole block. Amsterdam's tilted canal houses are a good example of how compactness can be helpful when something goes wrong. These houses are skewed because the old foundation systems have partially failed. Nevertheless, the tilted houses have persisted because the compaction of the block, as a system, has helped to support and buffer structural issues with particular buildings.

Achieving a balance in compaction is not easy because a city demands a certain stability to deliver the minimum requirements needed for it to keep on working. The dichotomy is that a city has to maintain its stability while also maintaining the capacity to produce spaces and land resources to respond to pressures to change. The paradox of the compact city is that the survival of its compactness requires the progressive sacrifice of spaces and land resources that could give it some flexibility. The process of increasing intensification of the texture of compact urban landscapes makes them more complex, more uniform, stable and consistent but less loose, diverse and resilient. The limit to how much intensification is too much lies at the threshold between having stability with some resilience and being stable while achieving rigidity.

From the resilience viewpoint, the development of mixed-use buildings with medium or high density, often promoted as a sustainable solution for the development of urban landscapes, can be questioned. The basic point of this criticism is not the mixed-use buildings as such but that there should be limits to such urban intensification before it makes the urban landscape so complex as to accelerate the transformation of the built environment into an irreversible rigidity and inevitable collapse. This happened in Victorian England during industrialization where the need to have workers within walking distance of the factories led to lines of back-to-back housing separated by narrow lanes, making housing dark and airless (Engels, 1845) and helping to spread disease. The cholera epidemics (caused by poor drainage) led to clearance and the establishment of parallel terraced by-law housing, with a street frontage and a small backyard for through ventilation (Swenarton, 1981: 13). This suggests that one relationship that can be inferred from the adaptive cycle is the presence of thresholds for density and intensity of land use. There comes a point where compaction produces an adverse social situation that then precipitates change. The more common change found in many modern cities is clearance of compact inner-city slum areas for high-rise housing for the relatively well-off. In terms of the resulting urban form, the latter will be much harder to change piecemeal in the future, with the only option demolition and starting again.

Streets can be used as a good parameter to measure connectivity and accessibility as is done in 'space syntax' approaches (Hillier *et al.*, 1976) but it is useless to measure the resilience capacity of a system if streets are used not to measure some sort of abstract degree of connection but rather the connectivity of some particular capital or potential, such as people. Having streets that are wide and difficult to cross, as in many modern Chinese cities, may provide connectivity in the abstract but it does not connect people together. Rather it encourages separation through car use, as in such streets driving is much more pleasurable than walking. For this reason the relationship between street systems, plots and building footprints becomes important. Plots also represent a way of understanding the distribution and organization of a capital, such as an agglomeration of building functions in a particular area, as happened with the medieval guilds, leading to specific areas of the city containing artisans in the same trade, such as the Shambles area of York which was once home to the city's butchers, or the way that income can be reflected in the built form of the city, as discussed earlier.

One thing to remember is that there are other options to compaction. Given that the modern idea of compaction grew up around reducing the use of the car to go to work, many cities in less developed parts of the world offer excellent examples of how subsidizing public transport makes such journeys possible. Since 2013 the price of a 'metro' ticket in Mexico City, population 8.9 million in 2010, is 5 pesos for a journey of up to 184 km (Sistema de Transporte Colectivo de la Ciudad de Mexico, 2016), making it one of the cheapest in the world. For comparison the equivalent cost in London is 80 pesos. The network of suburban railways and buses in Mexico City moves five million people per day (the London underground has up to four million passenger journeys per day; Mayor of London, n.d.). Although Mexico City does not have the cheapest ticket in the world when cost is compared to income, it is an example of how in a low-rise, spread-out city, moving people is easy if it is made cheap enough.

Moving people around cities in the developed world is often restricted in terms of the types of transport possible, whereas in the developing world the diversity of types of travel is much greater. Thus in an Indonesian city like Jogyakarta the central area streets contain cars, taxis, buses, motorbikes, scooters, bicycles and pedestrians as in a Western city, but also horse taxis, pedal rickshaws, horses and carts, as well as push carts. This greater diversity in the transport system introduces resilience into the urban fabric in a way that compacting built form does not necessarily achieve.

7.8 Conclusions

It is not enough to say that being compact is good. What is important is to make clear the goal to be achieved through compaction. As shown in the examples above if the goal is moving people other than by car then maybe public transport subsidies, leading to more transport use, might be a better way of reaching the goal. When it comes to behaving sustainably, transport measures are easy to assess in terms of the energy used per passenger kilometre. However, measuring the effect of compaction on the resilience of the city is a very complex task. This will be discussed further in Part 3 in the discussion of measuring resilience.

An important common point in resilience between designers and ecologists is an interest in assessing complex systems by analysing the 'texture' of their landscapes. However, the best results will only be acquired when this information is correlated with the behaviour and functions of different groups in the population of a landscape. In the built environment, maps and information about behaviour and function are still limited, even though such information is becoming more accessible and abundant through digitization. This makes the analysis of change more complicated. The study of the shape of a physical built environment is limited because concepts like intensity or density are hard to assess by measuring physical properties like area, length, etc. However, the texture of urban form can be studied with maps and this approach is becoming more common. The compaction of a built environment, its density and intensity, create a texture in the urban landscape. Through theories of resilience (see Chapters 3 and 10) it could be possible to link the study of the heterogeneity of a landscape with information about its complexity (Gunderson and Holling, 2002), richness and diversity, understanding that all of these are qualities that increase the general resilience of a system (Walker and Salt, 2006). The compaction of a built environment needs to be assessed in terms of its contribution to creating more or less heterogeneous landscapes, understanding that systems with more complexity tend to produce more heterogeneous landscapes, while simpler ones create more homogeneous landscapes.

Walker and Salt (2006) stated that the enhancement of the resilience of a system requires two things, tight feedbacks, meaning that when change happens we should be able to feel the consequences of change, and modularity, meaning that the components of the system are so arranged that if one fails the rest will not follow in a domino effect. The compaction of a built environment could be helpful in increasing resilience but too much physical building could compromise the redundancy of spaces and the production of opportunities (although putting as much building as possible on a given piece of land may be exactly what developers want to do to maximize profit and what may be too much for resilience may not be too much for a developer). A compact (well connected), intense but also low-density environment could also offer tight feedbacks, redundancy, modularity and opportunities for change. Perhaps an urban environment from medieval Europe, where buildings were close together along the street but loose behind, and where people moved about mainly by foot, could form a physical example of what this might be like.

Conclusion to Part 2

All the issues discussed in Part 2 could each have been the subject of a book. The purpose of this study of built environment aspects was to look at three issues – eco-cities, heritage and compaction – from the viewpoints of both sustainability and resilience. All three issues are clearly to do with sustainability. An eco-city should by definition be more sustainable than an ordinary or non-eco-city. Heritage has been linked to sustainability through the idea of making the maximum use of the resources that go into a building through making it last as long as possible. Compaction has also been linked to sustainability as a way of reducing resource use in the built environment by encouraging people to live nearer to work and use public transport rather than the car, while at the same time preserving valuable agricultural land at the city periphery.

However, as the discussion in this Part shows, having the idea of being more sustainable is not enough without also having a clear goal of what is to be achieved and how it is to be measured.

When it comes to thinking about resilience the pattern is somewhat different. The argument was made that eco-cities are not necessarily designed as the complex systems they are, but are diagrams of a simplified idea of a city. Only when the eco-city is complete and working will it be possible to say something about its resilience. However, when it comes to heritage, understanding the history of elements of the urban built environment (building footprints, plots, blocks and streets), which form the heritage of the urban area, can reveal something about the resilience of the built environment, but not necessarily anything about its sustainability. This suggests, as argued in Chapter 4, that resilience and sustainability are not interchangeable terms to be applied to a built environment.

Compaction of the urban environment, which is often argued for in terms of sustainability, can affect the resilience of the built environment. If there are too many buildings on an area of land then the system can be too rigid, with lost opportunities for change without moving to a completely new state. Sustainability and resilience converge in the discussion of compaction where many functions are found in the same area, which can lead to better sustainability outcomes through people not having to travel much for all the needs of everyday life, and this can also be a source of opportunities for change when it comes to resilience. In this way some low-rise, and to Western eyes, relatively undeveloped Asian cities may illustrate what it is to have an urban environment that improves both sustainability and resilience.

Bibliography

Anon. (1958). Homes without sprawl. *Home and Building* 21(3), 1 August, pp. 33–37.
Auckland Council. (2011). Population density: are we talking about the same thing? *Monitoring Research Quarterly* 4(1), pp. 1–4, available at www.aucklandcouncil.govt.nz/EN/planspoliciesprojects/reports/technicalpublications/Documents/mrq20110303.pdf, accessed 19 October 2015.
Auckland Council. (2013). The Proposed Auckland Unitary Plan, available at http://unitaryplan.aucklandcouncil.govt.nz/Pages/Plan/Book.aspx?exhibit=PAUPSept13&hid=161555&s=infill, accessed 6 November 2015.
Barrett, G. (1996). The transport dimension. In M. Jenks *et al.* (eds), *The Compact City*. London: E and FN Spon.
Berghauser Pont, M. Y. and Haupt, P. A. (2005). The spacemate: density and the typomorphology of the urban fabric. *Nordic Journal of Architectural Research* 4, pp. 55–68.
BP. (2015). BP Statistical Review of World Energy June 2015, available at www.bp.com/content/dam/bp/pdf/energy-economics/statistical-review-2015/bp-statistical-review-of-world-energy-2015-full-report.pdf, accessed 11 November 2015.
Bush, G. W. A. (1971). *Decently and in Order*. Auckland and London: Collins.
Calthorpe, P. (1993). *The Next American Metropolis: Ecology, Communities and the American Dream*. New York: Princeton Architectural Press.
Caragliu, A., Chiara, D. B., Kourtit, K. and Nijkamp, P. (2015). Smart cities. In *International Encyclopaedia of the Social and Behavioural Sciences* (2nd edn), pp. 113–117. Amsterdam: Elsevier.
Chadwick, E. (1842). *The Report from the Poor Law Commissioners on an Inquiry into the Sanitary Condition of the Labouring Population*. London: HMSO.

Case studies

Chen, H., Jia, B. and Lau, S. S. Y. (2008). Sustainable urban form for Chinese compact cities: challenges of a rapid urbanised economy. *Habitat International* 32(1), pp. 28–40.

Cheng, V. (2010). Understanding density and high density. In E. Ng (ed.), *Designing High Density Cities for Social and Environmental Sustainability* (pp. 3–17). London: Earthscan.

Chung, T. (2013). The measure of Hong Kong's *Urban Intensivity*: case study on Graham Street Market. In D. Radovic (ed.), *Intensities in Ten Cities* (Vol. 1, p. 136). Tokyo: Flick Studio.

Clastres, C. (2011). Smart grids: another step towards competition, energy security and climate change objectives. *Energy Policy* 39(9), pp. 5399–5408.

Congress for the New Urbanism. (2015). The Charter of the New Urbanism, available at www.cnu.org/who-we-are/charter-new-urbanism, accessed 7 April 2016.

Dixon, J. and Dupuis, A. (2003). Urban intensification in Auckland, New Zealand: a challenge for New Urbanism. *Housing Studies* 18(3), pp. 353–368.

Duarte, C., Van Den Wymelenberg, K. and Reiger, C. (2013). Revealing occupancy patterns in an office building through the use of occupancy sensor data. *Energy and Buildings* 67, pp. 587–595.

Dupuis, A. and Dixon, J. (2002). Intensification in Auckland: issues and policy implications. *Urban Policy and Research* 20(4), pp. 415–428.

Economist Group. (2015). Global Liveability Report and Ranking 2014, available at www.eiu.com/public/topical_report.aspx?campaignid=Liveability2014, accessed 11 November 2015.

Engels, F. (1845). *The Conditions of the Working Class in England*, available at www.marxists.org/archive/marx/works/download/Engles_Condition_of_the_Working_Class_in_England.pdf, accessed 19 October 2015.

EPA (United States Environmental Protection Agency). (2015a). Sources of Greenhouse Gas Emissions, available at www3.epa.gov/climatechange/ghgemissions/sources/agriculture.html, accessed 11 November 2015.

EPA (United States Environmental Protection Agency). (2015b). Overview of Greenhouse Gases, available at www3.epa.gov/climatechange/ghgemissions/gases/ch4.html, accessed 11 November 2015.

Farrer, J. and Nason, J. (2005). *Reducing Gwynedd's Ecological Footprint: A Resource Accounting Tool for Sustainable Consumption*. Cardiff: WWF Cymru.

Fookes, T. (2000). Auckland's urban growth management. In A. Memon and H. Perkins (eds), *Environmental Planning and Management in New Zealand* (pp. 263–273). Palmerston North: Dunmore Press.

Garcia, E. (2008). Urbanismo y arquitectura para el turismo de masas en las costas mexicanas: Ixtapa, un caso de estudio. Master in Architecture, Universidad Nacional Autonoma de Mexico, Mexico City.

Ghosh, S. and Vale, R. (2006). The potential for solar energy use in a New Zealand residential neighbourhood: a case study considering the effect on CO_2 emissions and the possible benefits of changing roof form. *Australasian Journal of Environmental Management (AJEM)* 13(4), pp. 216–225.

Ghosh, S., Vale, R. and Vale, B. (2007). Metrics of local environmental sustainability: a case study in Auckland, New Zealand. *Local Environment* 12(4), pp. 355–378.

Giridharan, R., Ganesan, S. and Lau, S. S. Y. (2004). Daytime urban heat island effect in high-rise and high density residential developments in Hong Kong. *Energy and Buildings* 36(6), pp. 525–534.

Guo, Y. (2013). A study of China. In R. Vale and B. Vale (eds), *Living within a Fair Share Ecological Footprint*. London: Earthscan.

Gunderson, L. H., and Holling, C. S. (2002). *Panarchy: Understanding Transformations in Human and Natural Systems*. Washington, DC: Island Press.

Hardwicke, C. (2006). Velo-city. *Alternatives Journal* 32(1), p. 40.

Hillier, B., Leaman, A., Stansall, P. and Bedford, M. (1976). Space syntax. *Environment and Planning B* 3, pp. 147–185.

Holden, E. and Norland, I. (2005). Three challenges for the compact city as a sustainable urban form: household consumption of energy and transport in eight residential areas in the greater Oslo region. *Urban Studies* 42(12), pp. 2145–2166.

Holden, E. and Linnerud, K. (2011). Troublesome leisure travel: the contradictions of three sustainable transport policies. *Urban Studies* 48(14), pp. 3087–3106.

Hunt, D. T. (1959). Market gardening in metropolitan Auckland. *New Zealand Geographer* 15(2), pp. 130–155.

IPCC. (2007). IPCC Fourth Assessment Report: Climate Change 2007, available at www.ipcc.ch/report/ar4/, accessed 11 November 2015.

Jacobs, J. (1961/2011). *The Death and Life of Great American Cities* (50th anniversary edn). New York: Modern Library.

Jurasovic, P. (2003). The environmental impact of new ways of working in the office: a life cycle assessment of the carbon dioxide emissions (CO_2) resulting from alternative ways of working in New Zealand. PhD thesis, University of Auckland.

Kelbaugh, D. (ed.). (1989). *The Pedestrian Pocket Book: A New Suburban Design Strategy*. New York: Princeton Architectural Press.

Matan, A. and Newman, P. (2012). Jan Gehl and new visions for walkable Australian cities. *World Transport, Policy and Practice* 17(4), pp. 30–42.

Mayor of London. (n.d.). London Underground, available at https://tfl.gov.uk/corporate/about-tfl/what-we-do/london-underground, accessed 22 March 2016.

Mensah, C. A. (2014). Destruction of urban green spaces: a problem beyond urbanization in Kumasi City (Ghana). *American Journal of Environmental Protection* 3(1), pp. 1–9.

Milman, O. (2015). Melbourne's urban sprawl: just how big can the city get? *The Guardian*, 3 September, available at www.theguardian.com/australia-news/2015/sep/03/melbournes-urban-sprawl-just-how-big-can-the-city-get, accessed 11 November 2015.

Moriarty, P. (2002). Environmental sustainability of large Australian cities. *Urban Policy and Research* 20(3), pp. 233–244.

Newman, O. (1972). *Defensible Space*. New York: Macmillan.

Newman, P. and Kenworthy, J. (1989). *Cities and Automobile Dependence: An International Source Book*. Aldershot: Gower.

Ng, E. (2009). Policies and technical guidelines for urban planning of high-density cities – air ventilation assessment (AVA) of Hong Kong. *Building and Environment* 44(7), pp. 1478–1488.

NZ Agricultural Greenhouse Gas Research Centre. (2012). *The Impact of Livestock Agriculture on Climate Change – Fact Sheet 1*. Palmerston North: Grasslands Research Centre.

Office of the Deputy Prime Minister (ODPM). (2003). Living Places: Cleaner, Safer, Greener, available at www.publications.parliament.uk/pa/cm200203/cmselect/cmodpm/673/673.pdf, accessed 6 May 2016.

Pamungkas, G. (2013). Kampung Naga, Indonesia. In R. Vale and B. Vale (eds), *Living within a Fair Share Ecological Footprint*. London: Earthscan.

Partners for Liveable Communities Australia. (2010. Defining liveability, available at http://livable.org.au/index.php?id=12, accessed 6 May 2016.

Pearl, H. (2015). Cycling the city: 'I have a dream Jakarta should be like Copenhagen'. *The Guardian*, 10 September, available at www.theguardian.com/cities/2015/sep/10/cycling-jakarta-dream-copenhagen-indonesia-bike, accessed 11 April 2016.

Reality Tours and Travels. (n.d.). Slum tours, available at http://realitytoursandtravel.com/slum-tour.php, accessed 6 May 2016.

Sevtsuk, A., Ekmekci, O., Nixon, F. and Amindarbari, R. (2013). Capturing urban intensity. Paper presented at the Urban Affairs Association, San Francisco, available at http://media.voog.com/0000/0036/2451/files/Capturing_urban_intensity.pdf, accessed 21 May 2016.

Sharbin, A. B. (2006). The social and environmental effects of residential infill development in New Zealand. Urban Development Strategy Working Paper 6, Wellington, available at http://wellington.govt.nz/~/media/your-council/projects/files/infill-social.pdf, accessed 10 November 2015.

Shelton, B., Karakiewicz, J. and Kvan, T. (2011). *The Making of Hong Kong: From Vertical to Volumetric*. New York: Routledge.

Sistema de Transporte Colectivo de la Ciudad de Mexico, Metro. (2016). Costo del boleto del metro, available at www.metro.cdmx.gob.mx/organismo/costoboleto.html, accessed 18 April 2016.

Smith, P., Martino, D., Cai, Z., Gwary, D., Janzen, H., Kumar, P., McCarl, B., Ogle, S., O'Mara, F., Rice, C., Scholes, B., Sirotenk, O., Howden, M., McAllister, T., Pan, G., Romanenkov, V., Schneider, U., Towprayoon, S., Wattenbach, M. and Smith, J. (2008). Greenhouse gas mitigation in agriculture. *Philosphical Transactions of the Royal Society B, Biological Science* 363(1492), pp. 789–813.

Swenarton, M. (1981). *Homes for Heroes*. London: Heinemann Educational Books.

Unwin, R. (1912). *Nothing Gained by Overcrowding*. London: Town and Country Planning Association.

Vale, B. and Vale, R. (2010). Is the high-density city the only option? In E. Ng (ed.), *Designing High-density Cities for Social and Environmental Sustainability*. London: Earthscan.

Vale, R. and Vale, B. (2013). Domestic travel. In R. Vale and B Vale (eds), *Living within a Fair Share Ecological Footprint*. London: Earthscan.

Vallance, S., Perkins, K. and Moore, K. (2005). *The Effects of Infill Housing on Neighbours in Christchurch*. Christchurch: Environment Society and Design Division, Lincoln University for Christchurch City Council.

UK Government. (2001). School run congestion is a major headache, say teachers. *M2 Presswire*, available from http://search.proquest.com.helicon.vuw.ac.nz/docview/445918538?accountid=14782, accessed 30 November 2015.

Walker, B. and Salt, D. (2006). *Resilience Thinking: Sustaining Ecosystems and People in a Changing World*. Washington, DC: Island Press.

Williams, K., Burton, E. and Jenks, J. (2000). *Achieving Sustainable Urban Form*. London: E and FN Spon.

Wilson, J. (2014). Canterbury region, Christchurch. In *Te Ara – the Encyclopedia of New Zealand*, available at www.teara.govt.nz/en/map/10370/the-expansion-of-christchurch-to-1926, accessed 10 November 2015.

Wood, A., Bahrami, P. and Safarik, D. (2014). *Green Walls in High-Rise Buildings: An Output of the CTBUH Sustainability Working Group*. Mulgrave: The Images Publishing Group Pty Ltd.

World Bank. (2015). Population density (people per square kilometre of land area), available at http://data.worldbank.org/indicator/EN.POP.DNST?page=1, accessed 11 November 2015.

WWF Cymru *et al.* (2005). *Reducing Cardiff's Ecological Footprint: A Resource Accounting Tool for Sustainable Consumption*. Cardiff: WWF Cymru.

Part 3

Measuring sustainability and resilience in the built environment

Introduction

This part of the book is also in three chapters and the book then ends with a separate discussion and conclusion that looks back at the whole process of unravelling the two concepts of sustainability and resilience when it comes to the built environment. The issue of investigation is whether ways of measuring the two ideas are so similar that the concepts are virtually the same, or whether the reverse is true.

Chapter 8 returns to thinking about measuring sustainability, something already considered in the discussion of building rating systems in Chapter 2. It looks at ways of assessing sustainability and concludes with thinking about measuring people and what they do rather than just assessing the environment in which they live. The aim is not to give concrete ways of measuring personal environmental impact, although these are referenced, but rather to think about what needs to be measured if humankind is really to meet the stringent targets of the Paris climate change agreement.

Chapter 9 begins by comparing qualities to seek for when investigating resilience in the built environment as proposed by various institutions. However, this reveals agreement but no way of assessing how much you need of the various parameters. It then returns to a discussion of the Panarchy as it might occur in a built environment. Using a case study, it explains how to mirror the approach of assessing ecological resilience by counting elements found in the built environment, and assessing how these change. This discussion continues in Chapter 10 by evaluating change in a case study built environment in an effort to determine its resilience. Chapter 10 concludes by returning to sustainability and whether methods for measuring it are the same as for assessing resilience.

8 Measuring sustainability

'He who buys what he does not need steals from himself.'

Swedish proverb

8.1 The issues

The world is full of indicators for measuring progress to sustainability but the problem is much simpler than would be thought from all these indicators (Figure 8.1).

The resources are the input from the sun and the Earth and the consumers are the Earth's inhabitants (flora and fauna). We might also note that the planet has two types of resources, those that are replenished in some type of short-term cycle, such as food crops and timber, and those which when once extracted and consumed cannot be replenished except at scales of geological time, such as coal and oil. The real problem in measuring sustainability comes from two factors – the dominance of human beings and the fact that resources are not allocated on a global basis but depend on national boundaries. Thus the simple problem of how many people and other living beings the planet can support is complicated by the fact local solutions are needed to this global problem. Thus there is insufficient sunlight falling on Finland even in the summer to produce all the energy it needs from renewables, and wind energy fails to work well in winter because of icing on the turbine blades (Tran Thuc Han, 2013: 69–70). This leaves biomass in the form of wood, which already forms 25 per cent of Finland's total energy supply (hydro and wind account for a further 3 per cent). The aim in Finland is to achieve 38 per cent of total energy from renewables by 2030 (33 per cent from wood), including reducing consumer demand for energy (Tran Thuc Han, 2013: 83). On the other hand, there are countries like Vietnam where the household demand for energy is not high but where the cost of renewables combined with an increasing population means it is equally difficult to see all energy coming from renewables and being able to meet present demands. In fact the prediction for the renewable proportion of fuel use in Vietnam falls from 50 per cent in 2008 (of which 46 per cent is biomass) to 21.5 per cent by 2030 (16.2 per cent biomass) (Tran Thuc Han, 2013: 73).

Then within any country there are the 'haves and have nots'. The ecological footprint (EF) of Indonesia as a measure of its national environmental impact is a good example. Overall the Indonesia EF is low, falling within the fair Earth share limit, this being what everyone is allowed if all the available land in the world is divided equally between all human beings, with some allowance for land for other species.

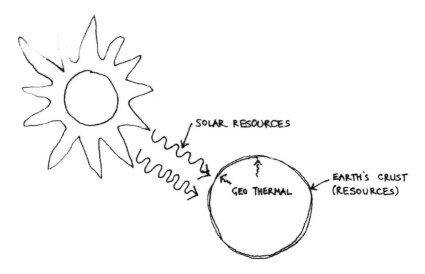

Figure 8.1 Inputs and outputs

In 2010 the Indonesian EF was 1.07 gha/person, which fell within the bio-capacity of the whole country of an available 1.12 gha/person. However, those living in the capital Jakarta on the island of Java have a higher average EF of 1.48 gha/person, while citizens of Indonesia living a subsistence life in remote rural locations, like Banten Province in west Java, might have an EF as low as 0.3 gha/person (Ministry of Public Works, 2010: table L13). Even within Jakarta there will be people with much lower EFs than others just because they are poor (Wardhani and Eldya, 2015). The question of whether measuring sustainability should allow for inequities, and who is to be on the 'have not' side of this becomes another problem. However, this is considering measuring sustainability in a holistic way, the ecological footprint being one version of this. It assumes that land is the ultimate resource for converting solar energy, whether into crops or directly to another form like electricity or hot water, as well as providing the platform for the human built environment. It deals in averages, and thus masks some of the complexities that are happening within the boundaries drawn round the land being measured, whether these are national regional or city boundaries. This has parallels with the multiple stability states found in resilience, since even a low average EF as in the Indonesian example above can mask the fact that some people's EFs are so low through poverty that their life is on the point of collapse.

To deal with equity issues the EF is sometimes coupled with other holistic measures such as the Human Development Index (HDI) (UNDP, 2015). This uses statistics of gross national average income, life expectancy at birth and education (expected years of schooling and mean years of schooling achieved on average) in combination as a single number to indicate the likelihood of the average citizen of a country living a long and healthy life, with education and an acceptable standard of living. As might be anticipated it is the nations with high EFs that tend to have high HDIs and vice versa, with the aim for global sustainability being to have a high HDI combined with a low

EF. In the latest Human Development Report (UNDP, 2014: 19), 75 per cent of the world's poor live in rural areas. This underlines both the attractiveness of migrating to cities, and the problem for sustainability that living in cities raises EFs. Moreover, in the developing world, and especially in Asia, this has led to population concentration in a few mega-cities, bringing with it time lost in commuting and increased health costs from urban air and water pollution (Henderson, 2002). The Human Development Report also states that there is positive correlation between countries with high HDI and EFs and emissions which are unsustainable, while both the developed and developing worlds have unsustainable water consumptions (UNDP, 2014: 45).

8.2 Measuring sustainability with carbon footprint

Holistic measurement of environmental impact is also achieved using the carbon footprint. Here sustainability is linked to climate change. Changing the climate is not a sustainable thing to do, so reducing the carbon footprint will help to mitigate unsustainable climate change effects such as global warming. The aim with the carbon footprint is to measure all the fossil fuel energy that goes into making human products, including buildings and urban infrastructure, and into human actions, such as driving or eating. A low carbon footprint indicates a reduced environmental impact just as does a low ecological footprint but they are not measuring the same thing and cannot be compared directly. Travelling by horse does not involve using fossil fuels directly, although some may be consumed in growing food for the horse and producing fertilizer for the land to grow this food. Travelling by car using biodiesel also involves no fossil fuels, although some may again have been used to grow the crop, like rapeseed oil, that is then processed (again maybe using fossil fuel energy) into biodiesel, and the car itself will take energy to make. So accepting that these additional amounts of energy are maybe both small and comparable, travelling by either horse or by car using bio-diesel could have a zero carbon footprint. However, when we look at the land needed to grow the crops a different picture emerges. A horse needs about 0.7 hectares and a biodiesel car 1 hectare for 10,000 km of travel (Vale, 2008). Admittedly, a horse carries one person or at most two, and the car four to five, but the horse still has a lower impact using the ecological footprint land measure. Hence carbon footprint and ecological footprint are two holistic measures for sustainability that measure different things and are therefore not directly comparable.

There are also qualitative aspects that might have to be considered. Unlike burning coal, oil and gas, nuclear power does not emit carbon dioxide directly in the conversion of radioactive materials to electricity but emissions are associated with extracting, processing and transporting the nuclear fuel, operation of the nuclear process, building and decommissioning a nuclear plant, operating the plant and dealing with the spent fuel (Sovacool, 2008). However, whereas most people are happy to have low carbon footprint solar collectors on the roof of their house, fewer people would jump at the chance of living next to a low carbon nuclear power station. The other issue of the carbon footprint is deciding on what is an acceptable level of carbon, since like nuclear power, all renewable energy systems have some impact in the way they are constructed and operated. This is shown in the carbon footprint of New Zealand electricity as it leaves the power generator (Table 8.1). These values can be compared with global averages for the period 2004–06 prepared by the UK government (Table 8.2).

146 *Measuring sustainability and resilience*

Table 8.1 Carbon emissions for electricity generation in New Zealand

Source of electricity	Emissions gCO$_2$/kWh	Reference
Wind	3.0	Rule et al., 2009
Geothermal	120.0	Rule et al., 2009
Hydro	4.6	Rule et al., 2009
Coal	720.0	MBIE, 2015: 6
Gas	420.0	MBIE, 2015: 6

Table 8.2 Carbon footprint of electricity generation based on 2004–06 global data, adapted from Baldwin (2006)

Source of electricity	Emissions gCO$_2$/kWh	Comment (high-low)
Coal	1070–766	Western Europe–Australia
Gas	662–398	US–Germany
Biomass	237–25	Direct combustion–gasification wood chip
Photovoltaics	110–35	UK–Southern Europe (greater operating hours)
Marine (wave converter and tidal barrage)	50–25	Emerging technologyUK–estimate
Hydro	34–3	Reservoir (dam)–run of river
Wind	29–4	UK offshore–UK onshore
Nuclear	80–3	Old tech–new tech (Sweden)

What Table 8.2 reveals is that using fossil fuels to generate electricity is something that needs to change if humanity as a whole is serious about mitigating climate change. However, the task is huge, as according to the International Energy Agency (IEA) in 2013 fossil fuels accounted for 67 per cent of global electricity with nuclear 11 per cent, hydro 16 per cent and other renewables 6 per cent (IEA, 2015a: 24). Indicators like carbon footprint reveal the deep problems of global society and the magnitude of trying to move to a low carbon sustainable future. The problem is exacerbated because the tables above deal only with electricity and most transport modes rely directly on fossil fuels. In 2013 total world energy came from 28.9 per cent coal, 31.1 per cent oil, 21.4 per cent natural gas, 4.8 per cent nuclear, 2.4 per cent hydro, 10.2 per cent biomass and waste and 1.2 per cent other (IEA, 2015a: 6); in other words, over 81 per cent of global energy was from fossil fuels. In their document prepared for CoP21, the 2015 climate change conference in Paris, the IEA (2015b: 3) stated the need for all renewables to rise from less than 20 per cent to 25 per cent of total world energy, with an increased share for natural gas and reductions for coal and oil, but this would in no way be a zero carbon future.

The carbon footprint used in this way is excellent at revealing the extent of the problem but it still only deals with energy and the energy that goes to make the world we live in. What it does show is which energy source we use is important. Most of us just want what happens when we use energy, or electricity (the car goes or the light comes on at night), and do not really care where that energy comes from, although we might care about how much it costs. The carbon footprint shows that we should care deeply about where our energy comes from. When it comes to availability of resources so that we can reap the benefits of having energy (being able to travel, having light in the darkness), the ecological footprint, which is also a holistic measure of sustainability, is more encompassing.

8.3 Measuring sustainability with the ecological footprint

The ecological footprint has been discussed in Chapter 2 and at the start of this chapter, so the discussion here is less about what it is but rather about how helpful it might be as a measure of sustainability. Like the carbon footprint, it is a holistic measure when based on national statistics and used to calculate the average EF of a country. Where regional or city statistics are available these can also be used to find average EFs. Very broadly, the published figures show that developed countries have much higher EFs than developing nations, that EFs rise as development occurs and that rural EFs are lower than city averages (Table 8.3).

Again, dealing in averages removes the problem from individual actions, so the impact of what we do every day is hard to see. However, the EF has two important characteristics. The first is it shows the problem globally and the second that it can be used in a bottom-up way to show personal impact. For designers it has the advantage that it is land-based and that land that is built on is considered degraded land. This means that every new building and road is reducing the available productive land.

Table 8.3 Comparative ecological footprints

Area measured	gha/person	Date	Reference
Selected nations			
USA	6.8	2011	www.footprintnetwork.org/en/index.php/GFN/page/trends/united_states_of_america/
The Netherlands	4.4	2011	www.footprintnetwork.org/en/index.php/GFN/page/trends/netherlands/
Brazil	2.6	2011	www.footprintnetwork.org/en/index.php/GFN/page/trends/brazil/
China	2.5	2011	www.footprintnetwork.org/en/index.php/GFN/page/trends/china/
Indonesia (2010)	1.4	2011	www.footprintnetwork.org/en/index.php/GFN/page/trends/china/
Cities			
Vancouver	4.0–7.0	2006/2005	Rees and Moore (2013: 12–13)[a]
Cardiff	5.59	2001	Collins *et al.* (2005)
Beijing	4.2	2008	Lin *et al.* (2010)
Jakarta (2010)	1.48	2010	Ministry of Public Works (2010)
Rural areas			
Gwynedd (2005)	5.25	2001	Farrar and Nason (2005)
Banden (2010)	0.3	2010	Ministry of Public Works (2010)

a The difference comes from the methods used to evaluate the EFs.

As a global measure national EFs are vital in showing how as a species humanity is living beyond the limits of what the planet can provide on a sustainable basis through its use of finite resources. Tracking the global EF shows that an increasing human population and a rising standard of living together mean that the day when humanity overshoots the resources it should consume in a year to be sustainable has moved back from early October in 2000 to mid-August in 2015 (Global Footprint Network [GFN], 2015). The result of this, according to the GFN, is depletion of fisheries, loss of forest cover, depletion of fresh water resources and increased CO_2 emissions, the latter as a result of using the stored reserves of fossil fuels. The GFN further points out that the effect of overshoot is probably worse for the poor as richer nations will buy in resources from elsewhere, while the poor are at risk from famine, resource wars and disease. This is not a resilient situation for the poor and not even for the rich. Like the carbon footprint, the global EF sends a big warning about the state of humanity. However, whereas understanding how much carbon use we have to reduce in order to meet a 2° or lesser rise in global temperature is hard to understand, the simple numbers of the EF are easy. For example in 2007 the world's average EF was 2.7 gha/person, whereas what would have been needed to live within the resources of the planet was an EF of 1.8 gha/person (WWF, 2010: 34). Another way of looking at the same thing is rather than one Earth, humanity needed the resources of one and a half Earths in 2007. This immediately shows the need to reduce human impact by one third.

The EF can also be broken down into components (Figure 8.2) showing where the impact is largest.

Whether rich or poor the largest component of the individual footprint is food. One of the perhaps unexpected issues of urbanization is that it tends to increase the impact of diet. If you are working long hours of physical labour, as many subsistence farmers do, it is possible to obtain enough nutrients by eating the desired number of calories from low impact food sources, such as vegetables and grains. However, an increasingly sedentary urban life means eating fewer calories than if you are working long hours doing hard labour. As a consequence the diet has to be richer to obtain the same nutrients, meaning there is a need to eat more nutrient-rich foods like meat, dairy and fish as well as vegetables and grains (Vale and Vale, 2009: 50). The other important aspect of the EF broken down into components is that part of it is not under the control of the individual but represents the EF of being a citizen of a particular country. This part accounts for the impact of government and the services government provides, such as schools and hospitals, motorways and warships. Here again it is the developed world countries that have the highest impact in terms of citizenship. This makes it harder for individuals in developed countries to try to reduce their personal EF to something closer to one planet living, or a 'fair earth share', as there is a substantial portion of the EF over which they have no control.

Like the carbon footprint, the EF is a way of seeing how far most of us have to go in terms of reducing our environmental impact. Using one of the many free EF calculators available online it is also possible to see the effect on the EF of possible changes you might make, such as driving less, not driving, not flying or becoming a vegan. As a tool for setting government policy, it is a business, as institutions like the GFN license their models for use by cities, regions or countries for use in modelling potential policy changes. The GFN do publish annual country by country EFs that show progress towards (or away from) sustainability, but for the individual these just make

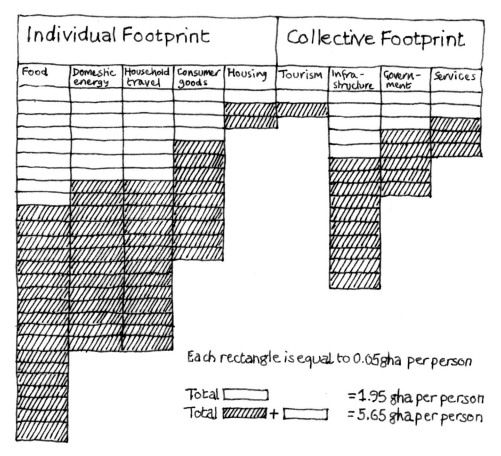

Figure 8.2 2005 EF of a citizen of Cardiff broken into components (based on Collins et al., 2005)

the position look more hopeless, as the Earth overshoot day occurs earlier each year. The EF is thus a curious measure, working at both top-down and bottom-up levels. It sets goals but leaves a gap between what is measured and how to reach those goals.

8.4 Measuring sustainability with indicators

Although it would seem the problem of finding a way to measure sustainability that would help to set policies for becoming more sustainable has led to the development of indicators in order to measure progress towards a lower environmental impact, in fact the indicators are as old as if not older than the ideas behind the ecological footprint and the carbon footprint. Indicators assume that the problem of working towards sustainability can be broken down into smaller pieces. Like the weak sustainability model (Figure 8.3) (see also Chapter 2), which sees sustainability happening when the three spheres of society, environment and economy intersect, indicators tend to be measures of social well-being (social sustainability), economic performance

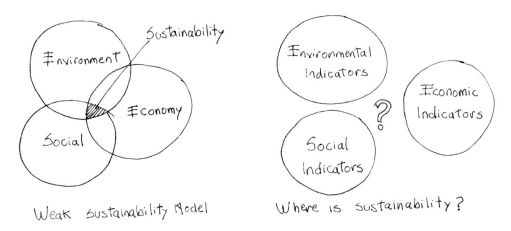

Figure 8.3 Weak sustainability model and indicator sets

(economic sustainability) and environmental performance (environmental sustainability), although quite how these are supposed to intersect is not entirely clear.

Indicators are also of two types. Predictive indicators look forward as a means of setting goals and retrospective indicators measure what has already happened (Braat, 1991). Obviously, in moving towards being more sustainable both types are necessary, since it is vital to know both where you are when you start and where you want to go. This position links to resilience, where it is also vital to know where you are starting from. However, measuring one aspect, like the quality of drinking water that arrives at the tap (a health/social indicator), does not tell you about the complex web of interactions that produced that particular water quality, such as the water source or sources (environmental indicator) and the cost of cleaning the water to an acceptable standard and piping it to the tap (economic indicator). Having good water quality (social indicator) could be at the expense of the environment through draining local aquifers, something that is really happening in many parts of the world (Dimick, 2014). This is like giving an old-fashioned clear hand signal when driving; it is no guarantee of being a good driver – it might be indicative of the care you take when driving but equally it might not – you might just be very graceful when waving your hand. The indicators indicate results but they do not talk about the cost of achieving them, nor who will pay that cost or whether if it is excessive it is an ethical expenditure. It is important to remember that a single number will not describe the whole reality of a complex system.

The other problem with indicators is that there are often a lot of them with no sense of priorities. From the start when Agenda 21 focused on the importance of indicators (United Nations, 1992: section 40.4), what emerged was a set of 134 indicators that related to its various chapters (Ghosh *et al.*, 2006). These were put into four categories (society, economics, environment and institutions) with sub-themes. Institutions were added because of the influence of governments, all with their own agendas, and the idea that 'Good governance towards sustainability… is not possible without appropriate institutions' (Spangenberg *et al.*, 2002). Each sub-theme was then subdivided into the driving force (1) behind the current state (2) and what policy measures could be adopted (3) to move towards sustainable development. This model looks simple but has problems. As Figure 8.2 illustrates, the risk is that a supposedly detailed description of problems and solutions becomes a map of individual goals but with no consensus about how these join together. Many good ingredients do not necessarily make a good cake. Taking the water example again, continually measuring how much water there is in local aquifers could lead to the situation where increasing domestic water consumption is seen as the cause behind the current state of having less water than anticipated, leading to policies for domestic water use reduction (low flow taps and shower heads). However, the cause of increasing water consumption might not be that simple but could be to do with increasing population, climate variation and reduced water entering the aquifers, or changing agricultural practices, leading to more demand for water upstream. Some aquifers themselves also change, for example as those by the coast become depleted they become more susceptible to salination by sea intrusion (Ergil, 2000).

However, it is the large number of indicators that makes the process really difficult to comprehend. The then UK Department of the Environment, Transport and the Regions (DETR) originally developed a set of 150 indicators that were then reduced to thirteen main ones that could be used to measure the overall progress towards sustainability. This is similar to the idea of important or key variables being the ones that drive change put forward by Gunderson and Holling (2002). However, such a simplification could also be misleading since the number of homes built on brown-field land is not necessarily an accurate reflection of the re-use of land (Ghosh *et al.*, 2006). For instance, in Detroit some vacant housing lots are now part of an urban agriculture movement (Kerrick, 2013: 10). By 2005 the UK government looked at sixty-eight indicators, with twenty priority indicators (National Statistics and Department for Environment, Food and Rural Affairs (DEFRA), 2005: 11), making it difficult to track progress from one set to another. Different countries have also developed their own sets of indicators. As an example, the Netherlands has three sets of indicators which are monitored – the present quality of life, available resources to indicate what future generations can have to shape their own life and the position of the Netherlands in the world in terms of the influence it has in moving towards sustainability (Statistics Netherlands, 2015: 18). Without an agreed way of comparing national indicators, or a holistic measure, progress in different countries is hard or even impossible to rank. Governments also care about looking good so national indicators may well be chosen to make things look as good as possible. There is also no general agreement about what progress is. Usually it is linked with an increase in wealth in monetary terms such as tax collected or jobs created (Kline, 2000) but wealth might equally be viewed as living within the means of the planet, and thus progressing towards sustainability. With large sets of indicators, progress is also hard to judge, although oversimplification of complex and dynamic situations when creating indicators could be equally misleading. All these complexities are equally apparent when it comes to measuring the sustainability of the built environment.

8.5 Measuring the sustainability of the built environment

The fundamental problem of measuring is that you can only measure what you can measure. As suggested in the discussion above, it is the complexity of the relationships between aspects of sustainability (environmental, social, economic) that are probably both the most crucial to know and difficult to discover. In a city is it more important to ensure there is land available for a healthy population of wildlife or is it more important to allow people to use that same land for growing food? The first is measured using environmental indicators and the second using social indicators, but how can both be equated so they can be compared directly? Is having two badgers in a park the same as growing enough potatoes for twenty-five households in poverty? The answer, of course, depends on whether you are a badger (the first is better) or a poor household (option two preferred). The first issue is, therefore, who benefits from doing the measuring of the built environment? The second issue is what does sustainability of the built environment mean? A clustered human settlement has to bring in resources from outside its immediate boundaries in order to function. Having a healthy (and sustainable) relationship with its periphery and hinterlands could be used to define the sustainable city. However, measurement of this regional balance is usually neglected in built environment indicators, and what is measured in the built environment often has a social or quality of life focus. For example, the early Boston Indicators Project was set up to build sustainable communities and had a focus within the built environment on better ecological health that would be a community asset and also improve the quality of life in the city (Kline, 2000).

The benefit of having urban indicators is in raising awareness of the issues involved in sustainability as much as trying to make existing urban settlements reduce their environmental impact. As the discussion of eco-cities demonstrated it is hard to see how it might be possible to make a truly sustainable urban environment without considering the sustainability of the region or nation encompassing it. Again, this reflects the need to look at relationships across scales, as demonstrated by the idea of the Panarchy in resilience thinking. Thus indicators such as LEED Neighbourhood are perhaps best viewed as guides to what we should be doing within an urban neighbourhood in a developed world community rather than as a blueprint for a sustainable built environment. LEED Neighbourhood (LEED-ND) is a points scoring checklist under (in version 4) the five headings of Smart Location and Linkage, Neighbourhood Pattern and Design, Green Infrastructure and Buildings, Innovation and Design Process and Regional Priority Credits (US Green Building Council [USGBC], 2015). The USGBC state rather tellingly that LEED-ND '... was developed primarily for application in situations where private developers pursuing environmentally sound principles would find it in their interest to obtain a green stamp of approval for their projects' (Welch *et al.*, n.d.: 2). The aim is to locate new developments so those living there have easy access to facilities and to use brown- rather than green-field land. Developments should respect the natural setting, which seems at first sight sensible to avoid destroying natural contours and agricultural land, but that would not be applicable if using brown-field land. Which is more important, respecting the natural setting or using brown-field land? If the aim is compaction and better access to public transport and other facilities then destroying natural or agricultural sites should not be an option. The issue is that LEED-ND is run by a business and developers pay to be certified so as to be able to display their green credentials. At the same time LEED-ND reflects the current process of urban development and the need to be able to move about the city for work and leisure, albeit with the encouragement (but not insistence) that this should be by public transport. This developed world model was illustrated in an exercise by Chicca (2013: 301–308) who showed how communities in India and China with very low ecological footprints would fail to score at all or only very low in a LEED Neighbourhood rating, concluding that LEED '... does not effectively assess the two major aspects of urban impact, food and energy' (Chicca, 2013: 306).

The possible value of indicators for the sustainability of the built environment is in alerting residents to the issues involved. However, existing indicators do not insist on real change to the urban fabric to make it truly sustainable; the car is still present in LEED-ND, even if confined out of sight to areas behind the buildings to remove on-street parking and make streets more walkable (Welch *et al.*, n.d.: 4). The other problem is that points scored for the various items in the LEED checklist may not be equivalent in terms of overall environmental impact. For example, one point is available for Access to Civic and Public Space and for Local Food Production (USGBC, 2015) but there is no guide as to how these issues have been quantified, or even advice on how much of each has to be provided. These details are only revealed either by paying to become a LEED assessor or when paying to have a project assessed. Similar problems of equivalency occur when assessing buildings.

The principles underpinning LEED-ND might be good for encouraging bottom-up initiatives in existing neighbourhoods, through showing what needs to be tackled, assuming that the things that are measured would actually make a difference. If action is undertaken by communities at the neighbourhood scale it could be much cheaper than building new eco-cities or eco-neighbourhoods, as the infrastructure is already built, existing community networks are established and so their common interests provide some continuation, and the whole city is already there and it has an identity as the home of people, more so than in many new developments. However, this bottom-up approach will not be good business for those selling LEED-ND certificates.

8.6 Measuring the sustainability of buildings

Because of the problems of assessing whole cities or whole neighbourhoods, when what is really being assessed is human behaviour, much effort has gone into indicators for individual buildings to reduce their environmental impact, both when initially constructed and over their operating life. Key building rating systems have already been discussed in Chapter 1, so the discussion here is about the approach taken to measuring the sustainability of buildings.

A building uses resources for its construction and operation, some renewable (wood, solar energy), some recyclable (steel, glass) and some non-renewable (stone, brick, natural gas). The building also has to provide adequate shelter for people, so has to be designed to work in both very hot and very cold climates, and all others in between. It has to provide appropriate sanitary conditions for those using the building. It also has to be maintained so as to have a long life, to make the resources that go into it last as long as possible. Its position within the urban fabric will also determine how people access it. All these issues therefore could become part of a building rating system that wants to promote sustainable buildings, in other words, buildings with the lowest possible impact on the natural environment.

A simple approach might be to ensure that all buildings are zero fossil fuel energy in use, and thus have a low carbon footprint, as this would be a first step in climate change mitigation. However, as discussed in Chapter 1 most sustainable building measurement systems are based on design intentions and not on the building in use, although there has been some move in this direction since the introduction of the Australian NABERS building rating system. Development of NABERS started in 2001 (the initial development team was Robert Vale, Roger Fay and Brenda Vale) and originally it was intended to be a regular annual assessment of building performance (once the building had been in use for at least a year so systems could be fine-tuned), recognizing how a building is used is as important, if not more so, than how it is designed. Prior to this in the UK, a series of Probe studies looked at buildings that claimed to be energy efficient and found a factor of six from the best to the worst in the CO_2 emissions/m^2 and an even greater factor of difference when it came to emissions per occupant (Bordass *et al.*, 2001). The Probe studies further highlighted the importance of good management of the building in use as key to energy better performance. However, as discussed in Chapter 1, most building rating systems up until now have only rated the intended design of buildings, leading to examples of buildings with excellent environmental ratings that do not perform as expected in use. For example, Newsham *et al.* (2009) in their analysis of the data from 100 LEED-rated medium energy use commercial buildings found that although overall the sample buildings used 18–39 per cent less energy on a floor area basis, 28–35 per cent of the rated buildings used more energy than their equivalent non-rated building. The other problem relates to where boundaries are drawn. In his analysis of the same LEED data for 100 commercial buildings, Scofield (2009) found that although when measuring energy used on site these 100 buildings saved 10–17 per cent of energy compared to conventional equivalents, when primary energy was accounted for by looking at the losses in generating and distributing energy, these LEED-rated buildings showed no savings when compared to comparable non-LEED-rated buildings. Since greenhouse gas emissions are associated with how energy is generated, this would seem an important factor to measure. This all suggests having a system that rates greenhouse gas emissions in use is the only safe approach to measuring the impact of buildings (Vale, 2012).

The other problem with the checklist approach to building rating is that, as discussed earlier, what is on the checklist is driven by trying to make the market accept being a bit greener. The checklist does not necessarily deal with what is required to make zero energy buildings. The new zero energy terraced houses by the Hockerton Housing Project (Martin, personal communication, 21 December 2015) have to be rated under the UK Building Regulations using the Standard Assessment Procedure (SAP) system (Department of Energy and Climate Change, 2014). Although these houses have a SAP rating of over 100 (on a scale of 1 to 100), they lose SAP points for not having gas heating, even though they are designed to have no heating at all and to generate as much energy as they consume though their roof-mounted photovoltaics. The other thing the predictive systems fail to address is the high variation of energy in use, even within the same building type. The Hockerton Project is monitoring their new terraced houses built in a neighbouring village, finding '… very big differences in energy and water consumption [per occupant] between different households' (Martin, personal communication, 21 December 2015). This leads on to the last way of thinking about measuring sustainability, which is to measure personal impact, and what this might mean when designing the built environment.

8.7 Measuring the sustainability of people

Ultimately, it is people and the choices they make in defining how they live that determine their impact on the environment. What built environment designers can do is to provide an environment that will support people in making choices that have the least impact. One way of aiding this process is knowing the impact of daily activities, for example, energy meters that display energy use immediately can be useful, rather than the traditional way of paying for what you have used long after you have used it. However, such displays need to be easily seen. Labelling is another way of showing the impact of potential purchases, but as yet such environmental labelling is in its infancy. Examples like the European Ecolabel are still only voluntary.

All these labels assume that you have enough money to be able to buy stuff. The poor seem to be the people of the world who automatically have a low impact. However, even decisions made by those who have little will not automatically be good for the environment. Moving from subsistence farming to growing crops like coffee may mean displacing wildlife or logging native forest in the search for more land on which to grow the coffee. However, the need to have more money through growing a desirable cash crop is understandable, given that food is treated as a global commodity, so if you cannot afford to buy food, you cannot afford to eat (Robbins, 2011: Section VI). The pressure, however, for 'foods' like coffee is coming from the richer developed world, not from the poor. This desire to show wealth through cultural practices, such as drinking coffee in countries that cannot grow it (ideally in liveable cities with a vibrant street life and coffee culture), or consuming an expensive delicacy like shark's fin soup (where the fins are harvested and the sharks are usually discarded; Passantino, 2014), are cultural practices that have an adverse and unnecessary environmental impact.

Behaving in an environmentally responsible way is thus accepting that one has to live within a resource limit, whether this is a carbon footprint or even better an ecological footprint. The current method of buying the equivalent of a medieval indulgence, whereby pardon for sins was secured for cash, to be redeemed when the buyer had been condemned to purgatory (Swanson, 2007: 114–115), is the carbon credit. This allows behaviour that generates greenhouse gas emissions, such as flying, to be offset against an activity that soaks up carbon, such as tree planting (capturing and storing emissions). In New Zealand, 1 carbon credit is the same as offsetting 1 tonne of CO_2 or equivalent emissions (carboNZero, 2015). Carbon credits can also be earned for using renewable sources of energy generation (to avoid emissions), reducing emissions through energy efficiency measures (also avoiding emissions) and methane capture such as taking the gas generated in a landfill site and using it (preventing the release of emissions). However, none of this deals with the real problem of moving all global economies to a renewable energy basis, or all resource use to a sustainable basis. Carbon credits allow for business-as-usual behaviour while reminding people what the important targets ought to be. We know if we want to go to heaven we should not sin, but like an indulgence, the carbon credits allow us to sin for a bit longer and avoid any unpleasant changes to our comfortable life. There is also a limit to how efficient it is possible to be in terms of using energy, and sequestering and storing carbon in trees. Trees only last as long as the harvesting cycle, unless all trees become building material and are not burned for fuel or left to rot.

If we truly want to measure sustainability then we have to realize that living within the resources of one planet with an ever-growing human population has to mean very big changes. We can count these resources just as we can count the people who use them (counting is also important for measuring resilience, see Chapter 9). We know what the problem is and that very large changes are required. However, without setting a goal as to what these changes might look like we cannot measure progress towards. At the moment all we are measuring is the path to perdition.

Bibliography

Baldwin, S. (2006). Carbon footprint of electricity generation. Parliamentary Office of Science and Technology, available at www.geni.org/globalenergy/library/technical-articles/carbon-capture/parliamentary-office-of-science-and-technology/carbon-footprint-of-electricity-generation/file_9270.pdf, accessed 10 December 2015.

Bordass, B., Cohen, R., Standeven, M. and Leaman, A. (2001). Assessing building performance in use 3: energy performance of the Probe buildings. *Building Research and Information* 29(2), pp. 114–128.

Braat, L. (1991). The predictive meaning of sustainability indicators. In O. Kuik and H. Verbruggen (eds), *In Search of Indicators of Sustainable Development* (pp. 57–70). Dordrecht: Springer Science+Business Media.

CarboNZero. (2015). Mitigate your greenhouse gas emissions, available at www.carbonzero.co.nz/options/mitigate.asp, accessed 10 December 2015.

Collins, A., Flynn, A. and Netherwood, A. (2005). *Reducing Cardiff's Ecological Footprint*. Cardiff: WWF Cymru, Sustainable Development Unit Cardiff Council and The Centre for Business, Relationships, Accountability, Sustainability and Society.

Chicca, F. R. (2013). Developing a label for excellence in design for urban sustainability. PhD thesis, Victoria University of Wellington.

Department of Energy and Climate Change. (2014). Standard Assessment Procedure, available at www.gov.uk/guidance/standard-assessment-procedure, accessed 10 December 2015.

Dimick, D. (2014). If you think the water crisis can't get worse, wait until the aquifers are drained. *National Geographic*, 21 August, available at http://news.nationalgeographic.com/news/2014/08/140819-groundwater-california-drought-aquifers-hidden-crisis/, accessed 10 December 2015.

Ergil, M. E. (2000). The salination problem of the Guzelyurt aquifer, Cyprus. *Water Research* 34(4), pp. 1201–1214.

Farrar, J. and Nason, J. (2005). *Reducing Gwynedd's Ecological Footprint: A Resource Accounting Tool for Sustainable Consumption*. Cardiff: WWF Cymru.

Ghosh, S., Vale, R. and Vale, B. (2006). Indications from sustainability indicators. *Journal of Urban Design* 11(2), pp. 263–275.

Global Footprint Network (GFN). (2015). World Footprint: do we fit the planet?, available at www.footprintnetwork.org/en/index.php/GFN/page/world_footprint/, accessed 10 December 2015.

Gunderson, L. H. and Holling, C. S. (2002). *Panarchy: Understanding Transformations in Human and Natural Systems*. Washington, DC: Island Press.

Henderson, V. (2002). Urbanisation in developing countries. *World Bank Research Observer* 17(1), pp. 89–112.

International Energy Agency (IEA). (2015a). Key World Energy Statistics, available at www.iea.org/publications/freepublications/publication/KeyWorld_Statistics_2015.pdf, accessed 10 December 2015.

International Energy Agency (IEA). (2015b). Energy and Climate Change, available at www.worldenergyoutlook.org/media/news/WEO2015_COP21Briefing.pdf, accessed 10 December 2015.

Kerrick, B. C. (2013). Borrowed ground: evaluating the potential role of usufruct in neighborhood-scale foodsheds. MSc thesis, Ohio State University, available at https://etd.ohiolink.edu/rws_etd/document/get/osu1366380928/inline, accessed 10 December 2015.

Kline, E. (2000). Planning and creating eco-cities: indicators as a tool for shaping development and measuring progress. *Local Environment* 5(3), pp. 343–350.
Lin, L., Gaodi, X., Shuyan, C., Zhihai, L., Humphrey, S., Shengkui, C., Liqiang, G., Haiying, L. and Ewing, B. (2010). China Ecological Footprint Report 2010, available at http://awsassets.wwfcn.panda.org/downloads/china_ecological_footprint_report_2010_en_low_res.pdf, accessed 10 December 2015.
Ministry of Business, Innovation and Employment (MBIE). (2015). *15 Energy in New Zealand*. Wellington: Crown Copyright.
Ministry of Public Works. (2010). *Ecological Footprint of Indonesia*. Jakarta: Ministry of Public Works.
National Statistics and Department for Environment, Food and Rural Affairs (DEFRA). (2005). *Sustainable Development Indicators in Your Pocket 2005 – Securing the Future – Delivering UK Sustainable Development Strategy*. London: DEFRA.
Newsham, G. R., Mancini, S. and Birt, B. J. (2009). Do LEED-certified buildings save energy? Yes, but… *Energy and Buildings* 41(8), pp. 897–905.
Passantino, A. (2014). The EU shark finning ban at the beginning of the new millennium: the legal framework. *ICES Journal of Marine Science* 71(3), pp. 429–434.
Rees, W. E. and Moore, J. (2013). Ecological footprints and urbanisation. In R. Vale and B. Vale (eds), *Living within a Fair Share Ecological Footprint*. Abingdon and New York: Routledge.
Robbins, R. H. (2011). *Global Problems and the Culture of Capitalism*. Upper Saddle River, NJ: Pearson Education.
Rule, B. M., Worth, Z. J. and Boyle, C. A. (2009). Comparison of life cycle carbon dioxide emissions and embodied energy in four renewable generation technologies in New Zealand. *Environmental Science and Technology* 43(16), pp. 6406–6513.
Scofield, J. H. (2009). Do LEED-certified buildings save energy? Not really… *Energy and Buildings* 41(12), pp. 1386–1390.
Sovacool, B. K. (2008). Valuing the greenhouse gas emissions from nuclear power: a critical survey. *Energy Policy* 36(8), pp. 2950–2963.
Spangenberg, J. H., Pfahl, S. and Deller, K. (2002). Towards indicators for institutional sustainability: lessons from an analysis of Agenda 21. *Ecological Indicators* 2(1–2), pp. 61–77.
Statistics Netherlands. (2015). *Sustainability Monitor of the Netherlands 2014 Indicator Report*. The Hague: Statistics Netherlands.
Swanson, R. N. (2007). *Indulgences in Late Medieval England: Passports to Paradise?* Cambridge: Cambridge University Press.
Tran Thuc Han. (2013). Sustainable patterns of living based on an investigation of footprint in Hanoi-Vietnam, Wellington-New Zealand and Oulu-Finland. PhD thesis, University of Victoria Wellington.
UNDP (United Nations Development Programme). (2014). *Human Development Report 2014: Sustaining Human Progress: Reducing Vulnerabilities and Building Resilience*. New York: UNDP.
UNDP (United Nations Development Programme). (2015). Human Development Report 2015: Work for Human Development, available at http://hdr.undp.org/en/content/human-development-index-hdi-table, accessed 11 December 2015.
United Nations. (1992). Promoting sustainable human settlement development. In *Agenda 21: Programme of Action for Sustainable Development* (Chapter 7). New York: UN Division of Sustainable Development.
US Green Building Council (USGBC). (2015). LEED v4 for Neighbourhood Development Checklist, available at www.usgbc.org/resources/leed-v4-neighborhood-development-checklist, accessed 10 December 2015.
Vale, R. (2008). Land use for sustainable personal transport. Session 4, Transport, Urban Structure and Development, China Planning Network Urban Transport Congress, Beijing, 19 July.

Vale, R. (2012). The ABCD Code – a new approach to low-carbon policy in urban planning. Paper presented at 2012 Conference on Urban Development and Planning, 12–13 June, Guangxi, China.

Vale, R. and Vale, B. (2009). *Time to Eat the Dog?: The Real Guide to Sustainable Living*. London: Thames and Hudson.

Wardhani, D. A. and Elyda, C. (2015). Jakarta sees rising poverty, widening income gap. *The Jakarta Post*, 29 January, available at www.thejakartapost.com/news/2015/01/29/jakarta-sees-rising-poverty-widening-income-gap.html, accessed 10 December 2015.

Welch, A., Benfield, K. and Raimi, M. (n.d.). A Citizen's Guide to LEED for Neighbourhood Development, available at www.nrdc.org/cities/smartgrowth/files/citizens_guide_LEED-ND.pdf, accessed 11 December 2015.

World Wide Fund for Nature (WWF). (2010). Living Planet Report 2010, available at http://d2ouvy59p0dg6k.cloudfront.net/downloads/wwf_lpr2010_lr_en.pdf, accessed 10 December 2015.

9 Measuring resilience

'The original is unfaithful to the translation.'

Jorge Luis Borges

This chapter presents a possible way of applying resilience theory to built environments and how it might be measured. The first part discusses the existing theoretical frameworks used inside and outside ecology to measure resilience. The objective is to map how various institutions are approaching this problem. The second part focuses on processes of change. The objective is to find the appropriate scale of analysis for the system. The idea behind this is to arrive at a set of nested systems at different scales, in other words, the Panarchy, and then to look for this in a built environment.

9.1 State of the art in the measurement of resilience

The measurement of resilience

There is no existing methodology for measuring resilience in the built environment, particularly when it comes to measuring things that matter for designers, like the size or shape of a block or a neighbourhood. Attempts to do this have looked at how well cities and urban areas could cope with disasters (Oddsdottir *et al.*, 2013; UNISDR, 2014; Winderl, 2014). This is an engineering resilience perspective based on the generation of technological solutions for improving the infrastructure of cities by looking at systems at different scales. Examples range from avoiding flooding by relieving pressure on storm water drains by inserting holding tanks or rainwater swales (street and neighbourhood scale), to changing a natural flood plain by embanking a river (city scale). However, as discussed in previous chapters, this will generate responses to particular natural hazards but does not account for ordinary changes in a city, like heritage loss, urban growth or the impact of cities on local ecosystems that in turn can increase the vulnerability of the built environment. Engineering resilience measurements will assess the possible impact of a flood on a particular urban slum but they will not measure the impact of social segregation (by income) and the vulnerability of slums to other agents for change, such as their removal to improve tourism.

Scholars in ecology have been developing their own ways of assessing changes to know more about resilience but there is as yet no unified approach. For example, Holling (1992) developed and used the Textural Discontinuity Hypothesis (TDH, see Chapter 3) to assess and understand resilience dynamics but the Resilience Alliance does not include the TDH in its theoretical framework. The point is that a single methodology that includes and considers all methods is not available. This is a problem for designers because authorities like city councils want to know how resilient a city needs to be, which implies tackling the entire resilience of a system. For designers the challenge is massive not only because cities are one of the most complex adaptive systems around but also because the references for measurements are changing, making them difficult to define. Therefore if a resilience measurement is needed, it is necessary to create a theoretical 'Frankenstein' (a theoretical built environment made out of the pieces we can measure) or to pick the variables that are assumed to be the most important and this of course depends on whose assumptions we use.

Frameworks to measure resilience in ecology

The Resilience Alliance assessment framework (2010) has many similarities with that developed by Walker and Salt (2006, 2012) (see Chapter 3), who also collaborated in making the Resilience Alliance framework. Two differences from Walker and Salt's work are the emphasis put on understanding the adaptive cycle, and using the dynamics across scales. This new framework was developed to help managers resolve resource issues through setting out the relationships between ecosystem services, stakeholders and the government. Table 9.1 summarizes the key steps of the Resilience Alliance framework and the methods of assessment.

The Stockholm Resilience Centre also produced a framework for measuring resilience (see Chapter 1). Their focus is on the resilience of ecosystem services produced by social–ecological systems, and this is 'defined as the capacity of SES [social–ecological systems] to sustain a desired set of ES [ecosystem services] in the face of disturbance and on-going changes in SES [social–ecological systems]' (Biggs *et al.*, 2012: 423). The decisions are potentially highly political considering that the importance, needs and demands are valued depending on the sector of the society affected. As a result the framework has two dimensions: properties to be managed in social–ecological systems (diversity, connectivity, slow variables), and attributes of the government (encourage learning, broaden participation, promote polycentric governance) (Table 9.2).

Frameworks to measure the resilience of cities

The Rockefeller Foundation pioneered the 100 Resilient Cities (2016) project. It differs from the Resilience Alliance and Stockholm Resilience Centre as its framework was especially developed for enhancing resilience in cities. Urban resilience was defined as the 'capacity of individuals, communities, institutions, businesses and systems within a city to survive, adapt and grow no matter what kinds of chronic stresses and acute shocks they experience' (100 Resilient Cities, 2016). The focus on growth suggests already that there could be a conflict with sustainability. There is no method by which to assess resilience, just a set of criteria (Table 9.3).

The City Resilience Framework (CRF) was developed by ARUP (2015a) and supported by the Rockefeller Foundation with the aim of understanding the factors and complexity that contribute to the resilience of cities. It consists of four dimensions and twelve drivers (Table 9.4).

The City Resilience Framework and the seven qualities established in the 100 Resilient Cities project were used to develop the City Resilience Index (CRI). The

Table 9.1 Criteria and assessment used in the Resilience Alliance theoretical framework

1. Describing the system

Criteria	Assessment
Identifying the main issues	List main issues and valued attributes.
Resilience of what?	List direct and indirect uses of key natural resources and the stakeholders that depend on them.
Resilience to what?	List the disturbances that have historically affected the system exceptionally or continually (periodicity), time for recovery, component affected, magnitude of effect, changes in the frequency.
Multiple space and time scales	List the scales above and below the focal system and describe how they interact with the social and ecological dimensions.

2. System dynamics

Criteria	Assessment
Adaptive cycle	Use timelines to identify changes in the system and possible drivers of the changes (specific measurements are not described).
Multiple states	Describe 3–5 key variables that determine the system's present and historical states (specific measurements are not described).
Thresholds	Describe and list thresholds and the drivers associated with them. Identify slow variables that are drivers (specific measurements are not described).

3. Cross-scale interactions

Criteria	Assessment
Panarchy	Describe what phase the system is in at the larger scale and its influence on smaller-scale subsystems.
Interacting thresholds	List thresholds of potential concern related to slow variables and describe them by scales and domain (social or ecological) assigning a level of certainty from 1 to 3.
General and specified resilience	For general resilience look for openness, reserves, tightness of feedbacks and modularity (specific measurements are not described). For the specified resilience list system components and observe decline in diversity in them (specific measurements are not described).

4. System governance

Criteria	Assessment
Adaptive governance	List key formal and informal institutions linked with the system. Describe whether they enhance or restrain flexibility. Identify the level of decision-making and if the rules and compliance are effective.
Social network	Map the social network by actors and roles. Assess the degree of centrality, number of relations and cohesiveness of groups (specific measurements are not described).

5. Acting on the assessment

Criteria	Assessment
Findings	Summarize each step.
Thresholds	Summarize thresholds and interactions by scale and domain.
Stewardship	Foster biological, economic and cultural diversity, stabilizing feedbacks and creative renewal; encourage social learning and adapt governance to changing conditions.
Transformation?	Make strategic investments to secure ecosystem goods and services; incorporate ecological knowledge into institutional structures; create social and ecological networks; combine different forms of knowledge for learning; provide incentives for stakeholder participation; identify and address knowledge gaps; develop expertise.

162 *Measuring sustainability and resilience*

Table 9.2 Summary of the Stockholm Resilience Centre framework

Principles	Measurements
Maintain diversity and redundancy. Diversity: variety (how many different elements), balance (how many of each element) and disparity (how different the elements are from one another). Redundancy: repetition of elements in a system to compensate for the loss of others.	Response diversity and functional redundancy are mentioned as criteria but measurements are not specified.
Manage connectivity. 'The way and degree to which resources, species, or social actors disperse, migrate, or interact across ecological and social landscapes' (Biggs *et al.*, 2012: 427).	Flows of energy, resources and information are mentioned as variables but measurements of connectivity are not specified.
Manage slow variables and feedback mechanisms Interaction across scales.	Measurements are not specified.
Foster complex adaptive system thinking. Understand behaviours that emerge that cannot be predicted from the analysis of subsystems in isolation.	No tools or processes are specified.
Encourage learning. 'The process of modifying existing or acquiring new knowledge, behaviors, skills, values, or preferences at individual, group, or societal levels' (Biggs *et al.*, 2012: 434).	The type of learning to be promoted, and its relationships with the scales and institutions are not specified.
Broaden participation. 'Participation refers to the active engagement of relevant stakeholders in the management and governance process' (Biggs *et al.*, 2012: 436).	Processes for participation are not specified.
Promote polycentric governance. 'Governance is defined as the exercise of deliberation and decision making among groups of people who have various sources of authority… In polycentric systems, each governance unit has independence… and each unit may link with others horizontally on common issues and be nested within broader governance units vertically' (Biggs *et al.*, 2012: 437).	Not specified.

Table 9.3 Key qualities of a resilient city by the 100 Resilient Cities project

Qualities	Description	Measurements
Reflectiveness	'Using past experience to inform future decisions.'	Not specified.
Resourcefulness	'Recognizing alternative ways to use resources.'	Not specified.
Robustness	'Well-conceived, constructed, and managed systems.'	Not specified.
Redundancy	'Spare capacity purposively created to accommodate disruption.'	Not specified.
Flexibility	'Willingness and ability to adopt alternative strategies in response to changing circumstances.'	Not specified.
Inclusiveness	'Prioritize broad consultation to create a sense of shared ownership in decision-making.'	Not specified.
Integration	'Bring together a range of distinct systems and institutions.'	Not specified.

Measuring resilience 163

Table 9.4 The City Resilience Framework (CRF) dimensions, drivers and measurements

Dimensions	Drivers	Measurements
Health and well-being	Meet basic needs. Safeguard livelihoods and employment. Ensure public health services are provided.	Not specified.
Economy and society	Promote cohesive and engaged communities. Ensure social stability, security, and justice. Foster economic prosperity.	Not specified.
Infrastructure and environment	Enhance and provide protective natural and man-made assets. Ensure continuity of critical services. Provide reliable communication and mobility.	Not specified.
Leadership and strategy	Promote leadership and effective management. Empower a broad range of stakeholders. Foster long-term integrated planning.	Not specified.

objective of this (ARUP, 2015b) was to develop a tool for governments to measure the performance of cities over time and perhaps provide a basis for comparisons between cities. The index adds fifty-two indicators that further describe the drivers in each dimension of the City Resilience Framework. The qualitative and quantitative assessment of each indicator is neither explained nor developed.

Who is measuring ecological resilience?

Table 9.5 looks at the relationship between key topics used in ecology to assess resilience and the institutional application of these concepts to measuring it. The institutions were taken from a list created by Schipper and Langston (2015), who compared frameworks that measure resilience, and then selected those on the list based on their potential use for designers. The institutions and frameworks are: Rockefeller Foundation's 100 Resilient Cities (100RC), ARUP's City Resilience Framework (CRF) and City Resilience Index (CRI), UK Department for International Development Building Resilience and Adaptation to Climate Extremes and Disasters framework (BRACED), USAID Measurement for Community Resilience (USAID), UN/ISDR Disaster Resilience Scorecard for Cities (UN/ISDR), GROSVENOR Research Report (GROSVENOR) and UNDP Community-Based Resilience Analysis (CoBRA) (Table 9.5).

There is a clear gap between the resilience theory developed in the science of ecology and its institutional practice. This means either the institutions are not measuring resilience or the methodologies developed in ecology are not yet suitable for application to complex systems other than ecosystems, like cities. Table 9.5 suggests that what is being measured is what can be easily measured. This is a similar situation to the discussion of measuring sustainability through using indicators.

At the moment, the way ecological resilience is hypothesized and explained looks too complicated for practitioners and also demands that researchers amass an immense amount of information. On the other hand, if institutions avoid resilience theory and methodology and use only the attributes that could potentially describe it, this results in measuring nothing at all. As Schipper and Langston (2015) asserted, the common

164 *Measuring sustainability and resilience*

Table 9.5 Institutions and their frameworks compared with key topics in ecological resilience

Institutions and frameworks	Key topics in ecological resilience					
	Adaptive cycle	Multiple states	Thresholds	Panarchy	Attributes and general resilience	Specified resilience
100RC	No	No	No	No	No measurements	No
CRF	No	No	No	No	No measurements	No
CRI	No	No	No	No	No measurements	No
BRACED	No	No	No	No	Indirectly related	No
USAID	No	No	No	No	Indirectly related	No
UN/ISDR	No	No	No	No	Indirectly related	No
GROSVENOR	No	No	No	No	Indirectly related	No
CoBRA	No	No	Yes	No	Indirectly related	No

point in all the frameworks is the repetition of attributes that are supposed to build resilience, at the same time assuming that more resilience is always better. These are attributes such as 'awareness and learning', 'options' and 'flexibility'. No things to measure are suggested to at least show how those attributes could be used.

For designers wanting to measure resilience in the built environment the available frameworks are not useful for achieving concrete results. The ecological hypothesis of how resilience works looks promising but the concepts somehow need to be translated so they can be applied to the built environment. The next part of this chapter considers this approach in more detail.

9.2 How to build an urban Panarchy

Framing problems

The Resilience Alliance (2010) suggests the first step in analysing a system is to define where it starts and where it finishes, in other words, establish its boundaries. A system in this case could be the urban landscape of a whole city, a neighbourhood, or just one block, and the relationship of each of these with the whole system. In the Resilience Alliance (2010) theoretical framework the limits of a system are defined in relationship to scales of time and space, along with the domains of each subsystem involved in the process of change being analysed (Holling, 1992). The boundary of a system is therefore related with the scale of the issue affecting the system. In urban landscapes, there are multiple issues linked with different scales, a factor that increases the complexity of defining the scale of the issue affecting particular urban processes of change. For example, a building is part of a street, but it is also part of a neighbourhood. If that building happens to be a local general shop, for those living in the street its closure is an inconvenience but a small one as they can still walk to the next local general store two streets away. However, if all the local general shops in a neighbourhood suddenly close, because their owners are forced out of business by the building of a new large supermarket selling cheaper food in the next neighbourhood, then the street changes (people will drive instead of walking to do their daily shopping) and the neighbourhood also changes as it become less desirable, lacking local shops, so house prices might drop. However, once all these changes have happened then we can analyse why they happened. Thus definition of the context of a problem can be approached by analysing the history of its economic, cultural or environmental development.

Scales in ecology and the built environment

The concept of using scales to frame changes as used by Holling (1992) and as suggested by the Resilience Alliance (2010) is not only geographical but also related with time variables. For example, the foraging scale of a mouse links the size of the mouse with the time it takes to get its food which is also linked with the area that it has to cover. In the ecological concept of scales, ideas of size (big and small) and speed of change (slow and fast) are assembled together, however this is not necessarily valid for the built environment, especially as scale is used in a different way.

Designers use scale in its geographic understanding, namely, to describe the size of something in relationship with something else. In order to draw a tourist map on a small piece of paper it is necessary to create an abstraction where a unit on the paper will equate to a certain quantity of units in real life. Designers take into consideration that different scales are linked with different contexts. For example, the human scale of a building will describe the size of a building in relationship to the human body, which is why small buildings seem cosy and large ones can intimidate. In contrast, the scales of a whole landscape are linked to geological time, urban scales deal with the whole city, and architectural scales with individual buildings where domestic and community life happens. However, in built environments the relationships that scales have with size (space) and speed of change (time) are not as clear as they are in ecology. Big houses can be inhabited by a single couple or overcrowded by numerous families, so although the building does not change, the effect of the number of inhabitants on local parking, vehicular use, etc. does (this suggests building function is probably important when thinking about resilience in the built environment).

One problem with finding boundaries to social-ecological systems is that human beings have a reach and impact in time and space that other species do not. While the latter may only forage in a limited area, human beings are no longer limited to gathering food or spending their lives in specific ecosystems. Now we forage the world; New Zealanders can eat bananas from the Philippines, live in Paris, work in London and take their holidays in China. If the global impact of human activities (that could be partially assessed using the ecological footprint) is considered as a way to define the scale of elements of the built environment, then a single-family house in the environment of Siem Rep could belong to a different scale than a single-family house in Melbourne, since Cambodia has a much lower ecological footprint than Australia. This could increase the problem of using scales in the same way in ecology and in the built environment. Since we live in social-ecological landscapes, the analysis of the built environment of cities provides information that is related with the behaviour of a community living in a particular place but that has to be read and understood while being aware of its limitations. This reality may push designers to create shortcuts with which to measure and analyse change in built environments without realizing the inherent danger of so doing.

Slow and fast

Instead of trying to define boundaries based on the impact of urban processes, another way of framing issues and establishing boundaries in an urban landscape could be by measuring the rate of change of its processes and linking them with specific units of analysis in the area being studied. One way of doing this is by analysing how units of the urban landscape change in time and space and comparing the results, so as to see at what scales the changes are operating. For example, changes in the transportation system of a city from being car-dependent to being car-free will probably take more time than changing the function of one street from accommodating cars to being pedestrianized. If the Panarchy theory is followed, slow change is linked with slow variables. These are things that change slowly in the long term, like the landscape or the climate, and for this reason they belong to big scales. Rapid change is linked with fast variables which are identified with small scales. The rate of change that the shape of a volcano with low activity experiences in one millennium is probably less critical than the rate of change of the skyline of a town in a hundred years. However, not all the volcanos and cities are the same, therefore measurements are needed to better understand what elements are working as slow and which as fast variables. This knowledge touches the core of the resilience theory since it is intrinsically linked with persistence and change. To discriminate processes of change and define fast and slow variables, the use of historical timelines is helpful in order to measure the speed of change of whatever variables are being observed. However, studying history does not necessarily reveal the kind of change that will occur in the future: the city of Coventry grew slowly over centuries but was destroyed in one night of wartime bombing which could not have been foreseen from its history up to then.

Timelines

In the Resilience Alliance (2010) workbook the generation of timelines is encouraged as a way to help in discriminating and bounding the different scales of a system and for understanding its histories and developments. The idea is to discover the drivers of the system at each scale and their impact on the landscape. A timeline should provide information about events and critical breakpoints that have shocked a system as well as information about the possible reasons that triggered the change. Radical changes, collapses and crises can be symptoms of a break in the capacity of a system to withstand internal or external pressures. A timeline, therefore, will help in describing the performance and development of a system, information that can be useful for understanding where thresholds occur. If the time spent on cycling from home to work is plotted on a timeline, it will be easy to observe the average time it normally takes. This average becomes a reference to know when someone is cycling slow or fast. Even though these numbers are only references and do not define a rule, they help in understanding how much is too much and make people aware of the risks when approaching these limits. While this chapter was being written, a large roadworks just outside Wellington, the capital of New Zealand, so increased journey times that many people stopped commuting into the CBD by car and opted to travel by train, meaning extra carriages had to be supplied. The journey time crossed a threshold which led to a behaviour change, one incidentally that is good for greenhouse gas reduction.

However, as explained in Chapter 6 on heritage, normally designers lack information on the complete series of events and history of what they need to analyse, whether one plot, one block or one specific street in the same neighbourhood. The other issue is that the histories of the economic, social and political changes of a country, region, state or city are not necessarily aligned, namely that when there is an economic change it might or might not be linked to a social or political change. For example, the 2009 American sub-prime mortgage crisis did not lead to a change in government housing policies (Wallinson and Pinto, 2012). At the same time, an economic change at a national scale (an increase in the tax on food) might not have the same impact in a rich neighbourhood as in a slum. Changes in the context of a place do not necessarily match or follow the same pace of changes in the morphology of urban landscapes. Nonetheless, the economic, social and political dimensions of an urban landscape do help to generate a qualitative approach to knowing something about the history of the people living in it.

In order to generate a timeline it is first important to identify the scale of analysis and domains, as explained previously. The Resilience Alliance framework (2010) suggests analysing key variables at three to five different scales of time and space (Holling, 1992). The first step to producing a timeline consists in creating parallel lines, where each one follows the evolution of discrete domains (economic, ecological) at different scales. The second step consists of placing major events that have perturbed the system along each timeline. The idea is to outline the break points and try to make connections between domains and scales. The third step consists of characterizing periods before and after a disturbance, for example by giving every identified era a different name. The investigation requires listing possible causes that have made a system vulnerable to a triggering event. The last step consists of looking for possible patterns of change. Patterns can be found in the frequency of disturbances, in the scales at which they have happened, and by looking at the intensity of the events and their impacts.

Timelines in the built environment

In order to get a more descriptive timeline of a certain built environment a designer can analyse how its form has changed (its morphogenesis). Conzen (1960) made fundamental advances in this field. Conzen's approach is based on the idea that urban landscapes develop in pace with societies (Kropf, 1993). Consequently, the analysis of the built environment allows an understanding of the processes that have shaped the urban landscape, and for this reason it is a tool for landscape management (Conzen, 1962).

Conzen (1960, 1962) used maps to compare changes in the form of urban landscapes and realized that, at least in Western cities, there were common elements that appear in all maps, namely streets, blocks, plots and building footprints, and these structures together create the urban landscape. Therefore he traced back and quantified changes in the form of these elements. He concluded that changes in urban landscapes occurred at different rates, in different quantities and, most importantly, that they generate a pattern of change that is not random but cyclical, something that he called the burgage cycle (Conzen, 1962; Whitehand, 2007). The process of building in-filling in the backyards of a medieval burgage (a form of urban rental property) was measured at different periods and Conzen found that the gradual filling up of the burgage followed different phases in relationship with discrete responses

168 *Measuring sustainability and resilience*

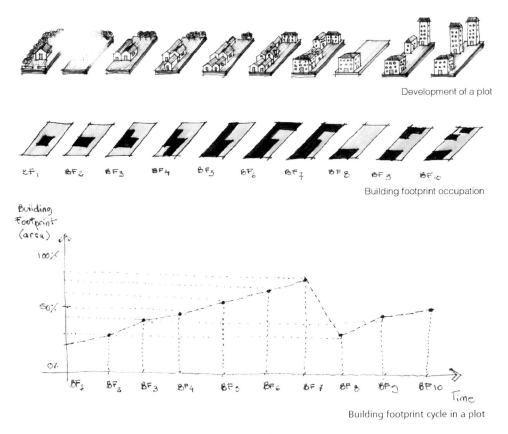

Figure 9.1 The burgage and the adaptive cycles

to social-economic forces. The phases expressed the level of building coverage in one plot. Conzen found that a fallow period (clearance and appearance of vacant land) tends to appear in plots that were previously fully built over. The fallow phase closes one burgage cycle and opens a new one (Figure 9.1).

In a conceptual way, the cycle of change described by Conzen is very similar to the adaptive cycle described by Holling, where the system becomes more complex and rigid until it either adjusts or collapses – the plot becomes more covered in building until the only way forward is to demolish one or a number of buildings and rebuild (adjust) or clear the whole plot and rebuild (collapse). Conzen's work suggests that an urban area, like an ecosystem, behaves as a complex adaptive system.

Another important conclusion from the work of Conzen was the understanding of the resistance to change possessed by each element of the urban landscape. Conzen found that streets, for example, are quite persistent in comparison with the shape or function of a plot. This information is important for designers that want to study the resilience of a built environment because it enables elements of the built environment to be identified as slow or fast variables.

As an example, the development of the plots, blocks and streets in the east part of the Auckland CBD (Figures 9.2 and 9.3) show the ideas of Conzen about the burgage

Measuring resilience 169

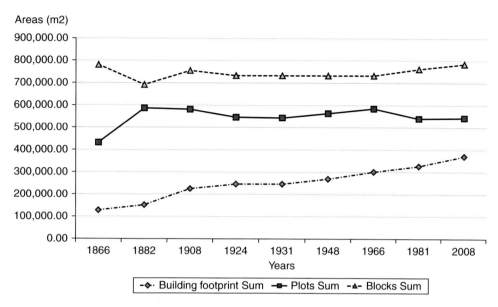

Figure 9.2 Development of total areas (sum) of building footprints, plots and blocks over time

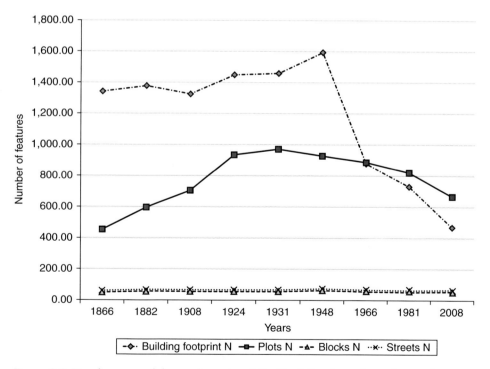

Figure 9.3 Development of the total number (N) of building footprints, plots and streets over time

cycle and the elements of the built environment as they appear in the history of the elements in this part of an urban landscape. Figure 9.2 shows a chart with three lines corresponding to the total areas of building footprints, plots and blocks (these are taken from the available maps and extrapolated as necessary). The three elements have developed in different ways. They are neither equal to one another nor linear in their developments. There is no intersection between the lines. Each one works at a different level in the same urban landscape. Therefore it might be possible to consider building footprints, plots and blocks as elements that belong to different scales. Figure 9.3 shows the total number of each element, namely, building footprints, plots and blocks compared with streets, in the same area at different times. What the chart shows is that the number of streets has persisted since 1860. What has been changing is the number of building footprints and plots, meaning that the infill process has not been linear and has both increased and decreased but at different times. This knowledge is not new to morphologists who study change in the built environment. However, it shows that Conzen's approach that recognizes the infilling process as cyclical has parallels with the way in which the adaptive cycle describes change in complex systems.

Something that is not yet clear yet in Figures 9.2 and 9.3 is the difference between crisis and collapse. More detailed study of each element would be required to investigate this further.

Changes, resilience and collapse

As noted in previous chapters, the difference between change and resilience behaviour is the latter involves an adaptation of something to something else. This implies that the system has adapted to a new reality and has buffered the disturbances caused by a crisis or other events. Observations will therefore be concentrated on discovering what is happening before and after a breaking point, or when the resilience of the system was no longer enough. The next step will be to see if the system has changed a little, a lot or completely. The idea here is to observe what is happening after changes have impacted on a system, and particularly if the system has kept or lost its identity. The challenge is to know what changes in the form and context of a built environment can be linked with adaptation to a crisis and which ones with a collapse. Changes that produce perturbations but do not change the identity of a system are coping with crisis. Changes that produce disturbances that change the identity of a system are the reasons for claiming a collapse. The recognition of a collapse becomes essential for defining where a cycle ends and a new one starts.

Tainter defined collapse as 'a rapid, significant loss of an established level of sociopolitical complexity' (1988: 4). In this definition complexity implies not only the quantity of variables, functions and interactions observed in a system but also their interrelationships with two qualities: inequity and heterogeneity. Inequity is associated with the difference in levels of a social structure where the lower levels have less access to resources. Heterogeneity is linked with the variety and diversity in a society. Tainter used the political state of a society as an indicator of its level of complexity. The hypothesis of Tainter is that in order to keep on growing, societies become very efficient in the development of problem-solving systems that can absorb the deficits that they produce in their processes of growth. A collapse emerges when the difference between the cost of becoming more complex and the cost of maintaining

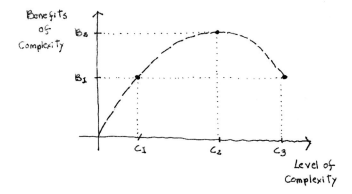

Figure 9.4 The cost–benefits of complexity (after Tainter, 2000). B1, B2, C1, C2, C3 are indicative of different levels of complexity and its benefits

the complexity already acquired arrives at a breaking point where negative marginal returns cannot be handled (Figure 9.4). As an example, Waiheke Island off the coast of Auckland is a tourist attraction but also has no sewage and mains water infrastructure. Water is collected off the roofs of buildings and stored in tanks and sewage is normally handled using a septic tank and drainage field. If the tank runs dry you have to buy water from a company on the island who own a borehole. Tank systems are good where owners know how to use them. However, an influx of tourists who do not have the experience of how to use such systems to keep them working could lead to an overload and a move to put in reticulated water and drainage systems. The cost of dealing with the overload created by the tourists who bring in money to Waiheke exceeds, in this case, the cost of putting in reticulated systems. The formerly robust decentralized system collapses, with a shift to centralized control (and presumably the business selling borehole water also collapses).

Tainter's analysis is useful for identifying when a system has collapsed and differentiating this point from a disturbance by observing how fast and how big were the changes produced in the system. In the example of Waiheke, the disturbance of having more tourists could first have to led to installing bigger tanks as a buffer against the less than careful use of water. When this was no longer sufficient, possibly because of having more tourists, or less careful tourists, then the move to a reticulated system of supply is a change in the system. The challenge then is to find a way to describe and quantify the degrees of complexity in a system, particularly in the urban built environment where each system is highly complex, far more so than the example of Waiheke Island above. Another important criterion to be developed is the assessment of how fast is a change that produces a rapid loss of a capital, property or quality, and how significant is the diminishment in the level of complexity. Measuring fluctuations of capital (such as buildings and infrastructure) could be a way of assessing disturbances and collapses. The important thing is to have clarity in what is being compared and the reference being used to measure the magnitude of change.

172 *Measuring sustainability and resilience*

Constructing and evaluating an urban Panarchy

The use of timelines, the studies of Conzen and the definition of collapse provided by Tainter are potential tools for having a better understanding of change in built environments, especially the kind of change that produces adaptations. However, the adaptive cycle of a system only tells the story of the changes that one scale of the system experiences at a time, while in the built environment there are many scales interrelated and influencing each other simultaneously. Urban designers, managers and researchers deal with large levels of complexity when trying to assess the dynamics of change in urban landscapes due to the multiple scales involved in all urban processes (Gibson *et al.*, 2000). Consequently, understanding the way each scale of the system works and how larger scales affect smaller scales (and vice versa) becomes a compulsory step in the analysis of the built environment of urban landscapes. In ecosystems, larger processes are slow and smaller ones are fast. However, in an urban system this rationality is challenged. Small elements of an urban system, like houses, that affect small quantities of land can change less frequently than governments or other forms of management that can have large effects at different scales through their top-down decisions.

In order to illustrate the production of an urban Panarchy, Figure 9.5 presents a very simple diagram. The hypothetical urban Panarchy has four scales that correspond to four units of analysis in the urban landscape (plot, block, quarter and city), and by inference to the social groups that they contain (family, neighbourhood, community and entire city), and to the role that these communities might play in the decision-making system of the city. The scales are linked because the plot illustrated in the smaller scale is contained in the block, the block in the quarter and the quarter in the city. At each scale, changes are exposed in a sequential manner to illustrate the way in which the land is progressively occupied by different buildings.

The benefit of building a Panarchy (Gunderson and Holling, 2002) is the understanding of the overall performance of a system. This performance can be assessed by comparing change in the structure and function of an urban landscape at different scales in space and time. The adaptive cycle was explained in resilience using two variables: the flow of a capital and its connectedness (Holling *et al.*, 2004). The flow of a capital can be measured as Conzen (1962) did in the burgage cycle by quantifying the aggregation of built area (building footprint) in the plot. This implies that the capital being considered is the built form. As mentioned in Chapter 6, the definition of what capital is to be observed is important because it defines the core of the study. In the Figure 9.5 example the objective of the urban Panarchy is to understand the resilience of the system to its own processes of development. It shows that small-scale changes happen more frequently than big-scale change. We can also see that the identity of the plot has changed significantly from start to finish but that the overall city has changed less with green space in its core being a persistent element of its identity.

The evaluation of the behaviour of the Panarchy of an urban landscape produces two basic scenarios. In the first, due to its resilience capacity, the system is adapting by buffering changes within and across scales. In the second, the resilience capacity of the system to buffer disturbances within and across scales has been exceeded, the system has collapsed and it starts a new phase in a different stability state (Walker and Meyers, 2004). It is important to remember that a system that does not change could stagnate. In the Panarchy this can be seen as a lack of change in big scales and

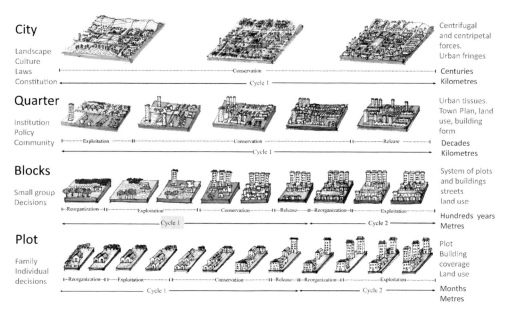

Figure 9.5 A hypothetical urban Panarchy

little change in the small scales, so all the variables start working as slow variables. Conversely, a system that is changing critically at all scales will be highly volatile and unpredictable, and in consequence all variables start working as fast variables. In both cases the scenario might or might not be desirable depending on the focus of the analysis.

The example sketched in Figure 9.5 corresponds to the first scenario where the resilience of the system has buffered changes across scales. In this case the buffering process can be seen in the number of cycles undergone at plot scale (2) against the city scale (1). The identity of the plot has changed from being occupied by a single detached house to being used by apartment buildings, however the transformation has not changed the identity of the city, which is still in the same cycle. The cycles and phases presented in Figure 9.5 are only indicative and have not been rigorously measured because the aim of this simple diagram was to explain how Panarchy can be used to understand and frame processes of change in urban systems.

The Panarchy could permit investigation of how quantity and speed of change can be linked with resilience. However, it does not provide a single number or indicator that can be used to compare two systems. What it does offer is a way of contextualizing change. From this point of view, the use of Panarchy in urban design might be the way to gain information about the general resilience of a system.

9.3 Assessing the texture of urban landscapes

Panarchy, complexity and heterogeneity

The Panarchy is a way to conceptualize systems by assuming that they are hierarchically organized through scales that are interrelated. A Panarchy that has many scales

174 *Measuring sustainability and resilience*

and is very diverse represents a more complex system than a Panarchy with fewer scales and less diversity. According to ecological resilience theory more complexity provides systems with more robustness and therefore they have more chances to deal with unpredictable change while remaining stable. One approach used by ecologists to analyse the complexity of ecosystems was looking at the qualities of their landscapes, especially their richness (how many species they have). The assumption is that richer systems are more complex than less rich ones (Garmestani *et al*., 2006). This complexity was expressed by the number of organisms and the diversity of species contained in one ecosystem. For example, the quantity and diversity of species in a subtropical forest is more than in a desert savannah. Richer ecosystems have richer Panarchies, with many elements and scales that produce more heterogeneous landscapes while less complex ecosystems are more homogeneous (Gunderson and Holling, 2002). The assumption is that by measuring changes in the form of a landscape it could be possible to have some insight into the complexity of the Panarchy that produced it.

As was shown in Chapter 6 on heritage, the complexity of a system is linked with its identity. If a savannah increases its complexity it becomes something else, just as when a subtropical forest is depleted it becomes something else. The landscape of Rangitoto, a volcanic island off Auckland, has changed its complexity from being a newly emerged erupting volcano to a hilly island that is home to more than 200 native species of plants (Department of Conservation, n.d.). Its complexity and identity (in a biological sense) have changed. Therefore, the observation of changes in the complexity of a landscape is a way of understanding transformations in the identity of a system. Paraphrasing Tainter, the complexity of an urban landscape will collapse when its heterogeneity experiences a significant loss in a short period.

Analysing the heterogeneity of urban landscapes: finding aggregations and discontinuities

Assuming that the heterogeneity of a landscape is linked with its complexity then its analysis is key to understanding the resilience of systems, so how can designers measure heterogeneity in the built environment?

In ecological resilience a Panarchy produces dynamic and hierarchical landscapes that are self-organized by clustering resources discontinuously (Allen and Holling, 2008; Holling, 1992). As a result a 'lumpy landscape' is formed by aggregations and discontinuities. The former can be understood as breaks in the continuity of a sequence of variables, like missing positions in a ranking. A simple demonstration is shown in the sequence: 1,2,3,4,…,7,8,9,10. There is a gap between the numbers 4 and 7 that discontinues the series. Another way of finding a discontinuity is to aggregate a group of numbers by the distance between them. In the example, a discontinuity will be produced when the distance between two numbers is bigger than 1. The groups of numbers between discontinuities are aggregations. In urban studies the concept of aggregations has already been used in morphological analysis but only to denominate a series of buildings (Caniggia, 2001).

Figure 9.6 illustrates the process of identification of discontinuities and aggregations using a morphological analysis of single-family houses, slab block dwellings of medium density and tall apartments of high density. In this example, elements of the built environment are grouped by size (number of people housed in a building), with

Measuring resilience 175

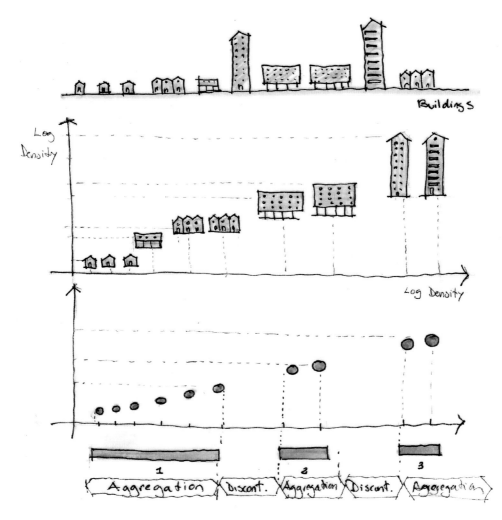

Figure 9.6 Aggregations and discontinuities in an urban landscape

small houses containing fewer people than large apartment buildings. The grouping is also related to land cover as the many people living in tall apartments have a smaller pro rata land footprint than people in single-family houses. As a result it is possible to obtain three different groups (or aggregations), pictured as grey bars in the diagram, and two discontinuities, which are the blank spaces between the grey bars. This system of clustering data could be used to count things in complex systems like cities that have many elements. Moreover, the aim of performing a clustering analysis is to create an abstraction to understand in a simplified manner the way in which a landscape is structured. In Figure 9.6 the result of the cluster analysis is a structure illustrated as three grey bars with two blank spaces. The final aim is to use these structures to make comparisons between landscapes or to analyse changes in the constitution of a landscape before and after a disturbance.

176 *Measuring sustainability and resilience*

In urban studies discontinuities can be linked with the interruptions in the continuity of a variable. For example, blocks are not normally the same size as the building footprint (if they were a single building would occupy the whole of a block). The absence of blocks of house size causes a discontinuity between the group of elements that are the size of a house, and that conform to an aggregation of house sizes, and the ones with the size of blocks, that generate an aggregation of elements of the size of a block.

In order to analyse the heterogeneity and discontinuity of urban landscapes it is necessary to consider not only elements that are built, but also those that are not built. The reason for considering unbuilt spaces as important elements in the analysis of the resilience of urban landscapes is that they constitute physical discontinuities in the built environment. They can be understood as a reserve of available space and therefore as a resource for the future. From this point of view, unbuilt spaces could be playing an important role in the control and self-organization processes of urban landscapes. Moreover, a network of unbuilt spaces could be related with the buffering of processes of change happening in the built landscape. Chapter 10 provides an example of measuring the heterogeneity of an urban landscape by analysing its open spaces.

The use of aggregations and discontinuities to assess resilience in urban landscapes

In order to explain the ideas around the use of discontinuities in the measurement of urban resilience, a hypothetical example taken from the Panarchy diagram illustrated in Figure 9.5 is used to show snapshots in the development of a block in Figure 9.7. The sketch at the top of Figure 9.7 represents a history of the changes in one block over a period of time. The subject of analysis is a block immediately before and after a disturbance. The moment in question, the disturbance, is encircled with a dotted line in the timeline. The analysis aims to understand the resilience capacity of the urban landscape to changes in the built density of its built environment. The disturbance is imaginary but due to the disappearance of houses, perhaps due to a fire or to the effects of an economic crisis. What we want to know is how critical the changes were for the resilience of the system. We also want to assess the quantity of change and whether the resilience of the built environment was such that it could cope with the changes. Therefore, the capital analysed is the built infrastructure. The same analysis could also be done by redefining the capital under analysis to be the open spaces.

The first step is to survey the built area of every building and make a cluster analysis to know the number of aggregations or class sizes that can be found in the block before and after the disturbance (assumed to be a fire). As explained in the previous section, the number of aggregations in the data serves as a reference to describe the organization and structure of the elements within the block. Charts in the middle of Figure 9.7 represent the clustering process as the buildings are grouped considering how type and density have influenced change in time and rank size.

Before the fire the urban landscape had four aggregations of buildings (grey bars with the numbers 1, 2, 3, 4). After the disturbance, the urban landscape has five groups of building type aggregations. Even if some buildings have been lost in the fire, it is possible to see that after the disturbance none of the four existing class sizes (grey

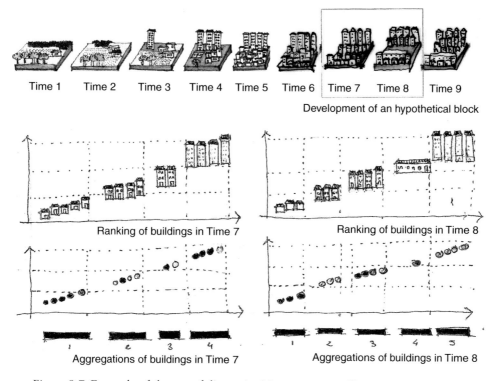

Figure 9.7 Example of the use of discontinuities to assess resilience

bars) has been lost, and moreover, a new class size has appeared. Therefore, the balance between the buildings lost during the fire and the buildings that appeared after the fire has not produced a decrease but rather an increment in the richness of the structure. One way of reading the information is that the fire has produced a change that produced the opportunity for a new type of building to appear. From this perspective the block has shown a resilience to the fire that can be seen in its ability to keep the structure stable while developing new opportunities to keep on enriching it.

The measurement can also be done in a more complex way by including building functions, for example by adding land use or building use to the information about each plot of the block. This functional richness can be measured both within and across scales (Allen *et al.*, 2005). In Figure 9.7 it could be possible to add the building uses to the analysis of the block to evaluate the richness, evenness and diversity of functions in each aggregation. Chapter 10 has a case study where evenness, richness and diversity are defined and used to assess the heterogeneity of a landscape. This measurement can be useful to quantify transformation in built environments that has been caused by functional changes. For example, the neighbourhood of Balmoral in Auckland is well known for its Asian shops and restaurants. Its identity is to be the Chinatown of Auckland. If the morphology of the built environment persists but the shops change ownership and start selling Indian food, the whole identity of the neighbourhood could shift dramatically. The problem is that land uses and the functions of buildings are difficult to track over time because maps with this kind of information are rarely available, particularly for studies that involve study over a long period of time.

9.4 Conclusions

The first part of the chapter looked at the current state of the art in the measurement of resilience from an institutional point of view. What emerged is a gap in the methods and measurements applied inside and outside ecology to assess resilience. Walker counted things found in ecological systems and used this knowledge as the basis for his resilience framework. Holling also based his theoretical work on resilience on counting elements in systems. This is something we can and should do as designers if we want to grapple with resilience. This is working from the bottom up, rather than the Rockefeller 100 Resilient Cities approach which is working from the top down, by basing its assessments of resilience on government policies rather than on the built environment. Conzen was the first person working in built environment research to count its elements, working back in the 1960s, and we still have much to learn from Conzen.

In the second and third part of this chapter the intention has been to translate and apply a number of the concepts developed in ecological resilience frameworks to urban landscapes. This translation has relied on theories from morphology, geography and history that have used similar concepts. Further research in the way of assessing resilience is needed but the only way of achieving this is by trying to measure it. It is important to put more effort into testing the assumptions and hypotheses generated in ecology before creating a new set of criteria, or a never-ending set of indicators, to measure resilience. By more measuring it will be possible to see what kind of advances designers may be able to make through the use of resilience, and also what the limitations are of applying the concept to the built environment.

Bibliography

100 Resilient Cities. (2016). 100 Resilient Cities, available at www.100resilientcities.org/ – /-_/, accessed 11 May 2016.

Allen, C., Gunderson, L. and Johnson, A. (2005). The use of discontinuities and functional groups to assess relative resilience in complex systems. *Ecosystems* 8(8), pp. 958–966.

Allen, C. and Holling, C. (2008). *Discontinuities in Ecosystems and Other Complex Systems*. New York: Columbia University Press.

ARUP. (2015a). City Resilience Framework (CRF), available at www.100resilientcities.org/page/-/100rc/Blue City Resilience Framework Full Context v1_2.pdf, accessed 10 May 2016.

ARUP. (2015b). City Resilience Index, available at https://assets.rockefellerfoundation.org/app/uploads/20160201132303/CRI-Revised-Booklet1.pdf, accessed 11 May 2016.

Biggs, R., Schlüter, M., Biggs, D., Bohensky, E., BurnSilver, S., Cundill, G. and West, P. (2012). Toward principles for enhancing the resilience of ecosystem services. *Annual Review of Environment and Resources* 37(1), pp. 421–448.

Caniggia, G. (2001). *Architectural Composition and Building Typology: Interpreting Basic Building*. Florence: Alinea.

Conzen, M. (1960). Alnwick, Northumberland: a study in town-plan analysis. *Transactions and Papers (Institute of British Geographers)* 27, pp. iii–122.

Conzen, M. (1962). The plan analysis of an English city centre. Paper presented at the IGU symposium on urban geography 1960, Gleerup, Lund.

Department of Conservation. (n.d.). Nature and Conservation, available at www.doc.govt.nz/parks-and-recreation/places-to-go/auckland/places/rangitoto-island/nature-and-conservation/, accessed May 18 2016.

Garmestani, A., Allen, C., Mittelstaedt, J., Stow, C. and Ward, W. (2006). Firm size diversity, functional richness, and resilience. *Environment and Development Economics* 11(4), pp. 533–551.

Gibson, C., Ostrom, E. and Ahn, T. (2000). The concept of scale and the human dimensions of global change: a survey. *Ecological Economics* 32(2), pp. 217–239.

Gunderson, L. and Holling, C. (2002). *Panarchy: Understanding Transformations in Human and Natural Systems*. Washington, DC: Island Press.

Holling, C. (1992). Cross-scale morphology, geometry, and dynamics of ecosystems. *Ecological Monographs* 62(4), pp. 447–502.

Holling, C., Walker, B., Carpenter, S. and Kinzig, A. (2004). Resilience, adaptability and transformability in social-ecological systems. *Ecology and Society* 9(2), p. 5.

Kropf, K. (1993). The definition of built form in urban morphology. Unpublished PhD thesis, University of Birmingham.

Oddsdottir, F., Lucas, B. and Combaz, É. (2013). *Measuring Disaster Resilience (GSDRC Helpdesk Research Report 1045)*. GSDRC, University of Birmingham.

Resilience Alliance. (2010). Assessing resilience in social-ecological systems: Workbook for practitioners. Version 2.0., available at www.resalliance.org/3871.php, accessed 10 May 2016.

Schipper, L. and Langston, L. (2015). A comparative overview of resilience measurement frameworks: analysing indicators and approaches. Overseas Development Institute.

Stockholm Resilience Centre. (n.d.). Sustainability Science for Biosphere Stewardship, available at www.stockholmresilience.org/, accessed 11 May 2016.

Tainter, J. A. (1988). *The Collapse of Complex Societies*. Cambridge and New York: Cambridge University Press.

Tainter, J. A. (2000). Problem solving: complexity, history, sustainability. *Population and Environment* 22(1), pp. 3–41.

United Nations International Strategy for Disaster Risk Reduction (UNISDR). (2014). Disaster Resilience Scorecard for Cities, available at www.unisdr.org/2014/campaign-cities/Resilience Scorecard V1.5.pdf, accessed 11 May 2016.

Walker, B. and Meyers, J. (2004). Thresholds in ecological and social-ecological systems: a developing database. *Ecology and Society* 9(2), p. 3.

Walker, B. and Salt, D. (2006). *Resilience Thinking: Sustaining Ecosystems and People in a Changing World*. Washington, DC: Island Press.

Walker, B. H. and Salt, D. (2012). *Resilience Practice Building Capacity to Absorb Disturbance and Maintain Function*. Washington, DC: Island Press.

Wallinson, P. J. and Pinto, E. J. (2012). Free fall: how government policies brought down the housing market. *The American Enterprise Outlook Series*, April, pp. 1–9.

Whitehand, J. (2007). Conzenian urban morphology and urban landscapes. Paper presented at the 6th Internathional Space Syntax Symposium, Istanbul.

Winderl, T. (2014). Disaster resilience measurements. Stocktaking of ongoing efforts in developing systems for measuring resilience, available at, www.preventionweb.net/files/37916_disasterresiliencemeasurementsundpt.pdf, accessed 11 May 2016.

10 Assessing resilience and sustainability

'Every line is the perfect length if you don't measure it.'

Marty Rubin

This chapter, which is in three parts, describes two examples of using the concepts developed in Chapter 9 to measure a built environment and learn something about its possible resilience, and then considers the relationship of this approach to measuring sustainability. The first of these examples looks at assessing an urban landscape in a case study of a part of the CBD in Auckland, New Zealand, using the Panarchy. The objective is to map the development of its urban form and correlate this with the events that have taken place in the history of this urban landscape, looking for the complexity and scales discussed in Chapter 9. The second example is about measuring the relative resilience of a built environment using the same case study. The third part of the chapter then considers the relationship between assessing resilience and measuring progress towards sustainability.

10.1 Assessing an urban Panarchy in the Auckland CBD

Understanding the history of the system

Chapter 9 outlined the importance of building timelines and plotting the history of a place at various scales, in order to understand how the system has changed. This approach is used here as a first step in building a timeline of the key events and processes that have characterized the development of Auckland, and the particular part of its CBD that forms the case study (Figure 10.1). The second step is to see whether using this historical approach makes it possible to define the key processes and events in the transformation of the shape of the urban area.

Timeline at the scale of New Zealand

It is difficult to find consensus in dividing the history of New Zealand into named periods; the literature used here (Hodgson, 1990; King, 2003; McLauchlan, 2005; Oliver and Williams, 1981) makes between four to six periods. The first period up to 1840 is dedicated to analysis of the Polynesian culture and the first settlement of New Zealand before the European arrival (McLauchlan, 2005). The second period (1841–1900) deals with the Land Wars and the beginning of a colonial economy (McLauchlan, 2005; Hodgson, 1990), which characterizes the end of this period of

Assessing resilience and sustainability 181

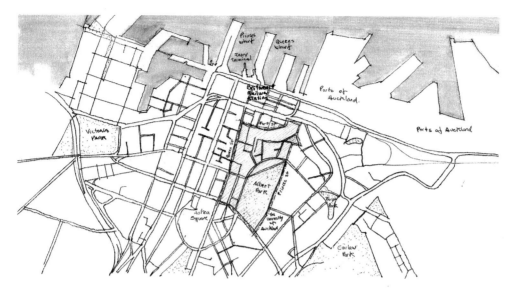

Figure 10.1 The case study area in the CBD of Auckland, New Zealand

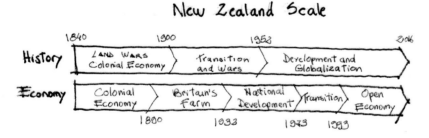

Figure 10.2 Timeline post-1840 at the scale of New Zealand

growth and violence (Oliver and Williams, 1981). The third period (1901–52) (Oliver and Williams, 1981) covers the transition from colonial to modern New Zealand. It includes the two world wars, depressions and political changes until just after the end of the Second World War. The fourth period (1953–2011) involves the development and globalization of New Zealand from just after the Second World War to the present (Oliver and Williams, 1981). This period has also been subdivided into two phases with an economic focus: before and after the 1970s. Before the 1970s, the country was described as experiencing a period of consolidation and prosperity (McLauchlan, 2005) after the difficult times of the Depression and the Second World War. After the 1970s, New Zealand settles into becoming part of a globalized world. Figure 10.2 looks at these events and periods in terms of general history and economic history. Ignoring the first period up to 1840, this gives three periods in the former and five in the latter.

182 *Measuring sustainability and resilience*

Timeline at the scale of Auckland

This analysis is based on the April 2010 report prepared for the Auckland Regional Council (Auckland Regional Council, 2010), and summarized below to show principal happenings. The report describes the development of the urban form of the metropolis from colonial times up to the present day. This chronological review draws a parallel between the key drivers of the context and their influence on the configuration of the urban form of the region.

Period 1 (1840–59)

The general character of Auckland in this first period was modest with a population of just under 3,000 people in 1842. Its inhabitants were focused on surviving and subsisting. Consequently, the buildings were temporary at best. To start with both the economy and the city's survival depended on the food the Maori supplied by canoe. However, around 1850 the expansion of the population and agriculture helped to consolidate the city.

Period 2 (1860–79)

Because of the Land Wars (settled in 1864) with the Maori, Auckland became a garrison town (McLauchlan, 2005: 31). The permanent community remained clustered in the Queen Street valley which led down to the harbour. The identity of the urban form of Auckland resided in this relationship between the harbour and the city. When the capital of New Zealand was moved to Wellington in 1865, the economy of Auckland faced big challenges. One response was development of the city to the south while expanding agricultural and forestry activities and another was the 1870 gold boom. This is a diversification of activities in response to the break in the city's dependence on government and military institutions. The first train ran in 1872.

Period 3 (1880–9)

In this period of economic expansion the railway produced a rapid extension of the urban areas incorporating new neighbourhoods in the urban fringe. This strengthened the centrality and importance of the Queen Street valley, making it the hub of transportation, commercial and industrial activities. New ferry services linked Queen Street with industrial and residential development on the other side of the harbour and the industrial belt alongside the railway, changing the focus of the city from the single link between city and sea that had characterized the settlement in the past to a more complex relationship, as suburbs grew up along both railway and horse-drawn tram lines.

Period 4 (1890–1929)

Auckland became the country's largest industrial centre in this period, while retaining agricultural activities on the periphery. The electric tram appeared in 1901 and this and cheap rail tickets for workers led to residential expansion along transport routes. This was also a time when the wealthier moved to more congenial

Assessing resilience and sustainability 183

outer suburbs, leaving the poor in the city centre, making the residential areas more homogeneous.

Period 5 (1930–49)

This period includes both the Depression and the Second World War. Car ownership and road-building became more important and the suburbs were consolidated along all types of transport routes. Electricity became more widely available as well as the provision of state houses for rent.

Period 6 (1950–69)

Auckland moved to becoming a large city that favoured car use with the introduction of a motorway system. This is a period of rapid peripheral growth. Industrial settlements and suburban developments brought about the loss of traditional centrality in the development of a metropolitan Auckland. Suburban areas absorbed population growth while the urban centre experienced population decline.

Period 7 (1970–2012)

Broad economic deregulation, intense change, the processes of entering a global economy, population growth and pressures on transport, housing and infrastructure all had an impact on the urban form of Auckland in the last forty years, which has continued to grow outwards, reliant upon roads.

Based on these periods, the timeline produced at this scale, the scale of the city (Figure 10.2), reveals similarities between the changes in periods that happen at the economic history scale and those that change the identity of the city in the same period. The latter have been expressed in terms used in the adaptive cycle and are based on key events (for example, collapse and shift happen after the capital is moved to Wellington and Auckland no longer has a function as a garrison town). A third timeline was added using the analysis of urban form summarized above.

What can be seen is that changes in the urban form periods are more frequent and of shorter duration, although almost all (there will have been demolition as well as building) are adding to the built capital of the city as it expands outwards. The identity timeline has fewer periods, perhaps because the idea behind identity is to cluster different dimensions of a system, like economy and urban form, into fewer periods that respond to when a particular identity persists. The only moment where the breaks between periods in all three timelines are clearly aligned is around 1970, which matches with economic deregulation and entering the global economy.

Timeline at the scale of the Auckland CBD

The information to create the timeline at the scale not of the whole city but just of its CBD was extracted from the same source used to develop the Auckland city scale combined with knowledge of the area. As stated before, it is usually challenging for designers to find historic information linked with specific changes in form at a neighbourhood, block or plot scale. The events and processes described below are shown as a timeline at the CBD scale in Figure 10.3.

184 *Measuring sustainability and resilience*

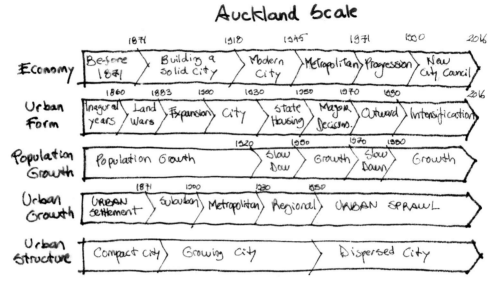

Figure 10.3 Timeline at the scale of Auckland (AKL)

(1840–50)

Shortland Crescent was the most important street. It linked the port with Britomart Point, the hill where the few government and institutional buildings were established (now Emily Place). Here there was Fort Britomart and the main church, St Paul's, Government House and the Albert Barracks. Princes Street was where the elite lived.

(1850–70)

The extension of Commercial Bay and the prolongation of Queen Street out into the sea as a commercial pier created a key social and commercial point in the city. Buildings were positioned around and on the sides of the Queen Street valley, highlighting the shape of the landscape. In this period Queen Street became the most important street, establishing a change of direction in the growth of the urban landscape. Fires in Shortland Crescent and available land in Queen Street made the shift possible.

(1870–1915)

The demolition of Britomart Point (early 1880s) and the Albert Barracks were major transformations of the urban landscape. At the street scale these changes produced the opportunity to develop Customs Street East, which created a new focus for the city, leaving Shortland Street (formerly Shortland Crescent) as a secondary focus. In adaptive cycle terms this could be seen as transition from the collapse of a conservation period to the reorganization of a new cycle.

(1915–69)

Land use in the central area underwent some change. For example, in 1930 former industrial sites behind Queen Street became warehouses. The impact of the motorcar on the urban landscape can be observed in the proliferation of garages (Albert Street, Shortland Street, Chancery Street and the Market Square), and also in the quality of the streets. The emergence of the High Street–Lorne Street system illustrates a tendency for having smaller pedestrian streets that appeared after the Second World War.

Period 5 (1970–2012)

The period is marked by a process of intensification of urban land. Aotea Square, built in 1979, became a landmark open space in the CBD, since Auckland had never before had a central space or main square.

Observations on the timelines

Historical periods at larger scales tend to be longer and fewer than periods at smaller scales. Periods tend to be shorter at all scales from the 1950s (Figure 10.4). The timeline in Figure 10.4 also reveals that it is difficult to link events and processes at larger scales with the history at smaller scales. Not all the transformations at the CBD scale can be explained as a linear consequence of processes and events that occurred at bigger scales, so there is no linear relationship between causes and effects across scales.

It is difficult to identify drivers of change in a complex timeline like that of Figure 10.4, and this suggests that for designers to have a deep understanding of a system, mapping all the information together will be extremely difficult. However, oversimplifying timelines may not provide useful information, which is why Figure 10.4 looks so complicated. When timelines at country and city scale are compared it is easy to find matching points (Figure 10.2), but adding the small scales (the CBD scale in Figure 10.3) makes it more difficult to find connections. This makes it complicated to define different phases in the adaptive cycle of the system. Moreover, what is being assessed here is not the change in the built environment but the change in its context. This suggests we need another way of trying to understand how the built environment changes in relationship to the adaptive cycle, and what are the slow and fast variables in the built environment.

Assessing change in a quantitative way

In the both methodology of the Resilience Alliance (2010) and Walker and Salt's framework (2006) the analysis and identification of slow and fast variables is seen as an important step in understanding thresholds and multiple states and to identify drivers of change. The theory of Panarchy (Gunderson and Holling, 2002) states that change at big scales happens less frequently than change at small scales. This implies that in the built environment designers will have to track two variables: quantity and frequency of change. The idea is to measure both how much and how fast the system is changing. Applying this to the case study, which covers the east side the Auckland CBD, one possible approach is to measure the frequency and quantity of change in building footprints (BF), plots (PL), blocks (BL) and streets (ST), which are called here

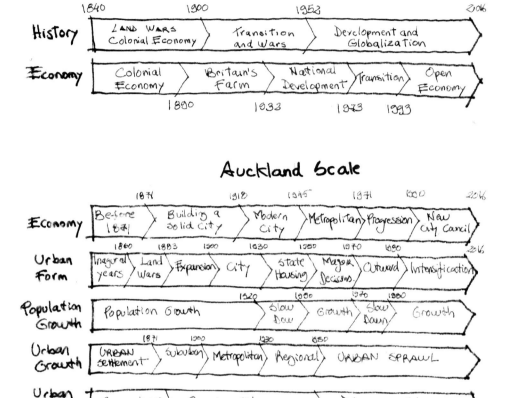
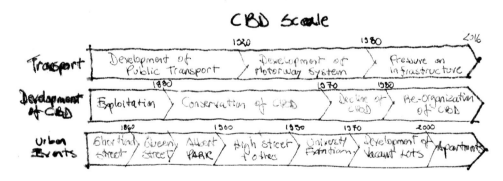

Figure 10.4 Auckland timelines at country, city and CBD scale

Table 10.1 Percentage of change in number of elements from 1866 to 2008

	1866	2008	Percentage change	Rate of change per year
Building footprints	126,758	373,329	195%	1.37%
Plots	457	665	46%	0.32%
Blocks	51	54	6%	0.04%
Streets	56	63	13%	0.09%

the elements of the urban landscape. The criteria for choosing these as variables is based on Conzen's approach, as explained in Chapter 9. The next step is to look for maps from which this information can be taken. For this part of the CBD maps are available for 1860, 1882, 1908, 1924, 1931, 1948, 1966, 1981 and 2008, although those for 1924, 1931, 1948 and 1981 have no data for building footprints. What happens to these between the dates of the maps has to be extrapolated.

There are two possible ways of measuring the quantity of change in the elements of the urban landscape; the first is to measure change in the numbers of each element and the second is to measure the total land area occupied by all the elements of each type and how this changes. Each form of measurement produces different results. In the case of building footprints, by measuring the area added to the total built area in a particular period it is possible to understand the quantity of change experienced in the urban landscape. However, for plots, blocks and streets, total areas of each variable will vary only up to the point the available land is totally built over. Not all land will necessarily be covered with buildings; there might be green space as another element in the urban landscape which remains because of laws that say it can never be built on. Beyond this point where all the available land is built on, the area of plots and blocks will remain fairly stable because the built environment is consolidated (change only occurs because of demolition and rebuilding). Consequently, it might be better to measure just the change in the number of blocks, plots and streets in the area in question in a period to have a better sense of the change. Because the measurement is focused on quantifying the percentage of change in the elements from one period to another, the units used for the measuring will not affect the result. By measuring the percentage of change in number of elements between periods it is possible to compare the quantity of change between blocks, plots, streets and building footprints. The percentage of change represents the difference between the value of a variable in one period and the new value of that variable in the next period.

Table 10.1 shows the percentage of change in the eight periods analysed across the full 144 years (1866–2008). The results show building footprints are the variable that has changed the most, followed by plots. Building footprints and plots are the fast variables that change more and at a faster pace than blocks and streets. If all the elements change at the same pace it could mean that the landscape is either stagnating (change in all variables is slow) or the system is quite volatile (all the variables are changing quickly).

Knowing which are the slow and fast variables it is then important to know more about the period by period changes in order to understand how the case study area is changing and whether any patterns can be identified. Table 10.2 shows the percentage of change in numbers of each element per period. The table also shows the

188 *Measuring sustainability and resilience*

Table 10.2 Percentage of change in the numbers of elements in the urban landscape

	1860–82	1882–1908	1908–24	1924–31	1931–48	1948–66	1966–81	1981–2008	Average change
Building footprints	19.71%	47.53%	9.28%	4.06%	9.28%	11.38%	8.85%	14.52%	15.58%
Plots	30.42%	18.46%	32.15%	4.18%	4.63%	4.31%	7.22%	19.20%	15.07%
Blocks	23.53%	1.59%	3.23%	1.67%	0.00%	0.00%	8.20%	3.57%	5.22%
Streets	8.93%	6.56%	0.00%	4.62%	3.23%	0.00%	3.13%	1.61%	3.51%
Average change per period	20.65%	18.53%	11.16%	3.63%	4.28%	3.92%	6.85%	9.73%	

Table 10.3 Average annual rate of change in the number of elements in the urban landscape

	1860–82	1882–1908	1908–24	1924–31	1931–48	1948–66	1966–81	1981–2008	Average annual rate of change in elements over all years
Building footprints	0.94%	1.90%	0.62%	0.25%	0.58%	0.67%	0.63%	0.54%	0.77%
Plots	1.45%	0.74%	2.14%	0.26%	0.29%	0.25%	0.52%	0.71%	0.80%
Blocks	1.12%	0.06%	0.22%	0.10%	0.00%	0.00%	0.59%	0.13%	0.28%
Streets	0.43%	0.26%	0.00%	0.29%	0.20%	0.00%	0.22%	0.06%	0.18%
Average annual change in all elements per period	0.98%	0.74%	0.74%	0.23%	0.27%	0.23%	0.49%	0.36%	

average change across periods, which gives a measurement of the overall change in the entire built environment. In this instance, this shows the percentage of average change decreased from 1860 to 1931 and then started to increase. However, the lowest average change occurred between 1924 and 1966, the period covered by the Depression and Second World War, which could be seen as events that affected the built environment of the Auckland CBD.

Table 10.3 takes the same information and extrapolates an annual value for the change occurring in the elements of the urban landscape. This information is presented graphically in Figure 10.5.

At first sight there are no obvious patterns in Figure 10.5 but just looking at the average change per period it is possible to infer that the system has three periods: the first from 1860 to 1924, the second from 1924 to 1966 and the third one from 1966 to 2008. However, there are doubts about the confidence in drawing this inference, given the few maps available. Nevertheless, there are common points with the timelines developed in previous sections. The 1970s continue to be a point of change. In Table 10.4 the last two periods, from 1966 to 2008, show a tendency toward growth in the percentage of change of the built environment after a period of stagnation, corresponding with deregulation and globalization, suggesting that if growth is what you

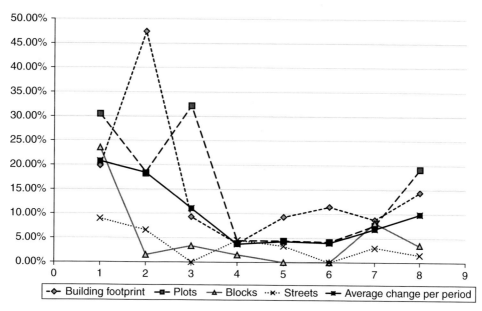

Figure 10.5 Plot of the average change per period and the rate of change per element in the case study area. The y-axis refers to percentage of change, and x-axis to periods. Period number 1 is 1860–82 and period 8 corresponds to 1981–2008

want the current system will provide it. Whether we want the consequences of that growth – climate change, increasing inequity and in Auckland an affordable housing crisis – is another matter.

In this case study each element of the urban landscape has changed in a discrete way. Therefore, the analysis of only one element of an urban landscape will not describe the dynamics of change of the whole system, proving that urban landscapes are complex entities. Blocks, plots, building footprints and streets are characterized by discrete rates of change in quantity and speed that are linked with their sizes. Small elements tend to change more and faster than big elements that change less and slowly. As a corollary, the number of larger elements in the urban landscape is less than the number of smaller elements. This relationship between size and number within the built environment reveals the presence of a hierarchy of elements in the urban landscape that can be compared with the Panarchy.

10.2 Assessing relative resilience in urban landscapes using discontinuities and aggregations

Assumptions and departure points

A Panarchy can illustrate the organization of a system and the relationship between its elements. Through the Panarchy it becomes possible to understand how the elements of a system vary in time and space (Allen *et al.*, 2014). It also shows how the

190 *Measuring sustainability and resilience*

elements are discontinuously distributed within and across scales. Chapter 9 explained how researchers in ecology use the link between the complexity of an ecosystem and the richness (number of different species in an ecological system) and heterogeneity (the way different species are distributed unevenly in the space occupied by an ecosystem) of its landscape to understand its resilience capacity. More complex systems should produce richer and more heterogeneous landscapes than less complex systems. Allen *et al.* (2005) proposed that the assessment of the discontinuous distribution of elements and functions in a system could provide a relative measure of its resilience. The assumption is that resilience is given by the way in which elements and functions are distributed in a system. A system that is resilient should keep its structure (functions and distribution of elements) even when some of its elements are lost during a disturbance. This approach will be probed in a second study of the same area of the Auckland CBD.

Defining the boundaries of the system

This analysis compares changes in diversity, where diversity is a quality that takes account of both richness (the number of different species in an ecological system) and evenness of distribution (how evenly this variety is distributed in the ecosystem) in the changes to the structure of the same small area of the CBD in Auckland, New Zealand. Because the intention of this exercise is to test a method using data from an existing built environment, the study was reduced in terms of number of periods to make the data more manageable. Considering the maps available with complete information for streets, blocks, plots and building footprints, the analysis is based on changes to the area within four historical periods: 1882 to 1908, 1908 to 1931, 1931 to 1966 and 1966 to 2006.

The variables

The first step in assessing the relative resilience is to define the key attributes of a system. Following Conzen's approach used above (see Chapter 9), the attributes to be measured are streets, blocks, plots and green space, both public and private. Private green space is calculated by subtracting all the building footprint areas in a block from the total block area. It was added as a new element of analysis because it is an important capital within the urban landscape and also because a green space is a physical discontinuity in the urban landscape that could possibly be linked with its resilience. The elements of the built environment were analysed based on their areas (m^2). The measurements were obtained by redrawing the original maps using QGIS, and exporting the resulting areas as an Excel table.

Finding discontinuities

There are multiple methods for identifying discontinuities in a database. In ecology, different methods have been tested including null models and simulations, cluster analysis, split moving window boundary and difference indices (Manly, 1996; Allen and Holling, 2001; Allen *et al.*, 2005). It is also recommended to use more than one method (Allen and Holling, 2001). As a first step, a single cluster analysis was used in this case study because software to do this is accessible for designers. The cluster analysis was conducted using the Weka (Waikato Environment for Knowledge Analysis)

Assessing resilience and sustainability 191

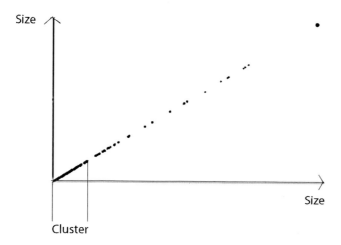

Figure 10.6 Visualization of a cluster analysis

software version 3.7.7. The software defines groups of variables that cluster around a few points in the database (Witten *et al.*, 2011). Calculations were made with the 'explorer' interface because this was more appropriate for non-experts.

The data input were areas (m^2) for blocks, plots and green spaces and length (m) for streets. These were collected from digitizations of building footprints (to obtain private green space), plots, blocks and streets previously done in QGIS and ArcGIS. The data (area of each element) was imported to Weka using a csv format (comma separated values). Options were tested until results satisfactory for the purpose of the analysis were achieved.

Figure 10.6 presents the information in a visual way. Here every dot represents a particular value of the area of an element. Clusters are found where the dots create a more continuous line made up of elements that have similar areas. There is clearly a cluster at the low end of the x-axis and then a brief break before the next cluster, which is a much shorter dark line, then there is a bigger gap and another rather 'gappy' line. The darker the line means there are more the dots in that particular cluster. The breaks between clusters can be considered as a discontinuity, just as species in an ecosystem can be grouped by weight (see Chapter 3). However, as the lines get lighter in the visualization the clusters are not obvious and that is why it is also important to have the information as numbers.

At this point the analysis will have produced the numbers of clusters in blocks, plots, streets and green spaces and the quantity of features contained in each cluster. The information can then be organized as a series of bars (aggregations or clusters) and gaps (discontinuities) to follow the examples from ecology. In Figure 10.7, aggregations and discontinuities in plots (I), blocks (II), streets (III) and green spaces (G) obtained in each year are illustrated chronologically using bars and gaps. The size of each bar is the range between the smallest area and the biggest area for that element contained in that aggregation. Gaps are distances between the biggest element of one aggregation and the smallest element of the next. The degree of grey for plots, blocks and streets and green space inside the bars represents the quantity of elements included in each aggregation. A black bar means there are lots of that particular size of element in that cluster or aggregation and a pale grey one means there are fewer elements of that size in the cluster. The area in hectares is shown along the x-axis and as the area increases the bars tend to get paler, indicating fewer large-sized elements in each cluster. The colours also respond to the percentage the elements of each cluster make up of the total, so the darkest cluster contains 80–100 per cent of all the elements. Using a diagram like Figure 10.7 begins to make it possible to visualize the quantity of aggregations and discontinuities in each element of the urban landscape and also the number of features contained in each aggregation. The diagram can be used for a qualitative analysis but it is still difficult to read. Its chief value, perhaps, is in seeing that each element of the built environment is organized and changes in a different way.

The objective of the cluster analysis is to identify the number of groupings of each element in the urban landscape and in this way describe its structure. However, it is clear from Figure 10.7 that this is difficult, and it would also be useful for designers to be able to identify visually which specific feature is in which cluster. Fortunately, this can be done using Weka. The processed data can be exported from Weka to Excel and reintroduced into QGIS or ArcGIS to make a map. A set of maps of the area of study are shown year by year in Figure 10.8. The maps for each year being studied form a row in the diagram and the elements are organized in columns of, from left to right, green spaces, streets, blocks and plots. As a result of the analysis, the maps in Figure 10.8 show the number of clusters for each element of the built environment. It is interesting to see in Figure 10.8 that the total area of green spaces diminishes across the years, but the number of clusters, in other words the number of groups of green spaces of a similar range of sizes, does not follow the same trend, as in 1882 and 2006 both urban landscapes have two clusters. The number of clusters is perhaps indicative of the richness of the urban landscape and this mirrors what ecologists were trying to measure in analysing the resilience of ecosystems by looking at how heterogeneous they were. In this case study we might assume that since the heterogeneity of the green space has not changed then this part of the system has shown some resilience, even though the total area of green space had decreased. However, this reduced overall area of green space might not be considered good if you are just looking at the built environment in terms of the ecological value it contains. It might also not be good to have reduced green area from the viewpoint of what might be useful for people. As discussed in Chapters 3 and 4 this highlights that resilience is not a goal but a property that can be either good or bad depending on the relationship between resources, people and government. After the 2010 earthquake in Chile the open spaces (squares, streets, undeveloped land and parks) in the metropolitan area of Concepcion were occupied by people '… as temporary habitable spaces, supporting a diversity of functions such as shelter, emergency services and the distribution of aid' (Allan *et al.*, 2013). The issue is to know how much green space is enough, something that only became apparent in Concepcion after the disaster.

10.3 Measuring relative resilience

The cluster analysis illustrated in Figures 10.7 and 8 provides information about the urban landscape and changes in the size and quantity of the elements that have been chosen for study. It gives information visually but does not provide numbers that could be used for comparing the textures of two urban landscapes.

Auckland

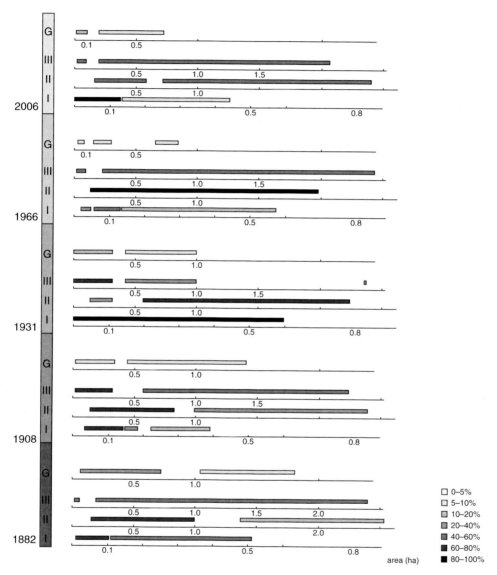

Figure 10.7 Illustration of the aggregations and discontinuities found in the cluster analysis of the elements of the urban landscape. I = plots, II = blocks, III = streets, G = green space

The first way of measuring two urban landscapes is by comparing their numbers of aggregations (clusters), understanding that more aggregations should mean a richer urban landscape. For example, in Figure 10.7 green spaces in 2006 have two aggregations (green bars) but three in 1966, suggesting the structure of green spaces in 1966 could have more resilience than in 2006 because overall things are more discontinuous

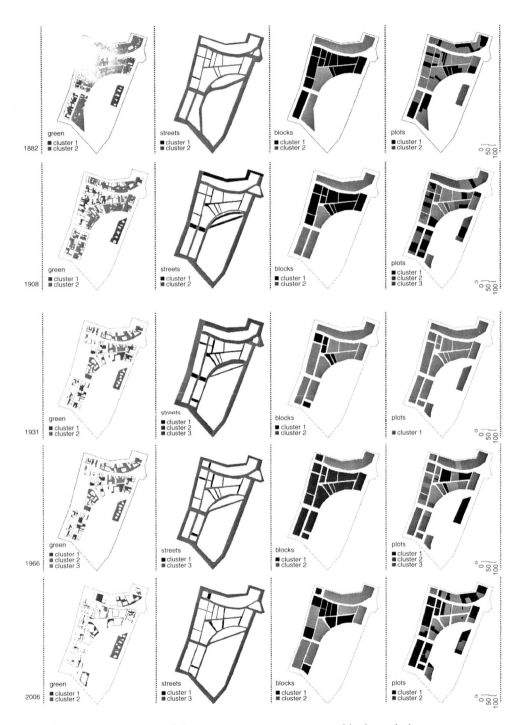

Figure 10.8 Mapping of clusters in green spaces, streets, blocks and plots

with two breaks between three aggregations, and a more discontinuous landscape is linked with being more heterogeneous, which in turn is thought to be more resilient. However, where two urban areas have the same number of aggregations then something else is needed to say which may be considered more resilient.

In ecology systems are examined in terms of order of the distribution of species within functional groups and systems can be compared by measuring richness, evenness and diversity within and across scales (Allen *et al.*, 2005). One hypothesis in ecological resilience stated (Peterson *et al.*, 1998) that a diversity of functions within and across scales provides systems with more redundancy and this in turn enhances their resilience capacity. In ecology, the definition of a functional group can be what animals eat and how they gather their food but in systems like cities it could be linked with the way the city functions (Allen *et al.*, 2005). In the analysis done here the functional groups are the different elements of the built environment, namely, blocks, plots, streets, green spaces, because they play different roles in the urban landscape and they change in discrete ways in time and space. Richness is linked with the number of aggregations found in the cluster analysis of plots, blocks, streets, and green spaces. In Table 10.4 the structure of the landscape in each year is analysed in terms of each of its elements, by considering the quantity of features in each element and the richness (number of aggregations), evenness (how equally these are distributed in the space) and diversity (which takes account of both richness and evenness) of each element per year. For example, in 2006 the element of 'plots' has two aggregations (A1, A2) with 179 plots in the first one and twenty in the second, therefore its richness is 2. In ecology a diversity index is a way of calculating the diversity of species in a particular community. Here, the Shannon-Wiener diversity index was used:

$H' = -\Sigma p_i \ln p_i$ where $p_i = 1/\log S$ (S= total number of elements).

This produced a diversity of 0.33 for plots in 2006.

In ecology, evenness is a measure of how even are the numbers of each species present in a given community. Here this looks at whether the number of elements in each aggregation is about the same or is different. Here evenness was calculated using the formula suggested by Pielou $J = H'/H'$ max $= H'/\log S$ where H' is the Shannon-Wiener diversity. This produced an evenness of 0.47 for 'plots' in 2006. Given the data were already in the form of Excel spreadsheets these calculations were not difficult to do. The results are shown in Table 10.4.

The information in Table 10.4 can be used in a variety of ways. Table 10.5 is a summary of richness, evenness and diversity for each year as a way to compare the resilience of the urban landscape in each period. Each average was calculated by averaging the data in Table 10.4 for each element. If every element of the urban landscape represents a different scale in the Panarchy, their averages would measure cross-scale richness, evenness and diversity in the system. In this instance, the period with the more heterogeneous structure and potentially the higher resilience was 1908 because it had the highest richness, evenness and diversity. These are the qualities that have been associated with ecosystem resilience (Peterson *et al.*, 1998). However, there has to be a caveat as these are also the things we can measure. Even in ecosystems the use of species richness as a measure of resilience has been questioned, especially for systems with multi-trophic food webs (where the 'waste' from one species becomes the 'food' for another (Downing and Leibold, 2010). The point

196 *Measuring sustainability and resilience*

Table 10.4 Measurements for assessing the relative resilience of the Auckland case study

Years	Auckland BE	A1	A2	A3	Features	Richness	Evenness	Diversity
2006	Plots	179	20		199	2	0.47	0.33
	Blocks	7	10		17	2	0.98	0.68
	Streets	9	10		19	2	1.00	0.69
	Green spaces	15	4		19	2	0.74	0.51
1966	Plots	37	64	10	111	3	0.82	0.90
	Blocks	17			17	1	0.00	0.00
	Streets	10	10		20	2	1.0000	0.69
	Green spaces	8	8	2	18	3	0.88	0.97
1931	Plots	119			119	1	0.00	0.00
	Blocks	6	9		15	2	0.97	0.67
	Streets	11	5		16	2	0.90	0.62
	Green spaces	12	4		16	2	0.81	0.56
1908	Plots	50	18	15	83	3	0.86	0.95
	Blocks	11	4		15	2	0.84	0.58
	Streets	12	7		19	2	0.95	0.66
	Green spaces	9	7		16	2	0.99	0.69
1882	Plots	64	43		107	2	0.97	0.67
	Blocks	12	3		15	2	0.72	0.50
	Streets	8	10		18	2	0.99	0.69
	Green spaces	13	3		16	2	0.70	0.48

of this analysis is not to say this is how to measure resilience in built environments but to see how the principles and ways of measuring resilience in ecosystems might be applied to built environments. Whether doing this is useful is another question entirely.

The same numbers from Table 10.4 could also be used to look at the heterogeneity of the urban landscape. Table 10.6 looks at the average values of the elements investigated in the case study over all years. It shows that streets, plots and green spaces are more diverse elements than blocks (there is more variety in the number of different sizes of these and in their distribution). Considering streets are the most diverse element, following the hypothesis that redundancy provides resilience, then streets should be the element of the urban landscape that vary the least over time.

The analysis presented in Table 10.7 compares the variance in richness, evenness and diversity in streets, green spaces, blocks and plots with the objective to see if there is a link between relative resilience and variability. If a diverse system has more resilience capacity to buffer disturbances then such systems should experience less change in their structures. Table 10.7 shows that streets are the element that has varied the least. This finding suggests a parallel with ecological studies that link resilience with diversity.

Something that it is important to observe in Table 10.4 is that the resilience attributes of the elements of the urban landscape change. This corroborates the idea explained in Chapters 3 and 4 that resilience it is not a goal or state that can be achieved, because within any system it is changing and is dependent on the context of the system (which as the timelines for the case study area of Auckland show is

Table 10.5 Averages for assessing relative resilience in the Auckland case study

Years	Average richness	Average evenness	Average diversity
2006	2	0.80	0.55
1966	2.25	0.67	0.64
1931	1.75	0.67	0.46
1908	2.25	0.91	0.72
1882	2	0.85	0.59

Table 10.6 Relative resilience of elements of the urban landscape

Element	Average richness	Average evenness	Average diversity
Streets	2.0	0.97	0.67
Green spaces	2.2	0.82	0.64
Plots	2.2	0.63	0.60
Blocks	1.8	0.70	0.49

Table 10.7 Variance in relative resilience of the elements of the urban landscape

Element	Average variance in richness	Average variance in evenness	Average variance in diversity
Streets	0.000	0.002	0.001
Green spaces	0.200	0.013	0.039
Blocks	0.200	0.165	0.079
Plots	0.700	0.157	0.161

also changing). So a period with high resilience could be followed by a period of low resilience.

Comparing Tables 10.6 and 10.7 shows plots were ranked third for average diversity in Table 10.6 but fourth for average variance in diversity in Table 10.7, whereas streets had the highest average diversity and lowest average diversity variance. It seems something has happened to plots. One possible explanation can be found in the fact that the diversity of plots diminished (Table 10.4) in the last period. This suggests there might be a relationship between changes in the diversity of plots and variability, and with further investigation this might be a way of looking at the resilience of a variable.

There is evidence that the relative resilience as analysed here could play a role in assessing the dynamics of change of the elements of a built environment. Even though blocks, plots and streets belong to different levels in the Panarchy their frequency of change could be affected by changes in the diversity of other elements within the Panarchy. The implication of this assumption is that designers will have to analyse the structure and distribution of the elements of the urban landscape of interest to have an understanding of the dynamics of change of the system. Applying resilience to an urban landscape could be a lot more complicated and time-consuming than looking for qualities in a checklist way, as described in Chapter 8.

10.4 Measuring sustainability and resilience together

The preceding case study makes clear that knowing how elements of the urban landscape change, although it may (or may not) teach us something about specific resilience, has little to offer about measuring sustainability. At the very least this underlines that these two concepts are very different and are never interchangeable. What remains for further analysis that may be more pertinent to sustainability is measuring function in terms of what activities take place in an urban environment and who does these (people). We know from experience that when a developed world suburb changes from being a place with local shops and schools, and where people walked, and becomes no more than a place to sleep because everyone drives everywhere, it is probably a lot less sustainable (more resources are used to support daily living) and less resilient because it has lost diversity of function. Ultimately, what sustainability is interested in is measuring the impact of people and how they live their lives, whether these are simple (in terms of limited use of resource types) as still found in many rural communities in the developing world, or highly complex as found in urban communities in the developed world who may be using a high number of disparate resources to support their lifestyles.

At first sight this seems to be running counter to the description of assessing resilience through looking at elements, which was based on greater diversity as being a sign of being more resilient. In the example above the urban communities with their complex heterogeneity should be more resilient than the simple urban communities, but experience (or at least Hollywood's Mad Max) tells us that when a crisis comes the rural community will survive just because it needs fewer resources for the lifestyle and these, and the skills to use them, will be close at hand. On the other hand, if in the name of sustainability we were to measure biodiversity in rural and urban communities it is probable that the low resource use rural one would have higher biodiversity than the developed world urban one. It thus all comes down to what you measure and the resilience of what to what.

This leads to the importance of not just measuring elements of the built environment but understanding where you are on the adaptive cycle at the point of measurement. This was the purpose of the long discussion of timelines in the first part of this chapter. The suburb with its local shops and facilities where everyone walks is not only more sustainable when measured by something like the ecological footprint (Field, 2011) but through having more functions (sleep, school, shop, social) within a small compass would also be more resilient to something like a steep rise in oil prices than the dormitory suburb with no local facilities that depends on the car. It also has room to buffer change in the way that a compact urban environment of high-rise buildings may not, even one that does contain a variety of functions, reminiscent of Le Corbusier's Unités d'Habitation. In that case its compactness and dependence on buildings that need lifts to operate means there is little room to accommodate change without moving to a new state (demolition and starting again with walk-up blocks of six or seven storeys as found in many European cities). What the application of resilience theory to urban environments perhaps shows most clearly is that at least in the developed world they will not be very resilient to the major changes indicated by moving towards living within the resources of one planet.

What is common between sustainability and resilience is the need for measuring what is happening to the flow of resources in a system and this needs more than just labelling things as being 'sustainable' or 'resilient'. What is also clear is that addressing climate change issues in the name of sustainability is going to lead to great change – how otherwise will an 80 per cent reduction in greenhouse gas emissions be achieved? Resilience theory shows not that we can build resilience into the built environment to resist this perturbation but that social-ecological systems will be moving to a new state. The hope is that we realize and start planning for this now rather than having it thrust upon us.

10.5 Conclusions

The importance of developing a quantitative historical analysis of an urban landscape is that it could provide a reference for the future management of the system being evaluated. To this end the Panarchy is useful for measuring change in urban landscapes over time and to see what has been happening at different scales. It is still difficult with this approach to define exactly where the system is in its adaptive cycle, although as discussed above this is important if we want to use any quantitatively based insights we gain from the analysis.

Discovering different levels of heterogeneity could be useful for defining how much diversity is needed in order to consider an urban landscape is sufficiently heterogeneous to be able to cope with change. This approach would be reinforced by undertaking a series of case studies similar to that described here, in the hope that this would give greater understanding of the dynamics of change as they relate to resilience in the built environment.

What we can observe is that what developers, planners and urban designers do could affect the distribution of sizes of plots and blocks (and streets) to produce more or less diversity. Immediately, this leads us into the realm of ownership, although as many people already know ownership will be overridden if the ultimate gains are in the interest of society, or at least society as government perceives it. Many new road schemes in developed countries depend on compulsory purchase or recompense for affecting existing land ownership.

What the analysis does provide is a picture of how the urban landscape has changed and how we read meaning into these changes needs more exploration. This is important as the increased urbanization of the global population, resource shortages and the idea of one planet living suggest a need to understand how cities truly behave and develop. The ability of a complex system to adapt to change that comes from internal and external pressures is the essence of creating a system than can sustain itself in the long term. The case studies in this chapter show that the application of resilience theory to urban landscapes is not as straightforward as it looks in the ecological theory as cities are very complex systems. Cities often appear as large grey stains on a map but as designers we try to dig into these stains looking for the many, many different shades of grey that form the many elements of a city at different scales, all of which are changing, persisting or disappearing. Only looking at plots, blocks, streets and green spaces is too limited to give a sense of what is really happening, but as we said earlier this is the result of dipping a first architectural toe into resilience, and you have to start somewhere.

Bibliography

Allan, P., Bryant, M., Wirsching, C., Garcia, D. and Rodriguez, M. T. (2013). The influence of urban morphology on the resilience of cities following an earthquake. *Journal of Urban Design* 18(2), pp. 242–262.

Allen, C., Angeler, D., Garmestani, A., Gunderson, L. and Holling, C. S. (2014). Panarchy: theory and application. *Ecosystems* 17(4), pp. 578–589.

Allen, C. R. and Holling, C. S. (2002). Cross-scale structure and scale breaks in ecosystems and other complex systems. *Ecosystems* 5(4), pp. 315–318.

Allen, C. R., Gunderson, L. and Johnson, A. (2005). The use of discontinuities and functional groups to assess relative resilience in complex systems. *Ecosystems* 8(8), pp. 958–966.

Auckland Regional Council. (2010). A brief history of Auckland's urban form, available at http://fdmcgeo.weebly.com/uploads/6/0/1/3/6013475/brief_history_of_auckland_urban_form_-_apr_2010.pdf, accessed 26 May 2016.

Downing, A. L. and Leibold, M. A. (2010). Species richness facilitates ecosystem resilience in aquatic food webs. *Freshwater Biology* 55(10), pp. 2123–2137.

Field, C. (2011). The ecological footprint of Wellingtonians in the 1950s. Master of Building Science thesis, Victoria University of Wellington.

Gunderson, L. H. and Holling, C. S. (2002). *Panarchy: Understanding Transformations in Human and Natural Systems*. Washington, DC: Island Press.

Hodgson, T. E. R. (1990). *Colonial Capital: Wellington, 1865–1910*. Auckland: Random Century.

King, M. (2003). *The Penguin History of New Zealand*. Auckland: Penguin Books.

Manly, B. F. (1996). Are there clumps in body size distributions? *Ecology* 77, pp. 81–86.

McLauchlan, G. (2005). *A Short Short History of New Zealand*. Auckland: Penguin.

Oliver, W. H. W. and Williams, B. R. (eds). (1981). *The Oxford History of New Zealand*. Oxford: Clarendon Press/Oxford University Press.

Peterson, G., Allen, C. R. and Holling, C. S. (1998). Ecological resilience, biodiversity, and scale. *Ecosystems* 1(1), pp. 6–18.

Resilience Alliance. (2010). Assessing resilience in social-ecological systems: workbook for practitioners. Version 2.0., 54., available at www.resalliance.org/3871.php, accessed 24 May 2016.

Section, A. C. D. (1969). *Auckland's historical background: its relation to central city planning*. Auckland City Council, Department of Works and Services.

Walker, B. and Salt, D. (2006). *Resilience Thinking: Sustaining Ecosystems and People in a Changing World*. Washington, DC: Island Press.

Witten, I. H., Frank, E. and Hall, M. A. (2011). *Data Mining: Practical Machine Learning Tools and Techniques*, 3rd edn. Burlington, MA: Morgan Kaufmann.

11 Conclusion

'It's funny. All you have to do is say something nobody understands and they'll do practically anything you want them to.'

J. D. Salinger

11.1 Confusion in sustainability and resilience

Resilience and sustainability are both subject to conceptual vagueness that can prove confusing for designers (present authors included). As stated in Chapter 1, without conceptual clarity it is difficult to know if designers are really engaging in sustainability or resilience, or effectively doing neither.

The use of resilience as a metaphor (Norris *et al.*, 2008; DeVerteuil and Golibchikov, 2016; Allan *et al.*, 2013) raises the issue of whether it is an apt metaphor. When it comes to metaphors we can believe in 'a river of hair' because hair has a flowing quality but not in 'an attic of hair' even though both hair and attics are at the tops of things. If resilience is applied to the built environment as a metaphor then it has to have qualities that make it appropriate for doing this. It is perhaps not enough to state 'When applied to people and their environments, "resilience" is fundamentally a metaphor' (Norris *et al.*, 2008). This book was an attempt to go beyond the metaphor and apply the theory of ecological resilience to the built environment. It set out to do two things: to distinguish between resilience and sustainability when it comes to built environments; to discover whether it is possible to apply the theory of ecological resilience to the built environment and if so how to do this. In the course of doing this the question of whether it is worth applying resilience to the built environment also arises.

Sustainability is a bit like Janus as it has two faces. The first is knowing that what we have to do (achieve an 80 per cent reduction in fossil fuel use to meet the Paris CoP agreement) means huge change in how we organize human societies on this planet. This is the utopian face of sustainability. The second is a practical face that says we have to do what we can, however small, such as taking your own bags to the supermarket. This is the pragmatic face of sustainability. The reality is we have to embrace both. Another issue with sustainability comes from the commercialization of the concept as found in various rating schemes and even in moves like making eco-cities, where the aim is still for developers to make money. We know what needs to be done, including devising an economic system that is no longer predicated on the idea of endless growth. However, the required change in human behaviour is hard to achieve in the short term, which becomes an excuse to do nothing. The idealism of sustainability seems impossible to practise in a society based on consumption. Instead of making true changes to how societies are organized, energy is wasted in developing palliatives in the form of technological gadgets and certifications to assess the performance of those gadgets. This will not help to change behaviour.

In the case of resilience confusion has arisen because there are gaps in the research on resilience. If it can be applied to the built environment then what do you count when it comes to knowing whether there is sufficient redundancy and tight enough feedback loops? If I choose to drive my car and the water starts to lap against my doorstep then I might understand the connection between greenhouse gas emissions and sea-level rise, but if I drive my car and it causes floods in Bangladesh then it is harder to make the connection (Milfont et al., 2014). The application of ecological resilience to urban landscapes is still a work in progress. Nonetheless, it will never come to maturity if institutions keep on selling resilience as a set of qualities and as a solution to temporarily fix and mitigate the lack of true changes toward sustainable behaviour.

Designers have little influence over the growth and final form of a city but they still have knowledge that can be useful for the other designers of the city: its people. The behavioural choices of people in a city could become a design force that could reshape and change the meaning of the built environment, and the relationship of the city to the rural landscape. If we decide to stop driving the children to school and find ways they can safely walk there and if we stop using the car to commute to work, then not only will this be part of greenhouse gas reductions, it could also stop new road building (if we also change who we vote for on the city council) and change the city from car dependency to one that is walkable (and probably better for cycling). All the nice words about walkable cities will only come to pass if there is behaviour change. This point is where the knowledge about resilience and sustainability might be important in understanding how to create urban spaces that can support this change.

11.2 Sustainability and resilience

As explained in Chapters 1 and 4 sustainability is a desirable goal while resilience (ecological resilience) is a quality of complex systems. Goals are achieved through actions. Properties like resilience are inherent. For the built environment this means the goal of being sustainable is to encourage people to behave in a way that minimizes human impact on the environment. This goal involves choices and actions to make this happen, and at present it is voluntary. However, a built environment has an inherent resilience whether we want it to or not. For this reason, the goal of a city cannot be to be resilient but to enhance the resilience of some part of the system, hopefully so that it will develop in a sustainable way.

Even though sustainability and resilience are conceptually different, they are compatible when it comes to surviving an environmental crisis (more global warming than we want) without losing our identities. In the light of what was said above, however, it may be that we cannot move to sustainability in the built environment without changing the identity of at least some urban environments. In the past when cities were smaller, were walkable and food was produced nearby and brought in to market and wastes were shipped back to the fields as fertilizer, the city was inherently more sustainable. There are small, lower-rise cities where this way of living could be recaptured without a change in identity, but there are also cities where such an arrangement would completely change the appearance and identity of the city. However, learning about the resilience of the built environment as a way of understanding how cities work as complex adaptive systems will be of little use if it does not have sustainability as a goal.

Sustainability can provide an ethical framework for designs that look toward enhancing the resilience of a city. As discussed in the Introduction, if Toronto is the most resilient city why is it so unsustainable in terms of its ecological footprint? If cities in the developed world are made more resilient what effect does this have on the developing world? At the same time the study of resilience can offer information about changes happening in a city that are not usually associated with sustainability. For example, resilience could be helpful for assessing the complexity of an urban landscape through the analysis of its texture in terms of the elements of its built environment and the relationships between these, which can be important for studies in sustainability to understand what level of complexity is acquired at which cost in resource terms. At the same time, looking at resources from a sustainable, or climate change mitigation, viewpoint could also be useful. It is no good promoting solar energy if having lots of Chinese PV panels on roofs in the developed world ignores the impact of the emissions from making these panels in an economy largely dependent on fossil fuels, especially coal.

A sustainable city is first a city

Dreams can be happy experiences or nightmares. In the same way ideal cities can contain hopeful ideas or dystopian futures. The ultimate compact eco-city clearly heads toward the construction of the city as a single mega-building where people do not use cars and could live and work in small spaces, but a building is not a city. As shown in Chapter 5, the failure of modern eco-cities is less related to the size of the enterprise but more with the understanding of what a city is, and how its economic foundation is fundamental to how it works as a city. Also more important than the aesthetics of a city, or its goal to be compact, eco or smart, it is its ethics – who is the city for and who is profiting from building it? If we truly embrace sustainability then we have to embrace it for everyone.

Designers love the idea of lots of change at once (which is misunderstood as being radical) even though this may often lead to satisfaction of the ego of the designer at the expense of the impact on the landscape. People do not like imposed, abrupt changes in where they live unless they are obliged to cope with these for the common good. Many changes to life occur, and are accepted, in extreme circumstances in wars, because winning the war is seen as a collective goal. Without the support of people no radical change is possible, however radical the design. Therefore, it is important to understand the pace of the development of a community and work with what is already there instead of imposing changes that will alienate people. This is something that the study of resilience teaches.

11.3 Applying ecological resilience to the built environment

When it comes to applying ecological resilience to the built environment the Panarchy reveals that the history of an urban system is a map of the opportunities that a place has already offered and that might or might not be available again. The persistence of some vernacular architectural traditions and the eventual disappearance of others show that in architecture and urbanism change is related with persistence. The role of inheritance in the persistence of the identity of an urban landscape is a good example of a change in the built environment that leads to a series of adaptations. Linking inheritance to the built environment highlights the importance of understanding that what is built in the present will be inherited by someone else in the future, along with the responsibility that goes with this.

This also requires understanding something about the history of the elements that make up a built environment. Plots are good example of an element that limits what can be built in a city and a plot is not something that is designed. However, without thinking about resilience the importance of plots may be underestimated. The analysis of changes in the form and use of the plot system is important for understanding how ownership and use of land gives the city shape, as well as seeing how inherited land subdivisions could encourage or limit the possibilities of new types of buildings. Plots are often forgotten in urban analysis but their geometry is important as shown in the example of the sausage houses in Argentina. As another example, the plot frontage is key when looking for diversity in the built environment, which is linked to its resilience, because it defines the ease with which plots can be subdivided, as well as forming the interface between the public and private realms.

The analysis of change through using the Panarchy and the identification of slow and fast variables are also important for designers. For example, if a designer alters things that will stay in the landscape for a long time, like streets, then it might not be a surprise that these changes trigger a series of other transformations in the urban landscape, either for good or bad. Any city which has had urban motorways carved through it will have experienced such transformations, through the divisions such motorways impose, and the change to land values around them.

The discussion above, through talking about the Panarchy, has assumed that it is possible to apply the theory of ecological resilience to the built environment. Cities are complex adaptive systems and so this seems reasonable. However, one of the reasons for looking for resilience is that we know we have future problems in trying to adapt to the effects of climate change, and also the effects of climate change mitigation in the changes this will impose on ways of living. We also know that to be sustainable in terms of living within the resources of one planet, we shall have to make changes.

What does a sustainable and resilient urban area look like?

At the moment the institutional answer to the question in the heading is a compact environment that is dense in terms of people per land area, and that has an intensity of use. However, these three concepts (compact, dense and intensity) are very different and hard to measure because elements that move, like people, and elements that are static, like buildings, are treated in the same way. Is it numbers of people or building area that are being compacted on to a small area of land? The answer may all depend on the time of day. The discussion is often not clear on exactly what is being compacted and when. The same processes and similar buildings in different cultures can also have different results. For example, in two compact built environments – San Miguel de Tucuman and Hanoi – the results are quite different because the cultures differ and this affects the process of change and types consolidated in the landscape.

From a resilience perspective, compaction and dispersion are both necessary qualities in a city. Compaction will provide stability and dispersion will provide opportunities for change without reaching a tipping point. Compaction may not be necessary for a sustainable built environment because changes in human behaviour and the organization of society, especially its economic basis, are more critical. What might be of more importance than building the Transit Oriented Development is to discuss how different forms of capitals (people, buildings, functions) could be tightened to obtain different degrees of complexity in different places. From this point of view, trying to measure what different levels of complexity mean for the resilience and sustainability of a built environment seems to be more useful than clustering buildings around bus stops or subway stations. From a resilience perspective what is useful to know is the points (thresholds) at which the complexity of a built environment stops producing the expected benefits in terms of sustainability. The other issue is to know when increasing complexity has to stop to avoid collapse.

You can measure only what you can measure

When it comes to measuring it is clear that resilience and sustainability are quite different because they have to be measured in different ways. Measuring is also not easy; there are no silver bullets or easy answers. Conversely, without measuring resilience or sustainability it is difficult to advance knowledge about either. The problem is that in built environments the information available on which to base measurements is often patchy at present. If what designers have to measure is people, because buildings tend to be used and built by them, then to know more about what people do and how they behave will offer useful input for understanding sustainability (Lawton, 2015) and probably resilience. The gaps in the data for measuring resilience are linked with the lack of maps and information related to land use functions. By measuring people it would be easier to build for them. This is complicated for designers that mostly design empty buildings without much thought to who might be using them.

11.4 Why it might be worth applying resilience in built environments

Obviously, if you are an organization or a university that is funded to investigate applying resilience to the built environment, then this is a worthwhile thing to do. However, this is at best a cynical view and at worst 'sour grapes'. The discussion in this book has assumed applying resilience theory to the built environment is worth doing. The task has then been to see how this might be done and how resilience might be measured, and thus unravel its meaning. In consequence, it is possible to make some useful observations about urban environments.

Cities are much more complex systems than ecosystems

The different degrees of complexity in ecosystems and cities could invalidate the theories in ecology for designers of built environments. The analysis and discussion in the previous chapters suggests that using an approach similar to that of Conzen, something might be learned about resilience in built environments, but we are still at the very early stages of being able to interpret this knowledge.

206 Conclusion

Although talking about urban ecologies is enticing and apparently applicable to landscapes – and cities have to sit within these landscapes – the resilience approach might be inappropriate for cities. Perhaps, as an alternative, designers will have to analyse cities as urban landscapes that depend on ecosystem services, which have their own scales and dynamics of change. This has fewer implications for the measurement of sustainability than for the measurement of resilience, since current research in resilience depends on the evidence and hypothesis developed in ecology, and assumes it could be applicable to the built environment.

This book has tried to develop a way of measuring resilience in the built environment along the lines of that used to measure resilience in ecosystems. This makes it different from current ways of applying resilience theory to urban environment. The problem with these is that confining the application of resilience to built environment labels, indicators, metaphors and wishlists makes it very difficult to find evidence of any advance in understanding what urban resilience is. It is important that designers see urban landscapes in the same way as geologists and meteorologists see things, as being in a state of movement. This leads to tracking changes continuously, and making analysis and designs accordingly. Ideally every council should have a department devoted to measuring how the built environment it has responsibility for changes. This implies defining what kind of changes are important to measure and why.

You have to know where you are before going somewhere else

When you want to use your phone to find instructions of how to get to a place, the first thing every application needs is your location. To move toward sustainability we also need to know where we are, and constantly update this information. Resilience is useful for developing a sense of awareness about the future using the past as the main source. Measuring resilience could help designers to understand the state of a system, and in turn this might inform the early stages of the design process. Particularly important is recognition of the drivers of change of a system because they establish directions for development.

Designing for persistence and change

Resilience is about understanding persistence and change as being one phenomenon. This is how complexity reveals itself through resilience. This dichotomy between change and persistence is also a starting point for analysing the built environment. Designers should ask themselves questions such as what is persisting in this system? What is changing? How can we observe persistence and change in the urban landscape? The big challenge is discovering how it might be possible to design while acknowledging persistence and change. A first step in this process is understanding each Panarchy in the built environment. The objective of an analysis of an urban area should be to understand what processes are critical and which are less so. What is interesting about the Panarchy is that the assumption behind it is that a few processes are key to understanding a whole system. As an example, the analysis in Chapter 10 showed how critical streets are when it comes to giving a built environment stability. If you change the street layout then expect others changes to happen.

Designers are not good at dealing with function and even worse at dealing with changes. When we design a building we expect it be such a masterpiece that it will remain in perpetuity. Changes can undermine the masterpiece of a designer and people may also interact with it in an unpredictable way (Brand, 1994). At the very least all buildings will need maintenance, which is a change. Put together, function and change represent what designers do not design. This could be understood as an opportunity or a threat for future designers but it is something we should acknowledge. From a designer's perspective, building resilience is about what we should not be building, so as to leave opportunities for introducing or buffering change in the future, and for this reason, it needs design. Since cities have resilience and have been very resilient (they are still with us) we have to be focused on making cities be cities for everybody. This is something we could and should be doing even without trying to measure resilience, but it is resilience theory that helps us picture why we might need to do this.

Maintaining lifestyles or sustaining life

If the expectation of making a better city includes having a built environment that sustains current resource-intensive lifestyles at the same environmental cost, then these expectations are probably not going to be fulfilled unless there is a drastic reduction in human population. Cities will be with us in a sustainable future but they will be recognized as dependent on their rural hinterlands and rural living will be as attractive, if not more so, than living in cities. Looking through the lens of resilience theory a sustainable city will be a place where people have the chance to survive resource volatility or scarcity, whether by producing more resources within the city limits or by a sustainable relationship with resource-producing places outside the city limits. This could be a big shift in the stability state of all our urban system towards a new regime, with a new identity for cities. From this point of view, the first resilience that cities will have to develop is not necessarily linked with natural hazards produced by climate change issues but with the transition to a less resource-intensive, cheaper and more sustainable complexity in cities. The good news for designers, if they are prepared to grapple with resilience and sustainability, is that the transition towards such a manageable complexity has to be designed in order to be affordable.

Bibliography

Allan, P., Bryant, M., Wirsching, C., Garcia, D. and Rodriguez, M. T. (2013). The influence of urban morphology on the resilience of cities following an earthquake. *Journal of Urban Design* 18(2), pp. 242–262.
Brand, S. (1994). *How Building Learn: What Happens After They're Built?* New York: Viking.
DeVerteuil, G. and Golubchikov, O. (2016). Can resilience be redeemed? *City* 20(1), pp. 143–151.
Lawton, E. S. (2015). Footprinting New Zealand urban forms and lifestyles. PhD thesis, Victoria University of Wellington.
Milfont, T., Evans, L., Sibley, C., Ries, J. and Cunningham, A. (2014). Proximity to coast is linked to climate change belief. *PLoS One* 9(7), p. e103180.
Norris, F. H., Stevens, S. P., Pfefferbaum, B., Wyche, K. F. and Pfefferbaum, R. L. (2008). Community resilience as a metaphor, theory, set of capacities, and strategy for disaster readiness. *American Journal of Community Psychology* 41(1–2), pp. 127–150.

Index

adaptation 45–49, 52–53
adaptive: capacity 43, 45, 64; cycle 37–38, 59–61, 86–87, 102–3, 112–13, 132–34, 160–61, 164, 168, 168–72, 198
affordable housing 77, 85, 189
Agenda 21 9, 150
aggregations 174–76, 191–95
Amsterdam, the Netherlands 134
Ancient Greece 22, 75
Angkor Wat, Cambodia 98
Annales School 52
Archigram 51
Arcologies 76
Auckland, New Zealand 96, 117, 127–30, 168–77, 180–90, 193, 196–97

Bangladesh 3, 203
Beijing, China 80, 82, 84
Black Death 39
biodiversity 129, 198
boreal forest 37
Boston Indicators Project 152
Brasilia, Brazil 72, 82, 83, 87
Braudel, F 99–101, 108
BREEAM 9, 10, 21
British new towns 74
Bruntland Report 17, 61
budworm *see* spruce budworm
burgage cycle 167–168, 172
bushfire 38, 45

capitals 125–27, 135, 171–72, 176, 206
Cardiff, Wales 130
CASBEE 9–10
carbon: credit 155; cycle 6; footprint 73, 145–47, 153, 155; neutrality 72, 76, 78, 80
cars 95–96
casa: chorizo 101–8, 112–13, 205; de vecindad 104, 107
Christchurch, New Zealand 96, 113, 117
China 7, 25, 72, 76, 80–89, 130, 152, 165
City Resilience Framework/Index 160, 163–64

Clean Development Protocol 9
climate change 9, 11, 24, 32, 46–47, 49, 50, 52–53, 78, 95, 116, 146, 153, 189, 198, 203–4, 207
cluster analysis *see* aggregations
collapse 23–24, 59, 61, 85, 87, 113, 134, 144, 166, 168, 170–71, 206; of cities 51, 53
colonial cities 96, 102–3
Concepcion, Chile 192–95
conventillo 105
Coventry, UK 125, 166
Conzen, M G R 63, 167–70, 172, 178, 187, 190, 205
crime 49, 73, 120
Curitiba, Brazil 73
cycling 25, 72, 83, 124, 166

da Vinci, L 75
density 69, 117–120, 176, 205; as perceived 119, 136
Detroit, USA 151
Dhaka, Bangladesh 3
Dharavi, India 126
discontinuities 174–76, 190–93, 195
diversity 40–41, 43–46, 52–53, 63, 84, 86, 132, 161–62, 170, 195–97
Dongtan, China 76, 88
Dresden, Germany 98

Earth 6, 31, 63, 143; overshoot day 148–49
earthquakes 8, 31, 43, 48, 96, 99, 100, 113, 193
ecological footprint 3, 8, 19, 60, 85–86, 88, 129–31, 143–45, 155, 165, 198
ecological resilience *see* resilience in ecology
ethics 49, 64–65, 204
engineering resilience 3, 33, 35, 47, 64, 76, 98, 159, 164
equity 27, 44, 64–66, 83, 120, 129, 144, 170, 189
European Ecolabel 155
evenness 195–97

fast variables *see* variables
feedback 36, 42–44, 136, 203; loops 98
Findhorn, Scotland 89
Finland 145
foxes 35–36
Freiburg, German 7, 71, 81, 98

GDP 25; carbon intensity of 81
General Motors 48
general resilience 43–45, 64, 161, 164
gentrification 119, 129
Genuine Savings Indicator 20
Global Footprint Network (GFN) 8, 9, 147, 148
governability 65
governance 44, 65, 150, 161–62
Greenest Neighbourhood competitions 66
greenhouse gas emissions 116, 127, 145, 148, 154–55, 203–4; reduction in 9, 71, 81, 116
Grosvenor Research Report 163–64
Guanajuato, Mexico 74, 75

happiness 16, 26
Hanoi, Vietnam 110–12, 126, 127, 130, 134, 205
Hartig, G L 18–19
heterogeneity 40–41, 133, 136, 170, 173–76, 190, 192, 195–96, 198–99
Hockerton Housing Project 154
Holling, C S 3, 11, 34–37, 40–41, 50, 58, 61, 63, 159, 168, 177
homogeneity 86, 133–34, 136, 183
Hong Kong 73, 117, 120–122, 124, 127, 131
Howard, E 75, 117, 132
Human Development Index 19, 144–45
humble heritage 101–110, 112
hydrological cycle 6, 39
Hygeia 75

identity 36, 41–42, 47–49, 77, 86–87, 95–103, 112–113, 119, 133–134, 173–74, 203–205; of Auckland 182–185
inequality 46, 49
inquilinato 104–10
inequity *see* equity
intensity 69, 119–23, 132, 136, 205
International Energy Agency (IEA) 24, 25, 146
International Living Future Institute *see* Living Building Challenge
International Panel on Climate Change (IPCC) 47, 71, 81

Jacobs, J 5, 132
Japan GreenBuild Council *see* CASBEE
Jevons, W 24, 88
Jogyakarta, Indonesia 135

Kampung Naga, Indonesia 18
keystone species hypothesis 37
Kyoto Protocol 9

Le Corbusier 74, 75, 80, 83, 125; Unités d'Habitation 198
LEED 9–10, 21, 152–54
Lincoln, UK 97; cathedral 58
Liveability 120–21, 125, 131
Living Building Challenge (LBC) 9–10
London, UK 101, 135, 165
lumpy landscape 133, 174

Mallet, R 33
Masdar, UAE 80
master plan 74, 75, 86
medium density housing 124
Melbourne, Australia 119, 125, 165
metaphor *see* resilience as metaphor
Mexico City 135
Miniplexion 76
Mr Micawber 16–17, 27
Modernist buildings 49
modularity 43–44, 63, 136
modulus of resilience 33
monotheism 22
More, T 71
morphology *see* urban morphology

NABERS 10, 153–54
Nachhaltigkeit 18, 20, 58
Napier, New Zealand 99
natural hazards 8, 32, 46, 48, 159, 208
neo-tube house 111
novelty 45, 53
New Urbanism 86, 123, 130
New York, USA 96, 126

Omega point 77

Panarchy: in ecology 37–40, 52, 59, 61–62, 65–66, 152, 187; in built environment 52–53, 86, 100–1, 161, 164–178, 180, 190, 196, 198–99, 205, 207; in Tucuman 108, 112; in Auckland CBD 180
pandas 35
Paris, France 97, 165; climate agreement (CoP21) 59, 72, 141, 146, 166, 202
pedestrian pocket 117
persistence 18–19, 32–35, 39, 42, 47–53, 61, 64, 67, 69, 75, 94–95, 110, 112, 205, 207
photovoltaics 78, 85, 154, 204
Plato 71, 76
plot ratio 118
Probe studies 154

public transport 4, 26, 47, 71–73, 78, 81, 83, 87–88, 117, 124–126, 128, 130, 136, 152, 182–3; subsidies 135

Rangitoto Island, New Zealand 174
rationing 16–67, 24
redundancy 36, 44, 52–53, 63, 133–134, 162, 195, 203
remember 39
renewable energy 62, 72, 74, 76, 81, 85, 129, 145, 155
revolt 39–40, 79
Resilience Alliance 11, 159–161, 164; workbook 166; framework 167
resilience: in ecology 34–41, 52, 112, 174, 192, 195, 201–4, 208; and identity 41–42; as metaphor 50, 52, 202; in psychology 34, 46
richness 136, 174, 177, 190, 192, 195–97
robustness 34, 64, 162, 174
Rockefeller Foundation 12, 160; 100 Resilient Cities 160, 162–4, 177
Roman Empire, 22, 23
rural migrants 5

San Miguel de Tucuman 96, 101–10, 205
sausage house *see* casa chorizo
scale(s) 36–37, 39–41, 44, 52–53, 61–66, 86, 99–101, 108–10, 159–62, 165, 167, 170, 177, 180, 199
self organize 63, 65, 174
Shannon-Wiener diversity index 195
The Shard 4, 26, 130
Sharp, T 5
shop houses 110
Sino-Singapore-Tianjin Eco-City (SSTEC) *see* Tianjin
smart cities 124
slow variables *see* variables
social capital 43–44, 63, 126
social-ecological systems 41–43, 53, 60, 66, 160, 165, 199; urban 11; resilience of 46
Soleri, P *see* Archologies
space syntax 135
specific resilience 43–44, 161, 164
sprawling cities 77, 117, 123, 125, 127, 131–32
spruce budworm 37, 58
Standard Assessment Procedure (SAP) 78, 154
Stockholm Resilience Centre 11–12, 41, 43–44, 160, 162
strong sustainability 15–16
sub-prime mortgage crisis 167
subsistence farming 16–17, 61, 136, 144, 148, 155

sustainability indicators 43, 143, 149–151, 163
systems thinking 60, 65

Tainter, J A 23, 170–71, 174
Teilhard de Chardin, P 76–77
Textural-Discontinuities Hypothesis (TDH) 40–41, 159
Tianjin, China 7, 80–88
thresholds 42–44, 45, 61, 134, 161, 164, 166, 206
tightness 43–44, 124, 126, 161
timelines 99, 166–172, 180–187
tipping points *see* thresholds
Toronto, Canada 3–4, 204
tourism 85, 97, 112, 126–27, 131, 159, 171
transformability 45, 47
Transport Oriented Development (TOD) 117, 124, 125, 127, 206
Tredgold, T 33
Tuareg nomadic life 98
tube houses 110–12

UK Department of the Environment, Transport and the Regions (DTER) 151
UK Department for International Development Building Resilience and Adaptation to Climate (BRACED) 163–164
UNDP Community-Based Resilience Analysis (CoBRA) 163–64
UN/ISRD Disaster Resilience Scorecard for Cities (UN/ISRD) 163–64
Unwin, R 118, 132
urban morphology 63, 80, 99, 108; analysis 174; morphogenesis 167
USAID Measurement for Community Resilience 163–64
utopia 27, 71, 72, 75; utopian future 59

variables 31, 35–37, 39, 44, 50, 65, 160, 162, 166, 168, 170, 173, 187–88, 205; key 63, 151
velo-cities 124
vernacular: architecture 18, 21, 39, 51; building tradition 10, 84, 205
Versailles 5
vitality 120
von Carlowitz, H C 18, 58
vulnerability 46–47, 64, 113, 159

Waiheke Island, New Zealand 171
Waisman, M 100–1, 107–8
walkable: built environment 83, 124; cities 124, 203; streets 153

waste: food 35, 196; disposal 24; management 18, 72–73, 75, 85, 103, 203; product 15
water: consumption 73, 81, 145, 151, 154, 171; quality 34, 150; rainwater 9, 37, 111, 159; recycling 71, 129; resource/supply 24, 62, 71, 73, 148, 150, 171; saving 26; virtual 16, 151
weak sustainability 15–16

Weka (Waikato Environment for Knowledge Analysis) 190–92
Wellington, New Zealand 100, 166, 182
Whitehill and Bordon 77–80, 117
Wren, C 53

zero carbon and zero carbon footprint *see* carbon neutrality

# Taylor & Francis eBooks

Helping you to choose the right eBooks for your Library

Add Routledge titles to your library's digital collection today. Taylor and Francis ebooks contains over 50,000 titles in the Humanities, Social Sciences, Behavioural Sciences, Built Environment and Law.

Choose from a range of subject packages or create your own!

Benefits for you
- Free MARC records
- COUNTER-compliant usage statistics
- Flexible purchase and pricing options
- All titles DRM-free.

Benefits for your user
- Off-site, anytime access via Athens or referring URL
- Print or copy pages or chapters
- Full content search
- Bookmark, highlight and annotate text
- Access to thousands of pages of quality research at the click of a button.

 Free Trials Available
We offer free trials to qualifying academic, corporate and government customers.

eCollections – Choose from over 30 subject eCollections, including:

Archaeology	Language Learning
Architecture	Law
Asian Studies	Literature
Business & Management	Media & Communication
Classical Studies	Middle East Studies
Construction	Music
Creative & Media Arts	Philosophy
Criminology & Criminal Justice	Planning
Economics	Politics
Education	Psychology & Mental Health
Energy	Religion
Engineering	Security
English Language & Linguistics	Social Work
Environment & Sustainability	Sociology
Geography	Sport
Health Studies	Theatre & Performance
History	Tourism, Hospitality & Events

For more information, pricing enquiries or to order a free trial, please contact your local sales team:
www.tandfebooks.com/page/sales

 The home of Routledge books

www.tandfebooks.com